PRAISE FOR *MORAL COMBAT*

"A fact-filled, persuasive, and witty debunking of the cyclical moral panic about video games."

—Steven Pinker, professor of psychology at Harvard University and author of *How the Mind Works* and *The Better Angels of Our Nature*

"A groundbreaking and vitally important book. It gets under the hood of how games actually work on our brains, and in the process it tells us more than any number of sensational news articles. This should be required reading for anyone who loves games or who loves someone who loves games . . . which is to say, everyone."

—Greg Toppo, author of *The Game Believes in You: How Digital Play Can Make Our Kids Smarter*

"What Chris and Patrick have done with *Moral Combat* is wonderful. They've taken the age-old debates of violence, addiction, and time dilation and presented a holistic perspective on the issue so that any lay person can truly understand the issues. As a filmmaker who's spent much of my career working on video game–related content, it's refreshing to finally see a book about games that gets it right."

—Jeremy Snead, founder of Mediajuice Studios and writer/director of *Video Games: The Movie* and *Unlocked: The World of Games, Revealed*

"Rigorous research is the essential foundation of good policies and good advice for parents. Unfortunately, when it comes to hot-button issues such as media violence, logic and rigor are tossed overboard in a frantic paddle toward favored conclusions. The results can be downright crazy. This book, from two highly respected academics, brims with fascinating detail on the history of media panics, the sometimes-shady 'sausage-making' of research, and collisions between agenda-driven scientists, doctors, judges, and politicians—with children's play as collateral damage. Even readers familiar with video game politics and history will find something to gasp about. And stressed parents may finally understand what their kids get out of those games, and how to manage them better."

—**Cheryl K. Olson, ScD, coauthor of *Grand Theft Childhood: The Surprising Truth About Violent Video Games and What Parents Can Do* and principal investigator for a major government-funded study of video games and youth**

"Apparently Markey and Ferguson's enjoying video games didn't distract them from writing a thoroughly entertaining analysis of whether we should be worried about the effects of violent video games. Gamers should buy this book for their parents, and parents should calm down teachers and pediatricians with a copy. Anyone interested in a great, skeptical takedown of bad science should get their own copy."

—**James C. Coyne, professor emeritus of psychology and psychiatry at the University of Pennsylvania**

"Markey and Ferguson shed needed light on a topic too often seen through the lens of our worst fears. This book delivers healthy doses of skepticism and scientific insights that broaden our understanding of 21st-century play. From political horse-trading to weak science, this book is a must-read for anyone interested in video games."

—**Andrew Przybylski, PhD, experimental psychology department research fellow at the University of Oxford**

WHY THE WAR ON VIOLENT

VIDEO GAMES IS WRONG

MORAL COMBAT

PATRICK M. MARKEY, PhD AND

CHRISTOPHER J. FERGUSON, PhD

BenBella Books, Inc.
Dallas, TX

BenBella

BenBella Books, Inc.
10440 N. Central Expressway
Suite 800
Dallas, TX 75231
www.benbellabooks.com
Send feedback to feedback@benbellabooks.com

Printed in the United States of America
10 9 8 7 6 5 4 3 2 1

Library of Congress Cataloging-in-Publication Data is available upon request.
978-1-942952-98-5 (trade paperback)
978-1-942952-99-2 (e-book)

Editing by Alexa Stevenson
Copyediting by Scott Calamar
Proofreading by Michael Fedison and Sarah Vostok
Text design and composition by Aaron Edmiston
Front cover design by Faceout Studios, Derek Thorton
Full cover design by Sarah Dombrowsky
Printed by Lake Book Manufacturing

Distributed by Perseus Distribution
www.perseusdistribution.com
To place orders through Perseus Distribution:
Tel: (800) 343-4499
Fax: (800) 351-5073
E-mail: orderentry@perseusbooks.com

**Special discounts for bulk sales (minimum of 25 copies) are available.
Please contact Aida Herrera at aida@benbellabooks.com.**

To all the politicians, activists, and scholars who have
foisted blame for all manner of social ills on to video games.
Without them, this book would not have been possible . . .
or necessary.

—PATRICK M. MARKEY AND
CHRISTOPHER J. FERGUSON

CONTENTS

LEVEL 1:

A BRIEF HISTORY OF VIOLENT VIDEO GAMES

The tiny beachfront town of Marshfield, Massachusetts, is ideally situated thirty miles outside of Boston on the shore of the Atlantic Ocean. In the summer, its population doubles as out-of-towners flock to the tranquil Victorian homes dotting the coast. Life in Marshfield during the warmer months means getting a tan while fishing and participating in a variety of beach-based activities. As the weather cools and the summer renters depart, the youth of Marshfield can be found cheering for their winning high school football team, hanging out at the local pizza joint, or wandering the small collection of downtown shops. What makes Marshfield unique is not what their citizens do but what they were forbidden to do—at least in public. For over three decades in this idyllic town, video games were banned.

In 1982, Marshfield's politicians and community leaders decided that outlawing this form of electronic entertainment was the best way to reduce criminal activity among the town's youth. Henceforth, the citizens of Marshfield would not battle zombies and dragons in *Ghosts 'n Goblins,* shoot evil agents in *Elevator Action,* or witness a fatality in *Mortal Kombat.* The US Supreme Court refused to hear an appeal from business owners the following year, essentially guaranteeing that the ban would remain in place. Residents of Marshfield tried, unsuccessfully, to have the ban lifted in 1994 and again in 2011, but it wasn't until 2014 that the thirty-two-year prohibition on video games was overturned—by a scant twenty-eight votes.[1]

Marshfield was hardly unique in its belief in the corrupting influence of video games, especially violent ones. Over the past four decades, American pundits and politicians have blamed violent games for just about every societal ill: school shootings, racism, obesity, narcissism, rickets (a skeletal disease), self-control problems, and drunk driving. Video games have been held responsible for homicides, carjackings, and rapes, for causing limbs to fall off (seriously), for learning disabilities, and even for the terrorist attacks on September 11th. Dozens of laws have been passed, federal hearings have been held, presidents have expressed their concern, and cases have been presented before the US Supreme Court, all in an effort to protect society from this digital menace. The fear surrounding violent video games is so prevalent that it is difficult to remember what it was like before we learned to be afraid of them.

SO IT BEGINS WITH A SMALL DOT AND TWO LINES . . .

The patrons of Andy Capp's Tavern had never seen anything like it. Sure, by 1972 they had heard of computers—hulking electronic brains used by banks and businesses—but few, if any, had seen a computer game you could play on a thirteen-inch black-and-white television set. There were no instructions on the machine, just the word *PONG* written in bold black text on the front. (See Easter Egg 1, at the end of the chapter.) The mysterious machine cost a quarter to play when other bar games, like pinball, only cost a dime. However, once a quarter was dropped into the slot, all became clear as a small white ball bounced quickly between two paddles. It was electronic Ping-Pong!

Unbeknownst to those clustered around the machine in Andy Capp's Tavern, they were among the first people to play the game. *Pong* was being test-marketed in this smoke-filled bar by a fledgling company called Atari, and it didn't take Atari long to realize they had struck gold. Eventually, over 35,000 *Pong* arcade machines would be sold, and millions of families would purchase the home version of the game to hook up to their own television sets. The video game revolution had begun, all thanks to a bouncing white dot of a ball and two lines for paddles (see Easter Egg 2).

Over the next five years, Atari and other companies such as Taito, Sega, and Midway would expand the themes of early video games. Many of these games were variants of *Pong*, like Atari's *Super Pong* or *Quadrapong*, but driving and war games also became popular during this time. Taito's 1974 *Speed Race* let players drive a digital race car using a steering wheel, and was the first game to feature scrolling graphics. In Atari's *Tank*, players each took control of a—guess—tank and tried to destroy the other's vehicle. Then, in 1975, Midway released the game *Gun Fight*, which was the first to feature human figures fighting each other using guns. In *Gun Fight*, players controlled dueling cowboys in an Old Western setting complete with cactuses, trees, and stagecoaches. Although the game depicted two people trying to shoot each other, it didn't generate much controversy. In fact, today *Gun Fight* is remembered as the first game to use a microprocessor, not as one of the first to feature violence against people.

Many of the early video game companies avoided producing violent games in an effort to sidestep potential controversy. Atari had an internal rule that their games must not display violence against people.[2] Alas, it wasn't a rule they were particularly fastidious about following. They released both *Cops n' Robbers* (a game set in the Roaring Twenties that allowed up to four players to shoot at each other as they controlled either "cop" or "robber" cars) and *Outlaw*, which was almost a direct copy of Midway's *Gun Fight*.

At the time, however, these games were not thought of as being particularly violent. One obvious reason was the technological limitations of early arcade machines and home systems. It was difficult to create a horrifying and realistic violent image in the blocky 160 x 192 resolution of an Atari 2600. Another reason for the lack of outcry was the games themselves, specifically the context in which the violence took place. Most were set in a stylized past or future—the Wild West, outer space, WWII. When they depicted crime, it was in the bygone gangland of Jimmy Cagney movies. These were already familiar subjects for entertainment. Movies and television regularly romanticized these events in *The Lone Ranger, The Dirty Dozen, Have Gun—Will Travel,* and *The Untouchables.* Before video games, children played "Cowboys and Indians," "Spaceman," and "Cops and Robbers" in suburban backyards across the country. Parents recognized this type of play as innocent fun—because they'd engaged in this same play themselves. As a result, when they saw their children virtually dueling in a virtual Old West, it seemed a harmless continuation of a timeless game. At the time, parents were more amazed that we could move images around our television sets than concerned with what those images were doing.

But as the video game market became more competitive, companies found that the novelty of moving a blocky character with a joystick was no longer enough to keep players interested. To hold their attention, and stand out in the now-crowded video game market, some game developers decided they would need to be as shocking as technology would allow.

FROM B MOVIES TO QUARTERS

A moviegoer in 1975 had some pretty impressive options for entertainment. They could watch a shark terrorize the resort town of
Amity Island in *Jaws,* learn how many times a swallow needs to
beat its wings in order to maintain airspeed (answer: forty-three)
in *Monty Python and the Holy Grail,* or marvel at Jack Nicholson's
performance in *One Flew Over the Cuckoo's Nest,* which would win
that year's Academy Award for best picture, along with those for best
director, actress, and screenplay. One release that failed to garner
any awards that year was a B-movie action flick called *Death Race
2000.* Set in the far-off year 2000, the film featured Sylvester Stallone
and David Carradine as competitors in a cross-country car race in
which points were awarded for running down innocent pedestrians. Teenagers were worth forty points, taking out a toddler would
get you seventy-five, and the "big score" was the elderly, who were
worth 100 points apiece. (As a bonus, while the women of 1975 may
have earned far less than their male counterparts in the workplace,
in *Death Race 2000* they were worth an extra ten points across the
board.) In one memorable scene, doctors casually move patients
from a geriatrics hospital into the street to be "scored" by one of the
drivers—something they call "Euthanasia Day."

Not surprisingly, the film ignited outrage among the public and
critics alike. Roger Ebert gave the movie zero stars and, foreshadowing the controversy to follow all violent media, noted that he was "torn
between walking out [of the theater] immediately and staying to witness a spectacle more dismaying than anything on the screen: the way
small children were digging gratuitous bloodshed."[3] As is often the
case, the public outcry and blistering reviews only served to make the
film more popular. The movie, which was made on a budget of only
$300,000, eventually earned nearly $5 million in ticket and rental sales.[4]

Recognizing the potential of such controversy to drive profits,
the computer company Exidy renamed the arcade game they'd been

working on *Death Race*. Although not officially based on the movie, there is no denying that *Death Race* was essentially an unlicensed spin-off of the film *Death Race 2000* (see Easter Egg 3). For a quarter, players were put behind the wheel of a crude-looking white car and given one minute to run over as many stick figures as possible. As in the film, hitting these figures earns players points—plus, they are rewarded by a high-pitched scream as each victim is replaced by a tombstone complete with cross. The game's arcade cabinet, featuring grinning skeleton grim reapers driving hot rods, only enhanced its sinister image, and it wasn't long before the game became more controversial than the film that inspired it. National media outlets and news shows like *60 Minutes* and NBC's *Weekend* covered the game and its "violent images" of blocky cars running over stick figures. Even the National Safety Council, an organization devoted to promoting safety and preventing accidental death, known mostly for its advocacy of things like seat belts, called the game "insidious," "morbid," and "sick, sick, sick."[5]

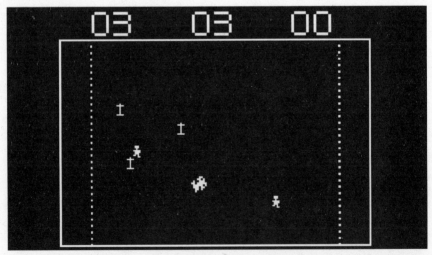

Exidy's Death Race—*the video game that almost caused a national panic*

Dr. Gerald Driessen, a researcher at the National Safety Council, became one of the first psychologists to publicly propose a link between violent video games and real-life violence when he suggested that the interactive nature of the game might cause a small proportion of the population to become violent when they got behind the wheels of *real* cars. He went on to point out that nearly 9,000 pedestrians were killed in the year *Death Race* was released, and that violence in interactive media is fundamentally different from television violence. "I shudder to think what will come next if this is encouraged," Dr. Driessen said gloomily, foreshadowing what advancing technology would eventually make possible. "It'll be pretty gory."[5] Predictably, the furor over the game caused its popularity to skyrocket; as more and more news stories were published, Exidy's profits increased, and sales of *Death Race* more than doubled.[5]

THE VIDEO ARCADE

Despite the wild success of a few games in the early- to mid-1970s, arcades were still in their infancy. Arcade *games* could be found in bars, pizza parlors, roller rinks, and elsewhere, but it wasn't until 1978, when Taito released the immensely popular *Space Invaders* in the United States, that arcades themselves really took off. This single game marks the beginning of the "golden age of arcades," which lasted until the mid-1980s when video arcades reached their peak popularity. It was a good time to be a gamer! Walking into your local arcade you were treated to a cacophony of sounds—from *Space Invaders, Asteroids, Galaxian, Missile Command, Berzerk, Defender, Battlezone, Pole Position, Rally-X, Frogger, Scramble, Dragon's Lair, Donkey Kong, Tempest, BurgerTime, Dig Dug, Joust, Q*bert, Zaxxon, Tron, Elevator Action, Spy Hunter,* and *Pac-Man* (to name a few).

While some of these games contained violence, parents were suddenly much more concerned about the seedy arcades their kids were playing in than what they were playing there. Keep in mind that arcades in the 1980s bore little resemblance to the family-friendly arcades of today—think *Dave & Buster's*—filled with ticket redemption machines and birthday parties. In the '80s, arcades were dark, foreboding places packed with sketchy-looking teens and young adults (granted, all teens are sketchy looking to some old folks). There was a constant din from both the game machines and the yelling of the patrons. Cigarettes dangled on the edge of arcade cabinets as youths competed for high scores in this *Lord of the Flies*–esque electronic dystopia. Your humble authors often frequented these dens of iniquity during their heyday in the mid-1980s. Much to our parents' dismay, our misspent youth mainly took the form of misspent quarters. By providing us with a venue in which to display our prowess at *Dragon's Lair* and *Spy Hunter*, video arcades were the sole source of our street cred (which likely explained our painful lack of success with our female peers). We also, fairly or not, blame arcades and our fellow patrons of these establishments for our adoption of unfortunate '80s hairstyles. (Markey favored the Flock of Seagulls look; Ferguson was pure mullet.)

Video arcades were blamed by the larger public for introducing a "bad element" into the community. In 1981, a group of 100 New Yorkers demonstrated outside an arcade in an effort to shut its doors. Their quarrel was not so much with the games inside but rather an increase in drug use and vandalism in the area.[6] As with the beachfront town of Marshfield, Massachusetts, which would enact their ban on video games the following year, this was not an isolated incident. Arcades were being shut down across the nation by activist parents intent on protecting their children from the dangerous influences lurking within these neon-drenched dungeons.

By the mid-1980s, arcade game profits had begun to decline, and over the next decade, thousands of arcades would close their doors. But the demise of video arcades was fueled not by parents, but by their children. The technological advances afforded by the Sega Genesis in 1989 and the Super Nintendo in 1991 allowed gamers to play close-to-arcade-quality games in their homes, and millions decided they'd rather fight aliens, drive sports cars, or be a star quarterback in front of their flickering TVs than at a video arcade. Although there are still arcades in the United States today, they are much less common, and focus on family entertainment or catering to the nostalgia of middle-aged adults eager to revisit the arcades of their youth.

And so as the '90s began, with arcades out of the picture and video games becoming a home-based activity—and thus one much more visible to parents—the public quickly refocused its attention and fear on virtual bloodshed.

THE YEARS OF VIRTUAL BLOOD: 1992 AND 1993

The publicity around games like *Death Race* and the dangers of arcades may have generated a general sense of unease about video games among the nongaming public, but three games released within a year of each other were about to ignite this unease into a full-blown panic. In 1992, if you went into your local bowling alley, movie theater, or pizza parlor, there's a good chance you'd see one of Capcom's *Street Fighter II* arcade machines (see Easter Egg 4), with a row of quarters lined up on the marquee. This immensely popular game almost single-handedly launched the "fighting game" genre, in which players engage in a series of one-on-one, close-combat fights. It didn't take long for other companies to launch their own fighting games in an effort to compete with *Street Fighter II* and get some of those quarters. Most of these games were fairly similar to each other, boasting colorful characters who could kick, punch, and string together special combination moves in an effort to defeat their opponent. However, in October of this same year, *Mortal Kombat* quickly set itself apart, taking both graphics and violence to an entirely new level.

Unlike *Street Fighter,* which was devoid of blood, *Mortal Kombat* was insanely vicious. Punching and kicking opponents splattered red pixels across the screen and characters could, quite literally, punch each other's heads off! But by far the most controversial gameplay element of *Mortal Kombat* was the "fatalities." While in other fighting games players would win by knocking their opponent to the floor, *Mortal Kombat* allowed gamers the chance to perform one final act of extreme violence on their defeated foe—murder. It wasn't unusual for a defeated player to find his character decapitated, immolated, electrocuted, impaled on spikes, or having his still-beating heart torn from his chest. Perhaps the most notorious fatality of all was the aptly named "spine rip," in which a character rips his opponent's head off with the spine still attached and holds it aloft, vertebrae dangling.

Adding to this was the relatively new technology employed in *Mortal Kombat,* which replaced the hand-drawn characters of other fighting games with the digital images of real actors and actresses. The photo-realistic characters in *Mortal Kombat* only heightened the realism of the violence: players were no longer punching or kicking a cartoonish opponent; they were punching and kicking actors like Daniel Pesina, who played the undead ninja Scorpion in the game. As you might expect, many parents were horrified the first time they saw their child rip the still-beating heart out of poor Daniel.

And while *Mortal Kombat* began as an arcade game, parents soon found this unsettling digital realism making its way into the family living room. The Sega CD was an accessory for the immensely popular Sega Genesis home-gaming console that, along with a few hardware upgrades, added the ability to play CD-based games. The main advantage of CD technology was that it allowed for an enormous increase in storage capacity. Whereas games had previously been around 8 megabytes in size, they could now reach an unbelievable 640 megabytes! Game manufacturers quickly took advantage of this additional storage space, not only by making games with improved graphics, but by incorporating full-motion digital video. Players were no longer limited to controlling a single digitized sprite, as in *Mortal Kombat*—now they could alter the sequences of entire interactive movies.

A game that took full advantage of this new technology was Digital Pictures' *Night Trap*. *Night Trap*'s game box harkened back to 1950s B movies, with a busty, frightened-looking blonde about to be attacked by a mysterious hooded man. "Non-Stop Action!" it promised, urging players to "watch the murderous action from hidden cameras" as "five beautiful co-eds are being stalked." While this sounds undeniably sinister, the player's job in the game was not to attack the hapless co-eds, but rather to protect them from a group of vampiric creatures called Augers by setting traps throughout their home. If players successfully foiled an Auger, they were treated to a brief movie scene in which the beautiful damsel in distress escapes from the creatures. If the player failed and an Auger snuck by the trap, a different scene would play, one of the helpless victim being attacked.

The actual violence in *Night Trap* was almost nonexistent. The special effects and acting (the most notable actress was *Diff'rent Strokes* star Dana Plato) were campy and exaggerated, more reminiscent of the low-budget vampire films of the 1950s than modern-day slasher movies. For example, in what became the most controversial murder sequence, we find one of the girls fixing her hair in the bathroom while dressed in a silky nightgown. Thinking a friend is hiding in the shower, she opens the door only to find one of the Augers; when she tries to escape, she is quickly surrounded by a pack of them (armed with a blood-draining machine—these were very modern vampires), who proceed to carry her away. There is absolutely no bloodshed, in this scene or any other. And remember, the player is not attacking the girls, but attempting to prevent them from being attacked. Regardless, the full-motion video scenes in *Night Trap* caused enough of an uproar to become part of the focus of a joint Senate Judiciary and Government Affairs Committee hearing on December 9, 1993, during which the game was called "sick" and "disgusting." It was suggested not only that *Night Trap* would encourage violence against women, but that exposing children to the game was akin to child abuse. *Night Trap* was eventually pulled from the shelves of major retailers, and Sega stopped selling it until a censored version, from which the controversial bathroom scene had been removed, could be created.

While senators in Washington were debating the dangers of *Night Trap*, a small software company in Mesquite, Texas, was set to release its newest game. On December 10, 1993 (the day after the Senate hearings), an employee at id Software uploaded a 2 MB file containing the game *Doom* to an FTP site at the University of Wisconsin–Madison. The game was being distributed as shareware, which allowed users to try out the first nine levels for free. If they liked it, they could send id Software forty dollars for access to the remaining levels. Within hours of being uploaded, *Doom* had made its way to players around the world, placing gamers in a first-person shooter perspective—instead of controlling a figure on the screen, the player *is* the figure, looking down the barrel of his own gun, the screen showing what the character sees as he moves through the virtual world. In *Doom*, this character is an unnamed space marine battling demonic hordes on the planet Mars. Within two years, an estimated ten million people were blasting demons and imps, and id Software was earning $100,000 a day.[7]

After learning that *Doom* had been installed on more computers than Windows 95, Microsoft decided to align themselves with the immensely popular game by rereleasing it for the Windows 95 platform (previous to this time, the game was mainly available on DOS). Then-CEO Bill Gates even created a promotional video for the release: it begins in the first-person perspective of *Doom*, moving through the familiar *Doom* corridors, blasting away with the iconic *Doom* shotgun. After the rampage is over, the camera pans back and you realize that the shooter is none other than Bill Gates, seen wearing a black trench coat and carrying a shotgun. Microsoft wanted so badly to tie themselves to the *Doom* brand, they even included a version of the game as an Easter egg (a hidden element usually accessible via an obscure sequence of keystrokes) in their Excel spreadsheet program—doubtless the most exciting thing ever to happen in Excel (see Easter Egg 5). Including the Windows version, the original *Doom* was eventually available on over a dozen different game consoles and operating systems. Subsequent sequels—and even a feature-length movie starring Dwayne "The Rock" Johnson—helped make *Doom* one of the most profitable video game franchises in history.

Doom was not the first of the first-person shooters. An earlier game from id Software, *Wolfenstein 3D*, allowed players to battle waves of Nazis from a first-person shooter perspective as they went about trying to kill a robot named Adolf Hitler. However, the more sophisticated graphics engine for *Doom* made it a huge step forward in immersing players in a true three-dimensional world. *Doom* was a fast-paced game in which players were forced to shoot quickly and kill often. It also allowed players to modify the game and create custom levels using what are called WAD files (short for "Where's All the Data?"), which could be shared among users. Many WAD files made relatively minor changes, such as altering weapons or adding extra levels. However, other files dramatically altered the game itself: in these modified versions of *Doom*, players could do everything from engage in a gunfight in the Old West to catch ghosts in a *Ghostbusters*-esque universe—there was even a WAD that let players kill the lovable/widely despised purple dinosaur Barney with a rocket launcher. Of course, with the freedom granted to gamers by WAD files came considerable controversy. A small minority contained pornographic images, replaced the game's demons with real-life people (typically politicians or celebrities), and later, even created levels where players could re-create horrific school shootings.

But perhaps the single aspect of *Doom* that most strongly influenced modern gaming was the introduction of online death matches. The goal in these matches was simple: kill (or, in gamer-speak, "frag") as many enemies as possible while keeping yourself from being fragged. What made this mode unique is that the enemies in question were not *Doom*'s computer-controlled demon hordes; they were other players—or at least their avatars. And unlike the multiplayer games of the past, gamers no longer had to be in the same physical location: thanks to increasingly widespread availability of phone modems, players could easily connect to friends' computers via a phone line or direct network and play against one another online. Soon gamers were networking computers in dorm rooms and offices around the country in order to hunt down and kill their coworkers and best friends in the virtual corridors of *Doom*. The amount of time employees spent playing this game became such a problem that many organizations were forced to make specific rules forbidding *Doom* death matches during business hours.[8]

Mortal Kombat, Night Trap, and *Doom* have become synonymous with video game violence and the public's fear of its dangers. After almost every horrific mass shooting, commentators are quick to invoke the name of at least one of these games. However, none of these were the most violent games of their day. Games like Epyx's *Barbarian: The Ultimate Warrior,* which let you behead foes with a broadsword to rescue a bikini-clad princess, or Monolith's *Blood,* in which the protagonist laughs like a sadist as he impales enemies on a pitchfork, featured just as much blood and gore.

The reason these three video games are singled out is because each popularized a new technology that the general public found shocking. *Mortal Kombat*'s digitized graphics seemed far more horrific than the hand-drawn graphics found in earlier fighting games. The movie-quality images in *Night Trap* frightened senators who had only previously seen *Pac-Man* gobbling dots (see Easter Egg 6). Fragging our friends in the impressive three-dimensional world of *Doom* was much more worrisome than virtually shooting them in Atari's blocky *Gunslinger.* It wasn't only the games that so bothered parents, politicians, and researchers—it was the advancing technology they embodied, which made the violence seem more realistic, and much scarier, especially to people unfamiliar with the technology.

WE RATE VIOLENCE

In the wake of controversies over *Mortal Kombat, Night Trap,* and *Doom,* the video game industry found itself in trouble. Responding to concerns voiced by media "watchdog" groups, the US Congress had not only held hearings on violent video games, they'd threatened federal regulation unless the industry did something to police itself. In response to this heightened governmental scrutiny, video game publishers and developers created the Entertainment Software Rating Board (ESRB). Much like the Motion Picture Association of America, which is responsible for film ratings, the ESRB is the nonprofit self-regulatory organization that assigns age and content ratings to video games.

A game's rating is determined by at least three trained "game raters" who work for the ESRB. The assigned raters sit around a large table, watching a DVD "highlight reel" created by the game publisher, containing all of the game's pertinent content. This includes typical gameplay, missions, and story scenes, along with the most extreme violent content. Afterward, the raters debate among themselves, ultimately choosing both a rating and "content descriptors." ESRB staff then reviews the raters' recommendation and may conduct a parity review to maintain consistency in rating assignments. Content descriptors are short phrases from a list created by the ESRB—things like "Animated Blood" and "Drug Reference." The process requires a majority consensus. Sometimes consensus is extremely easy to achieve: there probably wasn't much debate over whether or not *Mario Kart 8* should be rated E (for Everyone). Other times, raters may find it difficult to agree, especially for titles that seem to hover on the border between two rating categories. For example, the gloomy,

EARLY CHILDHOOD
Content is intended for young children.

EVERYONE
Content is generally suitable for all ages. May contain minimal cartoon, fantasy or mild violence and/or infrequent use of mild language.

EVERYONE 10+
Content is generally suitable for ages 10 and up. May contain more cartoon, fantasy or mild violence, mild language and/or minimal suggestive themes.

TEEN
Content is generally suitable for ages 13 and up. May contain violence, suggestive themes, crude humor, minimal blood, simulated gambling and/or infrequent use of strong language.

MATURE
Content is generally suitable for ages 17 and up. May contain intense violence, blood and gore, sexual content and/or strong language.

ADULTS ONLY
Content suitable only for adults ages 18 and up. May include prolonged scenes of intense violence, graphic sexual content and/or gambling with real currency.

ESRB video game rating categories

atmospheric *Batman: Arkham City* was rated T, while the remake of the fairly tame 2001 *Halo: Combat Evolved* received an M—despite these two titles having almost identical content descriptors (if anything, the T-rated *Batman* had more worrying descriptors than the M-rated *Halo*). Even the ESRB admitted that this was a case where the "M rating for *Halo* was undoubtedly at the lower end of the rating category spectrum and the T rating that *Batman: Arkham City* received was at the upper end of Teen."[9]

The game's developer may appeal a rating they think is unfair, but no game maker has ever done so. Instead, developers revise their games, toning down violent content in order to get a lower rating. In 2007, Rockstar Games (the company behind *Grand Theft Auto*) received an AO rating for their ultraviolent game *Manhunt 2*. Perhaps this should not have come as a surprise, given that the object of

the game was to quietly sneak up behind enemies in order to gruesomely execute them. However, because major retail chains refuse
to carry AO games and console manufacturers will not allow AO
games to work on their systems, such a rating would have effectively
banned the game entirely. To obtain a lower rating, Rockstar revised
the game by blurring the executions and completely altering one
particularly grisly variation that allowed players to perform an execution by ripping off an enemy's testicles while tearing out his throat
with a pair of pliers.[10] In the edited version, players would have to be
satisfied with using the pliers to beat their opponent to death. These
changes to the game were enough to earn the home console version
of *Manhunt 2* an M rating (the PC version of this game contains the
unaltered executions, along with the original AO rating). Thanks in
part to the controversy generated by the ESRB's initial concern over
the game's violent content, and the widely publicized alterations and
rating adjustment, the M-rated *Manhunt 2* went on to sell over 1.4
million copies worldwide.[11]

This episode caused some to question the accuracy of the ESRB
rating system, and less than a month after *Manhunt 2*'s Halloween
release, a group of US senators (led by Hillary Clinton and Joe Lieberman) sent an open letter to the ESRB challenging the integrity of their
rating process. However, there is little evidence to suggest such concerns are justified. Surveys have consistently found that both gamers
and parents tend to approve of the ESRB ratings assigned to particular games—in fact, people agree with the ESRB ratings about 95 percent of the time.[12] Not only that, but an undercover shopper operation
conducted by the Federal Trade Commission (FTC) found that the
ratings—and their associated age guidelines—are strongly enforced
by retailers.[13] In this secret operation, the FTC sent kids into stores
and movie theaters around the country to determine how easy it was
for children to consume adult media. As seen in the following figure,
it turns out that it was much more difficult for them to buy M-rated
video games than to access any other adult media, from R-rated movie

tickets to music bearing an "Explicit Content" label. Furthermore, of all the stores and movie theaters examined, the video game retailer GameStop was least likely to sell adult content to children. Only 9 percent of kids were able to walk away with a copy of *Manhunt 2* or *Grand Theft Auto* from this retailer, whereas a whopping 76 percent managed to buy DVDs of violent R-rated films like *Saw, Kill Bill,* and *Hostel* from Target. It therefore isn't surprising that parents believe the ESRB rating system is the most helpful and effective of all the entertainment rating systems, with 90 percent reporting that they find it useful.[14]

PERCENT OF CHILDREN WHO WERE ABLE TO PURCHASE

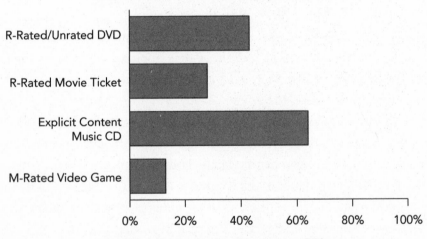

Accessibility of adult-related media content to children

THE LUST FOR VIRTUAL BLOOD

The adoption of the ESRB rating system turned out to be a double-edged sword for critics worried about video game violence. Although the ratings gave parents insight into which games might be particularly bloody, they also provided flexibility for game developers, who were able to produce games specifically for "Mature" audiences, games with more violence than some console makers would have previously allowed. For example, prior to implementation of the rating system, Nintendo strictly forbade games for its consoles from containing excessive violence, graphic deaths, or even mentioning words like "die" or "kill."[15] In an effort to avoid even the suggestion of death, it wasn't unusual for Nintendo games to refer to the number of "chances" or "tries" a player had left instead of "lives." Because of these rules, the version of *Mortal Kombat* released for the Super Nintendo system—predating the ESRB rating system—was censored by replacing blood with sweat and removing the game's signature violent fatalities. However, the year the ESRB rating system was adopted, Nintendo allowed *Mortal Kombat II* to be released on its home console in all its gory, unaltered glory. With a Mature rating, there was less need to worry about the PR ramifications of being associated with a controversial game. After all, Nintendo could assure irate parent groups that the game was not meant for children—it said so right on the box! As a result, Nintendo gamers could now join their friends on other platforms in slicing an opponent down the middle into two bloody halves.

Any concern the public had over the advent of fatalities on Super Nintendo was quickly eclipsed when the M-rated *Grand Theft Auto* was released for Sony's new PlayStation console. In *Grand Theft Auto,* players took control of a criminal for hire, performing various nefarious tasks for crime syndicates. The actual gore in the game was limited mostly to small pixelated patches of blood on the ground or a red tire track after striking someone with an automobile. What made the game unique was the unparalleled freedom it gave gamers, who could choose from a virtual smorgasbord of social deviance. For example, in one mission, players must drive around the virtual city in order to find and kill several rival gang members. They can accomplish this task in any number of ways: by running over the rivals with a car, gunning them down, or even bludgeoning them to death with a baseball bat. After getting their hands red with virtual blood, players learn the boss is feeling "horny" and are instructed to pick up a "bitch" in another area of the city and return her to head-quarters while avoiding a shootout. Gamers choose which missions to take on, and in addition are free to roam the virtual city, earning money by stealing cars or otherwise creating mayhem. Game mag-azines at the time praised *Grand Theft Auto* as innovative, techno-logically impressive, and extremely original, while also noting its "gleeful embrace of anarchy" and predicting that "wanna-be socio-paths" would have a lot of fun with the game.[16]

Over the next two decades, Rockstar, the company that devel-oped *Grand Theft Auto,* continued to embrace anarchy in a num-ber of sequels. With multiple light sources, dynamic perspective changes, and detailed, high-definition graphics, the latest iteration, *Grand Theft Auto V,* depicts a world so realistic it seems as if the player has just stepped out his or her front door. The ever-increasing hyperrealism of each installment of *Grand Theft Auto* is outpaced only by the escalation of the virtual violence—and by skyrocketing game sales. *Grand Theft Auto V* alone has sold more than 45 million copies and has earned over two billion dollars in revenue.[17] *Guin-ness World Records* recently recognized the game for breaking seven records: best-selling action-adventure video game in twenty-four hours, best-selling video game in twenty-four hours, fastest enter-tainment property to gross one billion dollars, fastest video game to gross one billion dollars, highest-grossing video game in twenty-four hours, highest revenue generated by an entertainment product in twenty-four hours, and most viewed trailer for a video game.[18]

Because games like *Grand Theft Auto* are so popular, many peo-ple forget that only about 11 percent of video games made each year are assigned an M rating.[19] But, like moths to a flame, peo-ple seem to be much more attracted to the relatively few M-rated games than they are to the more family-friendly games that make up the bulk of offerings. M-rated titles dominate the charts of the top-selling video games. In the past five years, more than 50 percent of the top-ten-selling video games were rated M. This lust for virtual blood has grown exponentially in the past fifteen years: when both the number of games sold and the violent content of those games is taken into account, the consumption of violent video games has increased more than 500 percent.[20]

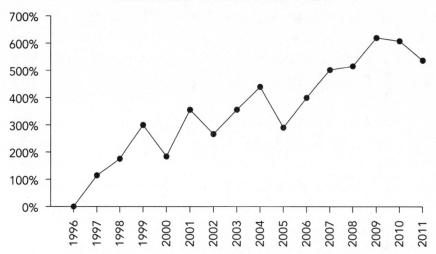

PERCENT CHANGE IN VIDEO GAME VIOLENCE CONSUMPTION

The increasing popularity of violent video games after the ESRB was created

Why are we attracted to such violence? In the real world, we go to great lengths to avoid the very situations we actively seek out in *Grand Theft Auto* and *Manhunt*. On the surface it seems illogical, but there are deep-seated reasons behind our attraction to virtual violence, and to understand them you need look no further than another form of media increasingly viewed on the flickering screens of computers—pornography.

It turns out that people, especially guys, like porn . . . a *lot*. It is estimated that in a single year, more than 100 million men in North America (about 80 percent of the male population over the age of fifteen) went looking for porn on the internet.[21] Researchers at the

University of Montreal even had to cancel a study examining the effects of pornography for lack of a control group—they couldn't find any men in their twenties who had never watched porn![22] Of course, the public's lust for dirty pictures is nothing new. The internet has made it much easier to obtain digital titillation than it was back in the days when youths were forced to search their father's sock drawer for the latest issue of *Playboy*. But porn has been around since the Paleolithic period, when our depraved ancestors created cave paintings of naked men and women with, er, exaggerated genitals and breasts. In our brains, sex equals reproduction, and in an effort to keep the human species chugging along, our evolutionary history has wired us (especially men) to be excited by the sight of naked people.

Our evolutionary history plays a similar role in our attraction to violence. We find playing a violent video game more exciting than, say, reading a book (well, except for this book, which is pretty exciting!) because violence has been an integral part of who we are as a species. If you found yourself walking down an ominous dark alley in the middle of the night, your heart would beat faster and your blood pressure would spike as your mind became alert to every sound and movement, creating sinister images out of the constantly shifting shadows. At this moment, you would certainly not be bored! After all, over the course of human history, vigilance in the presence of danger was crucial for survival.

In real life, the consequences are so dire that violence—or the threat of it—causes us anxiety, and so we avoid it. But our brains seem to understand that media violence is different. Violent video games provide us with the same intensity and stimulation as walking down that dark alley, but without the anxiety associated with the possibility of actually being brutally murdered. Our brains become excited by the graphic violence and the competition in *Manhunt* as if it were real, but because we also understand that it is not, we feel thrilled rather than frightened. The things that make a video game riveting, like single-handedly destroying an army of enemies in *Call of Duty*, are exaggerated versions of the things we find stirring in the real world—success, beating the odds, defeating an opponent. These games are essentially feeding into our basic evolutionary needs by providing us with supercharged (yet safe) versions of experiences we instinctually crave. In short, violent video games are popular because our minds are programmed to desire violent media. [23]

It might seem surprising that video games, which began only a little over forty years ago as a small white ball being struck between two lines, have morphed into something people simultaneously desire and fear. This didn't happen overnight. From *Death Race* and *Gun Fight* to *Mortal Kombat* and *Manhunt*, millions of years of human evolution and decades of developing technology all but guaranteed this would occur.

EASTER EGGS

I. Following the success of the prototype *Pong* machine placed in Andy Capp's Tavern, later versions of the arcade machine included three basic instructions: 1) insert quarter, 2) ball will serve automatically, and 3) avoid missing ball for high score.

2. *Pong* may have been responsible for starting the video game revolution, but it was not the first commercially available arcade machine. In 1971, Nolan Bushnell and Ted Dabney, who would later found Atari and create *Pong*, released the game *Computer Space*. Groundbreaking at the time, *Computer Space* allowed players the ability to control a crudely rendered rocket ship while attempting to shoot flying saucers. The game itself never reached the popularity of *Pong* due, in part, to its extremely complicated controls, which required players to use several buttons to control their spacecraft.[24]

3. Many early arcade games borrowed elements from films. *Computer Space*'s ships looked remarkably similar to the spaceships in *Flash Gordon*. But probably the first game truly based on a movie was Atari's *Shark Jaws*, released in 1975 as an unofficial tie-in with *Jaws*. This game was so strongly marketed as being related to the film that marketing material asked arcade owners to "cash in on the popularity, interest and profits associated with sharks." Even across the top of the cabinet, the word "shark" was so tiny in the title "shark JAWS" that it looked as if the game was simply called "JAWS"![25]

4. It is perhaps a bit sad that no one ever seems to discuss the first *Street Fighter* game. Released in 1987, it introduced the characters Ryu and Ken, who would appear in the over one dozen sequels. What was most unusual about the original game was that players could "punch" pressure-sensitive rubber buttons to attack an opponent. The harder a player hit the button, the harder Ken or Ryu punched their foes. Ultimately, the pressure-sensitive

buttons were removed from later versions of the game and the wild success of *Street Fighter II* caused the original *Street Fighter* to be slowly forgotten.

5. To access this hidden *Doom*: 1) open a blank worksheet in Excel 95; 2) select the entire 95th row; 3) tab to column B; 4) go to Help/About; 5) hold ctrl-alt-shift and click on the "tech support" button; 6) a window will appear with the level!

6. During the 1993 hearing on video game violence, it became painfully obvious most of the senators and expert witnesses who were worried about *Night Trap* had never actually played the game. At various times it was claimed that it was the player in *Night Trap* who was murdering the women and that, once successful, these women were hung on meat hooks and their blood was drained into wine bottles (neither of which is true).[2]

LEVEL 2:

TEACHING US
TO FEAR

Back in 2005, at the height of the Second Gulf War, then-senator Hillary Clinton held a press conference to focus national attention on the scourge that was putting so many of our nation's youth at risk: violent video games. Along with senators Joseph Lieberman, Tim Johnson, and Evan Bayh, Clinton was introducing the Family Entertainment Protection Act, a law that would have put the teeth of federal enforcement behind the existing Entertainment Software Ratings Board (ESRB) classification of video game content. While the age guidelines associated with these ratings were already enforced by major retailers—who were obviously invested in maintaining their family-friendly images—doing so was technically voluntary. The proposed bill would have changed all that: any retailer who sold an M-rated game (similar to an R-rated movie) to a minor would have faced fines and community service.

"It is almost routine in popular games for players to spray other people with Uzis, to drive over pedestrians, to kill police officers, to attack women, and in some cases even to engage in cannibalism,"[26] said Clinton. Referencing the work of several researchers[27] (since discredited[28]), she continued, "According to the most comprehensive statistical analysis yet conducted, violent video games increase aggressive behavior as much as lead exposure decreases children's IQ scores . . . Everybody knows lead poisoning is bad for children, well I want everybody to know that exposure to violent video games is also bad for children." Later, Clinton assured listeners that the legislation "is not about government censorship or regulation of content. Quite simply it is about protecting children and empowering parents. We need to treat violent video games the way we treat tobacco, alcohol, and pornography." Clinton wrapped things up by saying, "If you put it just really simply, these violent video games are stealing the innocence of our children."

Clinton's bill never made it out of committee and, in 2011, the US Supreme Court ruled that all such legislation was unconstitutional and that research evidence could not support claims that it was necessary.[29] The court declared that video games are art and that, if they are sometimes violent, this is no different from literature, film, or even fairy tales. But if comparing video games to lead poisoning seems bizarrely overdramatic, Clinton was hardly the only one making such inflammatory statements. Politicians seemed more passionate in their rhetoric about video game violence than they did discussing mental health reform, the war in Iraq, poverty, or any number of issues urgently affecting the lives of young people. Yet, unlike those exposed to lead, millions of children were playing violent video games and growing up just fine. What was going on here?

MORAL PANIC!

Your authors are the product of the 1980s, a period that produced the mullet, the Walkman, Cabbage Patch Kids, the Rubik's Cube, and the Smurfs (see Easter Egg 1). It also produced a number of great moral panics. People panicked over Satanism, *Dungeons & Dragons*, heavy metal lyrics, and microwave ovens slowly giving us cancer via harmful radiation (indeed, we still talk about "nuking" our food). What exactly is a moral panic? The term refers to a tendency for societies to develop overblown fears of an innocuous scapegoat or "folk devil," which is then blamed for a real (or often imagined) social problem. Put simply, a moral panic occurs when our fears of an object or activity greatly exceed the actual threat posed to society by that object or activity.

Moral panics can focus on just about anything. These days, they typically involve youth in some way, though they can center on any group—like women or the poor—seen as a threat to the establishment. For instance, in the late 1980s and early 1990s, the country was gripped by fears that Satanic cults were kidnapping young children and sexually abusing them as part of their rituals. This panic was fueled by the testimony of children detailing outlandish experiences with magic spells, animal sacrifice, and abuse orchestrated by a shadowy conspiracy of elite occultists. It is now believed that many of the children were influenced in their accounts by panicking parents or therapists and overzealous prosecutors, but not before criminal trials ensued and some reputations were forever tarnished. Perhaps the most famous example is the McMartin Preschool case, in which the proprietors of a day care center were put on trial for the sexual abuse of children in their charge. Many of the allegations were decidedly bizarre and included reports of secret tunnels under the preschool, that some of the abusers could fly, of orgies held at airports, and even that action star Chuck Norris was one of the abusers. Although the day care center's owners were ultimately acquitted, the trial went on for years, leaving the accused in jail for the entire duration.[30]

Some moral panics focus on kids themselves, typically over some ostensibly scandalous behavior. Many older adults have a general distrust of kids (particularly teens), and every generation seems to think the next has slipped to some new depth of moral depravity shocking in comparison to the idyllic memories of their own long-gone child-hood. This fear of youth has been termed *juvenoia*,[31] and some have found that catering to widespread fears of youth culture can be good business indeed. Take the legend of "rainbow sex parties." An idea popularized in the early 2000s, rainbow sex parties allegedly involved teen orgies in which girls would wear different shades of lipstick and take turns performing oral sex on boys, giving them, in effect, a rainbow of lipstick shades on their penises. This urban leg-end fed into parental fears of teenagers' hormones run amok (noth-ing new there), and gave television producers and the professionally outraged plenty of fodder. Alas, no evidence ever emerged that rain-bow parties were a real thing.[32] We are not saying that teens never do dumb, risky stuff, just that there's little reason to believe that this is particularly new to any generation, or that there's a sudden wave of previously unmatched depravity among teens.

Media has also been a rich target for moral panics. Very often when a new form of media or technology is released, society goes through a period of moral panic in which this media or technology is blamed for any number of social ills, whether real or merely per-ceived. These panics can be explained in large part by generation gaps in adopting new technology or media. The young are far more proficient at adapting to innovation than are the old. This can create a perception among older adults that they are losing control of the culture they helped shape—which, of course, they inevitably will—to the very youth they fear and view as morally bankrupt.

Even the Bible has been the source of a moral panic fueled by advancing technology. In Catholic Europe prior to the fifteenth cen-tury, most people were illiterate, and reading the Bible was reserved for the religious class. Books were largely created by hand, making them scarce to begin with, and Bibles were printed mainly in Latin (or Greek in Orthodox countries)—languages only taught to the educated elite. Ordinary folk learned about their religion through the teachings of their priest (though Masses themselves were often in Latin, so one imagines there was a fair amount of confusion). This was an intentional hierarchy—the notion of a direct relationship between a person and his or her God was an innovation yet to come in European religion.

In the fifteenth century, the invention of the mechanical printing press changed everything. Books were easier to mass-produce, and finally available to the masses: demand for Bibles in native languages (English, German, French, etc.) exploded. But the authorities, both religious and secular, were concerned that the common folk weren't equipped to read the Bible themselves. They believed commoners might misinterpret the Bible and get lost on the wrong moral path, ultimately fomenting rebellion, heresy, and the end of society as they knew it (granted, the Protestant Reformation was right around the corner, so these weren't entirely irrational fears). They introduced severe penalties for producing non-Latin Bibles, and men like William Tyndale who flouted them were charged with heresy and executed. It was a prototypical example of moral panic sparked by fear that new media will result in a loss of control over society.

In the five hundred or so years since then, we've seen countless innovations in media, arts, and technology. Almost any you can name has set off some form of moral panic.[33] Waltzes, when they were introduced, raised concerns that the close contact between dancers would provoke sexual immorality. In the nineteenth century, society elders were concerned about women reading novels.[34] It was thought that women were unable to distinguish reality from fiction (a refrain commonly heard today about youth), and that reading romantic novels would send them running off with stable boys en masse, neglecting their duties and leading to the collapse of the family. Immigrant and minority groups were also considered particularly "vulnerable" to the influence of movies and dime novels.[35] As the industrial revolution and educational reforms combined to create the concept of adolescence (before this, you were a child until you were old enough to work, and then you were an adult), young people increasingly became the focus of society's moral concern. Dance halls, short bobbed hair on women, new forms of music—especially those, like jazz and rock and roll, that originated within the African American community—were all sources of moral panic. The dangerous phonograph, the salacious radio, immoral moving pictures, and the surely corrupting television set: none escaped censure.

In the 1950s, society turned its eye to comic books. Like pulp novels, only illustrated and popular with children, most comic books of the time focused on horror, science fiction, or crime, and could be quite macabre. One psychiatrist, Fredric Wertham,[36] became well known for arguments that comic books caused not only juvenile delinquency but homosexuality. (Batman and Robin were secretly gay, you see. We're not making this up.) In 1954, Wertham testified before the Senate Subcommittee on Juvenile Delinquency, in hearings that led the government to threaten to regulate the content of comics (sound familiar?). The result was the Comics Code Authority, an industry self-censorship regime that persisted into the twenty-first century. The code eliminated all nudity, profanity, and any graphic violence from the pages of comic books. Words like "horror" and "terror" were not permitted in comic titles. Law-enforcement officials were never to be shown in a negative light, nor was any sympathy toward the bad guys allowed. Good must *always* triumph over evil, and criminals be punished for their misdeeds. This self-imposed censorship resulted in considerable changes to the comic book industry, with many companies that failed to adopt the code forced out of business. However, as time went on, society became less panicked about the dangers of graphic novels—moving on to fret over ever new threats to America's youth—and the comic book industry eventually abandoned the Comics Code. Today, not only are we no longer worried about the dangers of Batman, but it has recently been discovered that the person largely responsible for the moral panic over comic books, Dr. Wertham, overstated and potentially even fabricated much of his data.[37]

During the 1980s, the big concern was rock music, with many older adults convinced that rock bands—ranging from Cyndi Lauper (seriously, we're not making this up either!) to AC/DC and Ozzy Osbourne—were promoting suicide, violence, promiscuous sex, and occultism. Many were supposedly including subliminal or backwards lyrics that would entice listeners to all sorts of misdeeds. The name AC/DC (which is an electrical term—hence the band's signature lightning bolt logo) was said to be thinly veiled code for Satanism, standing not for "Alternating Current/Direct Current" but "Anti-Christ/Devil's Children." (Granted, it probably didn't help that the guitarist appeared with devil's horns on the cover of one album.) Cyndi Lauper's song "She Bop," an extended double entendre for masturbation, was condemned for encouraging sexual immorality. Apparently people were concerned "She Bop" might get teens running around masturbating everywhere (as if they needed Lauper's help for that).

All this naughty rock music prompted congressional action. In 1985, Tipper Gore, wife of then-senator Al Gore, and Susan Baker, wife of then-treasury secretary James Baker, founded the Parents Music Resource Center (PMRC), an advocacy group concerned about explicit lyrics in rock music. The group released a list of songs that highlighted their concerns, called the "Filthy Fifteen," with acts like Twisted Sister, Prince, and Def Leppard joining obvious deviants AC/DC and Cyndi Lauper. Leveraging their connection to Washington insiders, the PMRC then held hearings before Congress, hearings that became something of a show trial for '80s music. Many musicians testified against censorship, including John Denver, Dee Snyder of Twisted Sister, and Frank Zappa. After the usual array of pearl-clutching and scholarly hyperbole, the government threatened action and the industry prevented it by agreeing to slap CDs and albums with the "Explicit Lyrics" sticker we're all familiar with today.

This sticker is arguably one of the great failures of censorship efforts directed at art. After all, who would argue that there's less profanity or explicit content in music today than in the 1980s? The introduction of the sticker in the 1980s led some companies like Walmart to refuse to sell albums with the sticker, but this put few brakes on the music industry. Some argue that the sticker became a selling point, as telling people that they can't have something makes it forbidden fruit they only end up wanting more.[38] On the other hand, research hasn't always borne this out, with some studies suggesting that youth are more concerned with the perceived quality of the media than its warning labels.[39]

Around the same time Congress was discussing the dangers of Cyndi Lauper, several musicians, most notably Ozzy Osbourne, were sued by parents who held them responsible for the suicides of their teenaged children. In 1984, nineteen-year-old John McCollum shot himself while listening to an Osbourne album that included the song "Suicide Solution" (which is a song about the dangers of alcoholism, not a pro-suicide anthem). The family sued Osbourne and his record company, arguing that the song caused their son to kill himself. Had the courts agreed, this could have signaled considerable liability concerns for artists in all realms who touched upon edgy themes. However, the courts decided against the parents, ruling that music was not the cause of these suicides.[40]

Moral panic seems to be a constant in a society where nearly everything is always changing, but the moral panics of the past, from rock and roll suicide and Satanism to comic-book-inspired juvenile delinquents, all seem to pale in comparison to what has become the most famous moral panic of the late twentieth and early twenty-first centuries—violent video games.

VIDEO GAME MORAL PANICS

As we covered in Level One, people were blaming video games for society's problems long before Clinton held her press conference in

2005. As early as 1983, C. Everett Koop, the US Surgeon General, suggested that video games (he was mainly talking about *Asteroids*, *Space Invaders, Centipede,* and other popular shoot-'em-up games of the time) were a leading cause of family violence.[41] By 1993, Congress was threatening the video game industry with potential regulation or censorship, holding its *Night Trap* hearings and strong-arming the development of the ESRB ratings system.

However, it was not until the close of the 1990s saw a series of school shootings perpetrated by white suburban kids that "blame the game" really took off. Mass homicides were nothing new to the US, but when they'd happened before, news media put little effort into searching for societal causes and instead blamed the perpetrators. In 1993, Nathan Dunlap, a nineteen-year-old African American, visited the Chuck E. Cheese's where he'd worked as a cook before being fired. He ate a sandwich and played a video game called *Hogan's Alley.* Then he loaded a .25 caliber pistol in the restroom and hid there until the last customers had left for the night. Upon exiting the restroom, Dunlap went on a shooting spree that ended in the death of four employees. In the weeks following, the media and politicians focused on Dunlap's desire for revenge, his hatred and rage. An article quoted the police chief as saying, "This is just a tragic, tragic example of what can happen if something is not done about the level of violence existing with these kids today," but nowhere did anyone mention violent movies, television shows, or video games. Violence among minority kids in urban areas didn't often garner much attention, and when it did, the violence was blamed on the kids and communities themselves. But horrific acts of violence by white kids, supposedly coming from nice families, violated the prejudice that youth violence was a minority/urban phenomenon. Some scholars, such as James Ivory at Virginia Tech, argue that our racial prejudices about violence lead us to seek out external explanations when white kids commit crimes.[42] Therefore, if an African American youth, like Dunlap, commits a horrific act of violence, it is because he is full of rage or hatred, but when a "nice" white kid shoots up a school, he must have been brainwashed or under the corrupting influence of something outside himself—something like video games.

Perhaps the epitome of this was the 1999 Columbine massacre in Littleton, Colorado. On April 20th of that year, two teenagers, Eric Harris and Dylan Klebold, entered their school with the intention of destroying it. Both boys had a history of severe depression and issues with rage and anger.[43] For months they planned the attack on their school, hoping to eclipse the Oklahoma City bombing in scope. The two teens had initially intended to bomb the cafeteria and shoot surviving students as they left the school; however, when their bombs failed to explode, they were forced to improvise, and entered the building shooting. Over the course of about an hour, they roamed the halls shooting at terrified students and staff. All in all, twelve innocent students and one heroic teacher were ruthlessly murdered, and twenty-one others injured, before Harris and Klebold committed suicide in the school library.

The Columbine massacre set off a massive quest for answers. Why did two suburban kids commit such a horrific crime? Were they bullied and thus enacting revenge? Were they part of a sup-posedly antisocial goth "trench coat mafia" music culture? Were they reenacting scenes from the movie *The Matrix?* None of these explanations turned out to fit. Harris and Klebold weren't partic-ularly goth, nor did it seem that they were bullied any more than most kids, and links with *The Matrix* appeared to originate from the imaginations of observers rather than the perpetrators themselves. But Harris and Klebold were indeed fans of the violent video game *Doom*, which involved roaming mazes shooting at zombies and monsters. Primitive by today's standards, *Doom* nonetheless looked like the kind of "murder simulator" some anti-game activists had been warning about.[44]

With little doubt, the Columbine massacre was a pivotal event in cementing in the public's mind the notion that violent video games and school shootings were linked. It also created a cottage industry among scholars: violent video game research. As can be seen in the figure below, the number of research articles on the topic of violent video games begins to dramatically increase in the years after Columbine, continuing to soar to the present day.

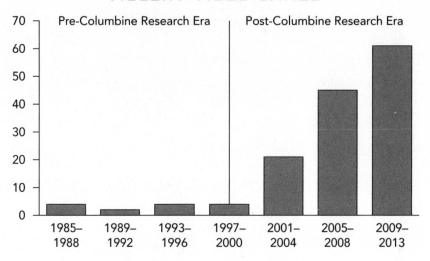

NUMBER OF STUDIES EXAMINING
VIOLENT VIDEO GAMES

Scholarly publications on violent video games by year

As is often the case for high-profile mass shooting events, the Columbine massacre led to hearings before Congress, and as would become predictable, these hearings suggested the blame for this horrific act lay with media violence.[45] Several scholars argued that media violence had an impact on society on par with the impact of smoking on lung cancer. For instance, prominent anti-game activist and social psychologist Dr. Craig Anderson testified before the US Senate Commerce Committee shortly after the Columbine massacre, saying, "[E]ven though one cannot reasonably claim that a particular act of violence or that a lifetime of violence was caused exclusively by the perpetrator's exposure to violent entertainment media, one can reasonably claim that such exposure was a contributing causal factor. More importantly for this hearing, my research colleagues are correct in claiming that high exposure to media violence is a major contributing cause of the high rate of violence in modern US society."[46]

How much research was there to support such a sweeping claim? Well, effectively none. So why, even without evidence, were politicians and some scholars so quick to blame violent media for the tragedy of Columbine? Because, in short, that's what a frightened and emotional public pays them to do. Both of your authors have children. We remember the days after the 2012 Sandy Hook shooting, in which twenty elementary school children were killed. Along with the national trauma of such a horrible act of violence, we recall our fear and sense of powerlessness at the thought of sending our kids to school with the possibility of not getting them back. When people experience such strong emotions, such a sense of powerlessness, it's only natural to try to reassert a feeling of influence over an event, even if that feeling is illusory. With these awful crimes, it becomes important for us to identify a culprit, and to look for ways to rid our society of that bogeyman to give us a sense of asserting control. Understandably, this causes us to turn toward authorities and political representatives to do something, anything, to prevent such a tragic event from happening again. For legislators, it helps if this bogeyman is something they can be forcefully against without losing votes. And since older adults control most of the power in our society—they are the ones who read the news, vote, and control the purse strings—their fears are the ones that count.

WHY WE PANIC

In an ideal world of rationally minded people, the process of testing a belief would be a logical, scientific one. A person might develop a hypothesis, understanding that it's only a hypothesis and that it may be wrong. Then the person would look for data to confirm or refute the hypothesis, being particularly attuned to the latter. Once all the data were in, the person would evaluate it dispassionately to see whether the hypothesis held up and, of course, would remain open to further data.

Were we all robots, we might be able to do this. Instead we are frail, emotional human beings who tend to latch on to cherished beliefs and hold on for dear life, whatever may come! As a substitute to testing those beliefs rigorously, we cherry-pick evidence that supports our predetermined beliefs and ignore that which does not. Cherished beliefs lead to pseudoscientific industries (among both scholars and advocates) that produce faux data to fuel those beliefs and stoke the flames of a moral panic.

The diagram above is of a moral panic cyclone (based on theories illuminated by David Gauntlett[47]) and demonstrates the basic way in which a moral panic begins and becomes self-perpetuating. To understand how it works, let's start at the top of the wheel, in box number one. Society (or at least the members of society who have most of the influence) comes to a decision, usually based on a "gut feeling," such as: *video games are bad*. Because these members of society control most of the money and votes, this sets up incentives for other elements of society to support those fears (box number two). Politicians call for action against video games. News media covers the supposed harms of video games with breathless concern. Should a young man, who happens to also play video games, do something horrible, news coverage and politicians will focus on the idea that video games likely contributed to this horrible something. This is all meant to serve a segment of the population that doesn't know much about video games, but doesn't trust or like this newer digital medium.

The trouble is, this pattern can have an influence on the scientific community. Scientists are, ultimately, human. We love to get grant money. We like seeing our names in newspaper headlines! We like the praise and adulation we get for "protecting children." Who doesn't want to protect children! Our professional organizations, such as the American Academy of Pediatrics and American Psychological Association, enjoy the prestige and influence that come with identifying social problems they and their members can "fix." To advance their agendas, politicians often call for research, while signaling what they wish the results of that research to be (box number three). For example, after the 2012 Sandy Hook shooting by twenty-year-old Adam Lanza, Senator Jay Rockefeller called for "research" by saying, "Recent court decisions demonstrate that some people still do not get it. They believe that violent video games are no more dangerous to young minds than classic literature or Saturday morning cartoons. Parents, pediatricians, and psychologists know better. These court decisions show we need to do more and explore ways Congress can lay additional groundwork on this issue. This report will be a critical resource in this process."[48] The "report" was to be a review by the National Academy of Sciences that examined the scientific literature regarding the influence of violent video games on children. But Senator Rockefeller made clear what he intended the results of the report to be. Under such intense political pressure, the scientific process can't hope to function effectively or objectively. This kind of political intrusion into science can only do damage, creating pseudoscience rather than reliable information.

The finalized politicized research is often oversimplified, exaggerated, and promoted breathlessly by news media and politicians (box number four). Witness Hillary Clinton's suggestion that video games have negative effects on our health comparable to those caused by smoking, alcohol, and lead poisoning. Such comparisons should have raised red flags of skepticism, and indeed, they have since been debunked. But at the time, they fit the alarmist narrative, and so people repeated them. Most people don't do much to fact-check information, even extreme claims, that corresponds with what they already want to believe. Bad science gives cover for advocacy and political agendas. Extreme claims make for great newspaper headlines and online "clickbait," and the general public only hears a select view from the research field. Sensationalistic language only further fuels society's unwarranted fear of this new technology (box one again), thereby creating an even greater moral panic. And round and round we go!

IDENTIFYING A MORAL PANIC

Science does identify real problems and threats to public health: global warming, say, or the dangers of smoking cigarettes. On one hand, how do you differentiate good science from pseudoscientific muck? On the other, how do you distinguish appropriate scientific skepticism from antiscience tin-foil-hatism? These are not easy questions. A lot of really bad science shows up even in peer-reviewed journals, so looking for the publication outlet of a scientific study isn't quite enough. Below, we offer a few guidelines that may help you identify a moral panic, and distinguish it from a true problem.

EXTREME CLAIMS COME BEFORE DATA

One indication that you may have entered the land of moral panic is that pundits and politicians are making shocking claims about some perceived threat to the moral fiber of society. This often takes the form of informing the public that today's youth are engaged in some immoral or harmful activity we wouldn't have dreamed of in our day. Look for language such as "Kids today are doing X younger and younger" or "shocking new trend in youth behavior" or "technology X is having a profound impact on our kids' behavior." Particularly when a stunning problem related to youth behavior seems to emerge from nowhere, this is often a sign that a moral panic is gearing up.

With video games, remember, politicians and anti-media activists were complaining about their supposed effects on violence long before there was data to support such claims. Video game research didn't really get rolling until the late '80s and, through the '90s, researchers were pretty honest about acknowledging there wasn't much evidence to support beliefs that even the most violent games were harmful.[49] That only changed after Columbine, when scholars heavily invested in criticizing violent television switched their focus to violent video games. We'll discuss this in more detail in the next chapter, but, in effect, the focus of scholarship changed to fit the moral panic. Beliefs about the dangers of video games came first, and then dubious social science capitalized on those fears.

Contrast this with other fields, such as research into climate change, or the influence of smoking on lung cancer. In these fields, the data built up first, facing initial skepticism among scientists and the public alike. The slow, steady accumulation of evidence eventually changed public opinion. In a moral panic, public opinion comes first, and specific types of research answers are then demanded. This brings us to our second guideline.

PUBLIC CALLS FOR RESEARCH SUPPORTING THE MORAL PANIC

One of the fundamental problems with moral panics, particularly longer lasting ones, is that they damage the scientific process. This happens when politicians or activists call for "studies" that will help them do something to fix the supposed crisis behind the panic. Watch for language from politicians calling for "research" that will help them understand how to best regulate media. In this case, research not into violence but into how video games contribute to it.

The 2012 Sandy Hook shooting provided rich examples of this. Just days after the tragedy, and with no official word of whether the shooter played violent games at all, Senator Rockefeller made his call for research into violent video games that would help "explore ways Congress can lay additional groundwork on this issue. This report will be a critical resource in this process." Calling explicitly for research that will move forward a particular agenda or policy goal is a recipe for pseudoscience. These rabid calls for one-sided research epitomized the era from the late '90s to the 2012 Sandy Hook shooting. The result was a huge pool of junk science that kept repeating the same basic research mistakes (poor measures of aggression, lack of standardization, lack of careful matching of games to ensure they only varied in violent content, and a failure to control for other variables in correlational studies), even after these errors in research had been pointed out again and again.

We're not the only ones to think so. The Supreme Court of the United States pointed out the very same thing in their decision in the 2011 *Brown v. Entertainment Merchants Association* (EMA) case, which considered whether regulation of violent games was constitutional.[29] Referring to several decades of accumulated research, the Court said, "These studies have been rejected by every court to consider them, and with good reason," going on to discuss how little such studies told us about the real world.

THE GOLDILOCKS EFFECT

Another thing to look for is questions along the lines of "Why can't kids just enjoy the media I enjoyed when I was young?" There's a great example of this in Fox News' coverage of *Mass Effect. Mass Effect* was a 2008 space-action game. Over the course of the thirty-plus-hours of gameplay, players have the opportunity to romance another character, potentially leading to a momentary tasteful sex scene toward the end of the game, in which a computerized woman's buttocks are briefly visible. The whole thing is about as titillating as what you might see in a PG-13–rated movie, but nonetheless it set off a firestorm, some pundits claiming the scene was the equivalent of hard-core pornography. A Fox News program featured a panel of "experts" discussing the controversy above the headline "SE'XBOX? New Video Game Shows Full Digital Nudity and Sex" (which, in fact, the game did not). One "expert" claimed *Mass Effect* would harm children's future sexual and social development, despite later admitting she hadn't bothered to play or even look at the game. Watching this panel, it was clear that the panelists were both unfamiliar and uncomfortable with this media. Said one: "This made me feel old watching this. Whatever happened to Atari and pinball and Pac-Man?"[50]

This attitude is typical of every generation: it's what we call "the Goldilocks Effect." Essentially, each generation thinks it got media "just right." The generation before us was too conservative, they were "stick in the muds" who just "didn't get" the music and media important to us. But these kids coming along next, well—they're totally out of control! And so the cycle repeats, generation after generation.

"SAVE THE CHILDREN!" MENTALITY

Saving children is obviously a good thing. We're not suggesting otherwise! But many moral panics adopt a defensive posture in which questioning the panic becomes tantamount to not caring for children. Granted, many moral panics actually *target* youth and portray them or their culture negatively, but they usually adopt the language of paternalistic protection while doing so. Those who argue against the panic are accused of either not caring about kids or of being in the pocket of a big, bad media industry.

Sadly, we've even seen this type of behavior among academic researchers. Some scholars, invested in promoting anti-media theories, have taken to implying that skeptics are the equivalent of "holocaust deniers,"[51] that they are "industry apologists,"[52] or are motivated by "building careers on contrarianism,"[53] rather than by a commitment to scientific truth. This type of language is characteristic of any ideological or religious system aggressively defending its beliefs from scrutiny by attacking critics personally. It's a warning sign that people are defending a belief system emotionally, not objectively subjecting it to reality testing as scientists should.

One of your authors (Ferguson) had an amusing run-in with this. Several months after the 2012 Sandy Hook shooting and in the midst of the ensuing (and ultimately misplaced) moral panic, Ferguson appeared on CBS's *Face the Nation* to discuss violent video games. The panel of guests also included a former FBI agent, a congressman, an advocate for the mentally ill, and Tim Winter, a representative of the Parents Television Council—the same anti-media advocacy group that blew a gasket over the brief exposure of Janet Jackson's breast during the 2004 Super Bowl halftime show. Everyone on the panel, with the exception of Winter, largely agreed that video games were not a cause of the Sandy Hook shooting. Winter's argument to the contrary was long on hyperbole but short on data. At the end of the segment, apparently realizing that he couldn't win on the facts, Winter referred to Ferguson, saying: "Sadly, just as the tobacco industry was able to find researchers to support their notion that their products weren't harmful, so, too, has the entertainment industry." "I'd like to respond to that!" Ferguson can be heard trying to interject, but he is cut off as the show ends.[54] (For the record, neither of the authors of this book have ever received incentives, financial or otherwise, from any media industry.) Failing to provide evidence of harm and then suggesting opponents are lining their pockets at the expense of children's health is the tactic of those without science on their side.

These are just a few of the red flags that might help identify a moral panic. In general, whenever society, through news media, politicians, and advocate groups, seems wound up about a supposed looming threat to morality—especially one involving media, our sexual behavior, or new naughty trends among youth—it's time to be suspicious. Unfortunately, moral panics can be damaging. As we saw with misplaced fears about Satanic ritual abuse, they can greatly damage the lives of individuals caught up in them. They routinely disparage youth and promote anti-youth attitudes among older adults, alienating young people in the process. But most crucially, they can distract us from more pressing issues. As we will learn in the next chapter, some researchers and organizations have used the public's panic over video games to secure funding to conduct questionable studies seemingly designed to further inflame the public's fear. For decades, these behaviors have distracted us from issues that actually *do* influence aggression and violence, such as poverty, mental illness, and educational disparities.

However, the story of the science examining violent video games is at a turning point. The moral panic set off by *Doom* and Columbine may have hijacked the scientific process, but in recent years a group of rebellious young scholars has begun to topple the well-established empire of anti–video game researchers . . .

EASTER EGG

1. Ferguson would like it to be known that he detests the Smurfs and did not agree to include a reference to the Smurfs in this sentence. Markey believes that Ferguson is simply a "Grouchy Smurf" for not recognizing all the Smurfy joy the Smurfs bring to the Smurfy world of Smurfy nostalgia. "La la la-la la la, sing a happy song."

LEVEL 3:

SCIENCE WARS

Back in 2000, the Pulitzer Prize–winning author Richard Rhodes wrote an article in the *New York Times* discussing the limitations and overstatements of the television violence research field.[55] As Rhodes noted, media research is often characterized by crude and clumsy research designs, matched in dubiousness only by the alarmist rhetoric of scholars claiming that media causes violent crime. In response to Rhodes' article, researchers Rowell Huesmann and Leonard Eron, longtime critics of violent TV, wrote a rather perturbed essay not just defending their work (which would be natural), but personally attacking Mr. Rhodes.[56] They wrote:

> "It is also clear that Mr. Rhodes is not an unbiased observer. He has a conflict of interest when he writes on violence. Not only is his own ego wrapped up in the view that he has been damaged by being abused as a child, but his own financial well-being depends on the sales of his book, *Why They Kill* which takes the viewpoint that media violence is unimportant and being violently abused is important . . . Finally, if he were really an unbiased observer, he might discuss the evidence that

individual differences in testosterone plays a role in aggression. But as one who has publicly confessed to taking testosterone regularly, that might have been hard for him to do."

In fact, Rhodes' book *Why They Kill*[57] isn't about media violence in particular, although he does mention some of the same critiques of the research included in his *New York Times* piece. His use of testosterone, it happens, is treatment for a medical condition.[58] Finally, accusing someone of being incapable of scholarly objectivity because he was abused as a child, disparaging the victim's view that his abuse was damaging, and suggesting that his status as a victim is a matter of "ego" are all indefensible, and outright bizarre when you consider those writing are *psychologists*. How could aggression researchers be so, well, mean?

Within the world of video game research, a David and Goliath battle is under way. The Goliaths are a well-organized, politically connected, and well-funded group of senior scholars who have been linking violent video games to horrific acts of real-world brutality for over thirty years. As you will learn in the coming chapters, there is no epidemic of real-world violence associated with video games. But there is one place where the association between video game violence and aggression is indisputable: in the halls of universities around the world, among researchers studying the topic.

To the outside observer this might not seem like such a big deal—just nerd-on-nerd violence—but the stakes of these conflicts are high for everyone. They influence court decisions about what kinds of media can be censored or regulated. People have been sentenced to jail or gone free based on the testimony of video game scholars. And millions of dollars of taxpayer money has been spent fighting these battles, funding biased scientific studies that may do more harm than good.

The anti–video game giants are being challenged by a rebellious group of younger, pro-game researchers, many of whom grew up surrounded by Atari, Nintendo, and PlayStation systems. Theirs is an epic struggle for truth as they attempt to challenge the much more powerful anti–video game empire. This is not a battle fought on strange planets by lightsaber-wielding Jedis; it is fought in the pages of scientific journals, in the media, and in courtrooms (and regrettably, there are no lightsabers). But while it may not be as thrilling as the battles in *Star Wars*, it does bear some interesting similarities to events that occurred in that galaxy so far, far away.

HOW THE EMPIRE WAS BUILT

When I left you, I was but the learner; now I am the master.
—Darth Vader, Sith Lord

Every story has a beginning: Anakin Skywalker was transformed into the Emperor's evil henchman Darth Vader; a pair of psychological researchers inadvertently started an anti–video game empire. In 1986, two scholars from Princeton University published one of the first studies to experimentally investigate the effects of violent video games on aggression.[59] By this time video games had captured the interest of the nation—it was understandable that these researchers wanted to explore how violent video games might affect children. However, it quickly became apparent that these researchers understood little about video games or the people who played them. The "violent" game these scientists chose for their study was *Missile Command* . . . for the Atari 2600. For those who are not familiar with this game, there is actually no violence in it at all. There are no people or life forms of any kind. Players move a small X around in an effort to protect "cities" (blocky bits along the bottom of the screen) from a missile attack. No blood, no gore, just lines, Xs, and an occasional flash of light. Nonetheless, the researchers concluded that Atari 2600's *Missile Command* had "measurable consequences" for the aggressive behaviors of children.

You may not be surprised to learn that this unusual study did not exactly take the scientific community by storm, sending flocks of scholars scurrying to examine the dangers of playing the Atari 2600. Over the next decade, only one or two studies came out each year that examined violent video games. Even the authors of the *Missile Command* study never published another article on the topic. However, following the tragic events at Columbine High School, a group of senior researchers quickly took advantage of the public's outcry (and outpouring of funding) to revive the field of study. Studies of violent video games increased 1170 percent in the post-Columbine world—launching the start of the anti–video game research empire.

Most people are surprised to learn the details of how this video game research was actually conducted. Some studies have done little more than ask people what types of games they like and how they feel. Seriously, that's it! The following box provides a sampling of some of the actual questions researchers have used to determine whether video games cause "aggression." As you will notice, these questions are not concerned with real acts of violence. Instead, they are focused on whether a respondent might be a bit of a jerk (e.g., "to say nasty things about a person behind his/her back is OK"), feel like being alone (e.g., "I feel unsociable"), or—oddly enough—politically conservative (e.g., "any nation should be ready with a strong military at all times"). Obviously, any conclusions one might draw about aggression—much less actual violent behavior—from such studies would be dubious.

Some researchers have tried to be a bit more systematic, conducting experimental studies. These usually involve asking one group of people to play a "violent" video game, while another group plays a "nonviolent" video game. Exactly what qualifies as a violent video game has varied widely among researchers. *Grand Theft Auto, Doom, Call of Duty,* and *Mortal Kombat* are obviously violent and have all been used in violent–video game research, but so have games that seem much more innocent. For example, anti–video game researchers have said that *Missile Command,* the arcade space-shooter

A SAMPLING OF ITEMS VIOLENT–VIDEO GAME RESEARCHERS HAVE USED TO DETERMINE IF RESPONDENTS ARE AGGRESSIVE

- I tell my friends openly when I disagree with them.
- To say nasty things about a person behind his/her back is OK.
- When people annoy me, I may tell them what I think of them.
- I am suspicious of overly friendly strangers.
- Children should be spanked for temper tantrums.
- Our country has the right to protect its borders forcefully.
- I feel unsociable.
- Any nation should be ready with a strong military at all times.
- War in self-defense is perfectly all right.
- I feel willful.
- To spread rumors about others is totally OK.
- To show someone up in front of others is totally OK.
- War is often necessary.
- The person running the study was not very courteous.

* Items are typically answered on a 1–5 scale with higher scores indicating you are more aggressive.

Zaxxon, the cartoonish game *Ty2*, (rated E), the exaggerated version of baseball in *MLB Slugfest* (rated E), the game *Herc's Adventures* (rated E—in which the main character employs cartoonish attacks such as "pepper breath"), and even *Pac-Man* are violent video games.

Typically, after a short play session of around fifteen minutes, participants in these studies have their aggressive thoughts or behaviors assessed, either via survey or by giving them a chance to perform some "aggressive act." Using this methodology, some researchers have found that individuals who play violent video games are more likely to expose others to loud, irritating noises, report feeling more hostile on a questionnaire, give longer prison sentences to hypothetical criminals, and even give hot sauce to people who do not like spicy food. Other researchers can't find these effects. And while these various outcomes might be related to unfriendly thoughts and behaviors, it is quite a leap to imply that the desire to expose others to loud noises or hot sauce translates to a propensity to commit homicide or violent assault.

Not only are researchers guilty of overgeneralizing and extrapolating the findings from such studies (does anyone really think that a willingness to say "nasty things" behind a person's back tells us anything about whether someone is likely to become a school shooter?), but they sometimes get sloppy with how they conduct these experiments in the first place. For instance, one popular method researchers have used to measure aggressiveness after playing a violent video game is to give the subject a chance to "blast" someone with an irritating noise. Specifically, after their game-playing time is over, subjects are allowed to select both the *duration* and the *intensity* (on a scale of zero to ten) of a white-noise burst administered to another person.

The problem is that there is no agreed-upon way to score this measurement of aggression. For example, researchers have scored aggression as the sum of the *intensity* and *duration,* the product of the *intensity* and *duration,* the log transformation *duration* (ignoring the intensity . . . and if you don't remember from high school math what a log transformation is, don't worry, you're not missing much here), and even the square root of the *duration* score multiplied by the *intensity* score. Confused yet? Altogether, there are at least 140 different ways researchers have scored this measurement! Recently, German scholar Dr. Malte Elson was able to demonstrate that, depending on how creative a researcher gets in scoring this measurement, it is easy to make violent video games look like they increase aggression, decrease aggression, or have no effect whatsoever . . . using the *same sample*.[60, 61]

Suppose, for the sake of argument, we look past these methodological problems: How "big" of an effect do these studies show video games have, even on such mundane outcomes as exposing others to irritating noises, feeling unsociable, or giving hot sauce to a person who does not like spicy food? Numerous scholars on both sides of the video game debate have examined all the research done on this topic, working to get a sense of the average effect video games have on slight forms of aggression. So how much do video games seem to affect people's minor expression of aggression? Given the extensive media coverage and the dire concerns expressed by policy makers and others, you might guess that playing violent video games increases aggression by around 40 or 50 percent. Even if you are a bit skeptical, you might imagine that surely video game researchers must have found at least a 10 percent effect. It turns out you'd be wrong—by a lot. On average, research suggests that only 0.4 percent to 3.2 percent of the variation in minor forms of aggression can be explained by violent video games[62, 63] (see Easter Egg 1).

Keep in mind that these small effects are based on studies that have almost exclusively relied on self-reports of aggressive behavior or employed proxy measurements of aggression. And usually, it's kind of obvious what participants are "supposed" to do in these studies—subjects may very well be giving researchers the responses they think they want rather than behaving as they normally would. Even if we take this research at face value and say that playing a violent video game may make some people more likely to afflict others with loud noises or hot sauce, these are actions with minimal repercussions—unlike, say, committing rape or aggravated assault. As such, it is likely that even the extremely small effect found by some studies linking violent video games to minor forms of aggression far exceeds the effect of violent video games on real-world aggressive behaviors. In short, these studies might suggest it's a good idea to keep an eye on our friends who play violent video games if they are going to make us a taco, but they give little insight into whether video games pose a public health risk. Then again, given inconsistencies between studies, dubious measures of aggression, the bizarre list of games researchers have called violent, and other methodological issues, maybe even our tacos are safe, and the whole thing is utter rubbish.

HOW THE EMPIRE GREW STRONG

Fear is the path to the dark side.
—Yoda, Jedi Master

The obvious question is this: Given that there is very little scientific data linking violent video games to acts of violence, why are so many people so worried about these games? As we learned in Level Two, the simple answer is fear. Parents are scared. According to one survey, more than 60 percent of parents believe a school shooting is likely to happen in their own community.[64] However, there is a major disconnect between this fear and reality. The chance a child will be killed in a school shooting is 0.000001 percent. Although such events are undeniably tragic, they are much rarer than many of the potential dangers our children face every day. It is more likely that a child will die in a plane crash (0.01 percent), from a bee sting (0.001 percent), on death row as a convicted murderer (0.0008 percent), by being struck by lightning (0.0007 percent), from a dog bite (0.0006 percent), or even in a tragic fireworks accident (0.0002 percent).

And while studies may have failed to demonstrate a link between violent video games and actual violence, you would never know it from the way these studies are reported to the public—by the media, and even by the scholars themselves. When society is in the grip of a moral panic, as we are with violent video games, major stakeholders in society are pressured to both validate and address the fear. These stakeholders include politicians, who court votes by looking serious on moral issues, and news editors, who rely on salacious clickbait headlines to garner sales. After all, which would you be more likely to click on: "Scientists Say Video Games Creating Generation of Sociopaths" or "Video Games Don't Really Influence Us Much, New Study Finds"? In the aftermath of three recent school shootings, nearly 5,000 newspaper articles were published that discussed video games in the context of the events.

We'd like to think all scientists hold themselves to a higher standard, but, unfortunately, remaining above the fray does not pay well. Scholars can get grant funding, professional prestige, and newspaper coverage for their work by tying their research to the current moral panic, and the more extreme their statements, the more coverage they receive. Social science during a moral panic begins to look and behave less like an actual science and more like a convenient way to benefit from societal agendas.

The following box presents just a small sampling of times when researchers have linked violent video games to horrific acts of violence in the media and in scientific journals. Keep in mind that none of these statements are backed by any research examining real violence; all appear akin to sensationalistic attempts to exploit actual horrific events in order to provoke interest in these scholars' research.

Some of these quotes are examples of scholars making true statements that are, alas, irrelevant to the study they have conducted. For example, the first quote is correct: Eric Harris and Dylan Klebold did assault Columbine High School in Littleton, Colorado, murdering thirteen and wounding twenty-three before turning the guns on themselves. However, the quote appears in a study that did not investigate any violent outcomes; it instead related media use to various self-report assessments of mood, such as irritability (e.g., "I think I have a lot of patience") and the likelihood that participants would expose a hypothetical person to an irritating noise. (It's worth noting, too, that the quote completely mischaracterizes the military's use of video games; see Easter Egg 2.) In a similar manner, the second quote accurately reports that Germany was shocked by a school shooting in which seventeen people, including the shooter, were killed. Nevertheless, it is unclear what this tragedy has to do with the study, which assessed whether playing a violent game made subjects more likely to endorse opinions such as "To spread rumors about someone is totally OK."

EXAMPLES OF A MORAL PANIC: QUOTES FROM RESEARCHERS LINKING VIOLENT MEDIA TO HORRIFIC ACTS OF VIOLENCE

"On April 20, 1999, Eric Harris and Dylan Klebold launched an assault on Columbine High School in Littleton, Colorado, murdering 13 and wounding 23 before turning the guns on themselves. Although it is impossible to know exactly what caused these teens to attack their own classmates and teachers, a number of factors probably were involved. One possible contributing factor is violent video games. Harris and Klebold enjoyed playing the bloody, shoot-'em-up video game *Doom*, a game licensed by the U.S. military to train soldiers to effectively kill."[65]

"In April 2002, Germany was shocked by an unprecedented school shooting in which 17 people, including the assailant, were killed. It was soon established that the 19-year-old killer, a former pupil at the school who had been expelled some weeks prior to the attack, had not only been fascinated by firearms but had also spent much of his time playing violent electronic games."[66]

"Paducah, Kentucky. Jonesboro, Arkansas. Littleton, Colorado. These three towns recently experienced similar multiple school shootings. The shooters were students who habitually played violent video games. Eric Harris and Dylan Klebold, the Columbine High School students who murdered 13 people and wounded 23 in Littleton, before killing themselves, enjoyed playing the bloody video game *Doom*. Harris created a customized version of *Doom* with two shooters, extra weapons, unlimited ammunition, and victims who could not fight back—features that are eerily similar to aspects of the actual shootings."[67]

"Recent school shootings (e.g., Columbine High) and the September 11, 2001, terrorist attacks on the World Trade Center and Pentagon have refueled the long-standing debate about the effects of exposure to media violence. Although this debate appears unresolved in the public arena, the scientific literature leaves little doubt about the effects of media violence on aggression behavior."[68]

"Overall, an estimated 10% to 30% of violence in society can be attributed to the impact of media violence."[69]

"The impact of media violence on real-life aggressive behavior is stronger than many commonly accepted public health risks and nearly as strong as the link between smoking and lung cancer."[65]

A few of the quotes are more than just misleadingly irrelevant, they are irresponsible misrepresentations of statistics—or, to put it in layman's terms, rubbish. Despite the fact that none of their studies actually examined violence, these scholars have happily implied that violent games cause mass shootings or that the effects of violent games on society are a public health crisis on par with smoking and lung cancer.[70] Consider, for example, the quote about 10 to 30 percent of violence in society being attributable to media. We're in the difficult position of trying to explain where such a nonsensical number came from. To say "they made it up" wouldn't entirely be fair . . . better to say that a selective, creative, and arguably self-delusional application of misguided statistics was at play. But, either way, these numbers in no way reflect reality.

BUILDING THE DEATH STAR

That's no moon, it's a space station.
—Obi-Wan Kenobi, Jedi Master

In *Star Wars*, the Empire has constructed the Death Star: a moon-sized battle station that can destroy a planet. This super laser was built to consolidate the Empire's growing power and more directly control society through fear. Recently, the anti–video game empire has been attempting to consolidate the views of a vocal minority of senior researchers into something more powerful than the sum of its parts: a policy statement. Just like the Death Star, these statements are tools to centralize power and create fear in the public. Policy statements are typically released by scholarly guilds, such as the American Psychological Association (APA), to promote policies that benefit their members. Often these statements are warnings about some supposedly dire situation facing society, one that can only be solved by the organization's professionals. In the

Star Wars prequels, Emperor Palpatine orchestrates the overthrow of the Old Republic in order to give himself the opportunity to restore order during the Clone Wars—Palpatine creates a problem, and then rushes in to "fix" it, reaping most of the rewards himself. We're not suggesting research psychologists are Sith Lords, but this particular parallel is undeniable.

In 2005, the American Psychological Association released their first policy statement on violent video games. It declared that a "comprehensive analysis of violent interactive video game research suggests such exposure a) increases aggressive behavior, b) increases aggressive thoughts, c) increases angry feelings, d) decreases helpful behavior, and e) increases physiological arousal."[71] This conclusion was based on studies like those described earlier involving hot sauce and questionnaire responses such as "When people annoy me, I may tell them what I think of them," and "I feel unsociable." The statement was written by a task force made up entirely of anti-media researchers.[72] Effectively, these scholars reviewed *their own work* and declared it beyond further debate, something your authors would love to be able to do one day. The policy statement did not discuss any of the methodological limitations of these studies (like the fact that none actually examined violence). What's more, although there were numerous studies that failed to find any link between violent media and violence, the statement neglected to mention any of these, referencing no research that would have contradicted its conclusions. By failing to inform the public of contradictory findings in the literature, the policy statement is not only misleading, it is also actively dishonest.

Unfortunately, the APA does not seem to have learned their lesson. In 2013, responding to criticisms of the 2005 policy statement, the APA agreed to appoint a new task force to reconsider the evidence on video game violence.[73] Unfortunately, this new seven-member task force was once again stacked with those already possessing strong anti-game views. One member had previously coauthored a highly politicized report discussing the dangers of video games. Two members had signed an amicus brief supporting the regulation of violent video games in the 2011 *Brown v. EMA* case. Another had signed a petition statement implying a link between violent media and mass shootings. And another had spent much of his career attempting to validate the widely criticized laboratory measures of "aggression" used in much of the video game literature. Once again, no scholars who had previously expressed skepticism about media effects on violence or laboratory aggression measures were invited to participate.

The other problem with the APA's video game task force was that its members were just, well . . . old. It's impolite to ask people their age, but we can infer the ages of the task force members by looking at the years in which they graduated from college. Sure, some might have been child geniuses (and some late bloomers), but let's assume most people graduate with their bachelor's degree around age twenty-two. Based on this logic, the average age of the task force was about sixty-two, with no one under fifty years old! This means most of the task force members were forty-somethings when the first PlayStation was released and pushing fifty by the time the Xbox rolled out. This is particularly troubling as studies have indicated that older researchers—those who did not grow up surrounded by Nintendo and other gaming systems—are much more distrustful of video games than younger scholars.[74] If you want an alarmist statement on a new form of art or media, the go-to group is always the same: older adults who don't use, understand, or value that media.

One thing to remember about groups like the APA is that they are not neutral parties. They are professional advocacy organizations, not objective observers. These groups are, in effect, trying to sell their professions to the public. This is just good business, and it isn't necessarily sinister. But once you see them as guilds promoting their professions, seeking influence, and looking to increase grant and funding opportunities for their members, you'll begin to understand why they may not always be transparent about scientific data inconvenient for their political positions. It's to their advantage to find problems their members can fix, not to be honest when data suggest there may not be a problem at all. Indeed, it isn't too surprising to learn that the 2015 APA policy resolution concludes with an appeal for more funding to support its members doing further research into violent video games!

There is also a conflict of interest in that these organizations both produce politically loaded policy statements and also publish research. Such organizations may be tempted to selectively publish research that supports their policy positions and reject research that does not. Then, to complete the circle, task forces or committees producing the policy statements are often reviewing research from the professional organization's own journals. They are likely not as keen to criticize the quality of research in their own journals as outside organizations might be. Think of it like Microsoft assembling a committee to determine whether their Xbox system or Sony's Play-Station is the better console. Is a Microsoft committee ever going to decree the PlayStation to be a better product? No. Expecting groups like the APA to criticize their own products, upon which they depend for money, prestige, membership loyalty, and political influence is about as likely.

Perhaps the most striking example of how all this works comes not from video games, but from allegations that the APA colluded with the Bush administration to change their ethics code in order to allow psychologists to assist with harsh interrogations (i.e., torture) of detainees during the war on terror (perhaps our lighthearted comparison with the Empire was less far-fetched than we thought).[75] The APA's decision to allow psychologists to participate in harsh interrogations had always been controversial (they were the only medical organization to allow their members to participate), but in 2014, *New York Times* journalist James Risen exposed communications between the APA and CIA detailing jerry-rigged meetings between specifically selected APA members and government officials. The meetings had been designed to ensure that the ethics code would be changed to allow for participation in these interrogations—without most APA members being involved in (or even aware of) the decision-making process. After Mr. Risen's story was published, the APA announced an independent investigation into the claims.[76] In July 2015, the independent investigation (typically referred to as the Hoffman report, after the lead investigating attorney) confirmed that the APA had indeed colluded with the Department of Defense to allow for the torture of detainees.

This revelation has become an incredible crisis point for American psychology. A few heads did roll at the APA as a consequence of the Hoffman report, but whether the organization's systematic governance problems have changed much remains to be seen. We doubt it. Our point is: stacking meetings to influence policy is normal behavior for the APA and groups like it. And if the APA is willing to gerrymander their own ethics code to allow torture, why would we think they're telling the truth about video games?

The dubious nature of the APA's task force on violent video games recently prompted 238 psychologists, media scholars, and criminologists to write an open letter asking the APA to retire its policy statements on video game and media violence, as the statements are misleading and outdated.[77] Other independent groups that have looked at both the APA policy statement and the research literature have begun to acknowledge that the research on video games is inconsistent and methodologically flawed. These groups include the governments of Australia,[78] Sweden,[79] and the United Kingdom,[80] as well as the US House of Representatives[81] and multiple US courts. Even Common Sense Media, an anti-media advocacy group, acknowledged the issues in a 2013 review of the research.[82]

The anti–video game empire might have succeeded in using questionable policy statements to harness the power of fear, but there is a growing group of scholars challenging such practices.

Certainly some of these rebels are older adults who have been in the field for many years, but most are younger researchers who grew up in the video game era and, regardless of whether they are gamers themselves, understand both how games work and how they fit into modern culture. These scholars are changing the nature of the field.

THE REBEL ALLIANCE

This is Red Five, I'm going in.
—Luke Skywalker, Jedi Master

In the spring of 2015, renowned psychologist Philip Zimbardo went to the UK to promote his new book. Zimbardo is best known for the Stanford Prison Experiment, in which he randomly assigned students to be either prisoners or guards. To Zimbardo's surprise, the guards in the study began to treat the prisoners with horrible cruelty, and the experiment had to be discontinued when a research assistant complained. This famous study is illustrative both of some uglier facets of human nature and dubious ethics in psychological research. In his new book, Zimbardo alleges that boys and men are experiencing a crisis, brought on by everything from women teachers to video games (Zimbardo is also a former president of the APA—yes, the same APA that created the anti–video game policy statements).[83]

Appearing on the BBC, along with several young gamers and Oxford psychologist Dr. Andrew Przybylski, Zimbardo claimed that the isolating nature of games was damaging the brains of boys. In the interview, the eighty-two-year-old Zimbardo appears to have little idea how video games actually work. For instance, the young gamers point out that most games are now played socially, not in isolation, and that there are many women and girl gamers. But the most effective rebuttal to the bollocks Zimbardo tries to sell the audience comes from Dr. Przybylski, who notes that Zimbardo misrepresents much of the research he refers to and fails to note other data, such as falling youth violence rates that contradict Zimbardo's claim of a "crisis."[84]

Dr. Przybylski is a young father and so, like any parent, is concerned about issues that affect children. Back in the mid-2000s, he'd begun investigating what motivated kids and young adults to play video games. Dr. Przybylski's research is fascinating because until then, believe it or not, few people had bothered to ask *why* either kids or adults played video games in the first place. He found that people tended to play video games that helped them meet motivational needs that weren't being met in real life, such as socialization, feeling they can make their own decisions, or feeling able to do something useful and have an impact on the world. This makes sense. If you're an adult in a job shuffling papers from one side of the desk to another, or a kid filling out boring quizzes and papers, it may be hard to feel a sense of agency and motivation. But band together with some friends in an imaginary world, slaying monsters or shaping whole narratives, and those needs can be met in a concrete way, even in virtual reality.[85]

What Dr. Przybylski couldn't find was evidence that violent games promoted aggression in players. Indeed, when Dr. Przybylski tried to replicate past studies that had been used to "prove" the dangers of violent video games, he couldn't do it. Violence in video games had no effect on players' aggression. Instead, what Dr. Przybylski found is that past video game researchers had made a huge mistake: they confused the effects of violence with the effects of frustration. During most video game studies, participants play a game for only about fifteen minutes. Since players are often asked to play video games they haven't played before, and many violent games are more complicated and difficult to master than nonviolent games, any links between violent video games and aggression seem to have been the result of frustration experienced by players, and *not* the violent content. Dr. Przybylski showed, in his own work, that if the experiment controls for this frustration, by manipulating frustration levels in the game and comparing violent and nonviolent games with equal levels of frustration, no effect on aggression is seen.[86] In other words, when past experiments found changes in aggression after a session with a violent video game, it was not a result of violence, but of the experimenter not understanding video games and the experience of playing them.

Initially, Dr. Przybylski had difficulty publishing this research. An early draft, sent for review at a prestigious journal, was met with harsh criticism. The journal had sent the draft to anti–video game researchers, who chastised the paper as potentially harmful to the social agenda to save children from video games. Dr. Przybylski persisted, adding new studies and resubmitting to the same journal, where—much to the displeasure of the anti–video game empire—the paper was ultimately accepted. Today, Dr. Przybylski is one of the foremost experts on the effects of video games.

Dr. Przybylski's experiences running the gauntlet of anti-game researchers are not unique. In 2005, Dr. Dmitri Williams, a scholar at the Annenberg School for Communication at the University of Southern California, published a groundbreaking study along with colleague Dr. Marko Skoric. The study found that even long-term and repetitive exposure to violent video games did *not* increase aggression.[87] This was not the first study to show results of this sort—indeed, warning notes had been sounded in the literature for years, though few listened.[88, 89, 90] But Dr. Williams' paper was one of the first questioning the link between video games and aggression that actually received widespread media attention. What came next was, perhaps, predictable: anti-media advocates tried to discredit Dr. Williams' study and even threatened his career. One scholar (with a bit of a history for personal attacks on those who disagree with him) singled Williams' paper out for criticism in a 2007 review of the literature, giving it a particularly oily feel by saying the study was "frequently cited by game manufacturers."[91]

Although Dr. Williams is now a respected, tenured faculty member, he still speaks about the bullying he received from senior anti–video game researchers during this time, when he was a young faculty member without tenure:

"The stronger reaction was really about the field and what I'd 'done to it.' One critic suggested to me that I'd ruined years of progress. I think what he meant was progress in getting policy makers to focus on harmful media. What took me aback was the sense that some set of answers were more appropriate than others. I mean the data tell the story, and so the story is what it is. I didn't set out to help or hurt anyone. I wanted to find out the truth, and in my one study the truth wasn't a fit for the storyline to date. It could have gone the other way, and I'd have been fine with that. But it didn't . . . As it was, it was kind of a scary time. I'm this very green, junior scholar with established heavyweights making very threatening statements to me."

There is an irony, of course, in researchers who profess to be concerned about aggression in children being so aggressive themselves. So much for modeling good behavior.

Like it or not, this is sometimes just the way academia works. Behind the scenes, science is often about politics, social agendas, personalities, and ego. Senior scholars are often reluctant to let go of their outdated beliefs. After all, their whole careers, their whole lives, have likely been devoted to establishing one theory as fact. And if that one theory is wrong, what do they have to show for any of it?

As we learned in Level Two, new media is often distrusted by older people who did not grow up with it, and scientists aren't immune to this (your authors may end their careers complaining about some new media that hasn't even been invented yet!). It takes a generation of new scholars willing to stand up and push against resistance from the establishment, publish good data, and insist that the data drive the story. Drs. Przybylski and Williams are just two examples. Others include Paul Adachi, who has found that controlling for competitiveness in games makes the effect of violent content vanish;[92] Morgan Tear, who has found that violent games do not influence prosocial (helping) behavior;[93] and Malte Elson, who demonstrated the inadequacy and poor validity of the traditional methods used in video game research.[60] These young scientists are hardly alone—the number of studies finding that violent video games have no harmful effect has been skyrocketing in recent years.[94, 95, 96, 97, 98, 99, 100] Indeed, there have been so many that for scholars to claim studies consistently show any effect can hardly be anything but deliberate dishonesty or impressive levels of self-delusion.

The writing is on the wall for the anti–video game empire. To be sure, the old critics of video games are still publishing questionable research that fails to examine anything related to truly violent behavior. Indeed, with a careful eye, you'll see the same research names come up again and again! But once a field has gotten to this point—a tug-of-war between old and new, between the establishment and the up-and-comers—the battle is over. There's no budding rebellion among young scholars against the concept of global warming, or that smoking causes lung cancer. But the idea that violent video games can be meaningfully and reliably linked to harmful outcomes is falling apart from within the scholarly community. Even Dr. Williams, who is no longer a young researcher but an established expert with years of experience, predicts that the change in thinking about video games will have little to do with science in the end, but rather is simply a consequence of age, time, and death:

"It's a massive change in generations and the mainstreaming of the medium that's essentially swept this debate off to the side. Teens who were told games were stupid are now parents, teachers, and policy makers, and they're out of the gaming

closet now. The war is over, and it was won through demographics and simpler, accessible, portable technologies."

Time, as ever, fixes these moral panics over media. Today, few
people take seriously Fredric Wertham's long-ago warnings about
comic books causing delinquency and homosexuality. The same is
true of claims that the music of Ozzy Osbourne and Cyndi Lauper causes suicide or sexual mayhem, despite what Tipper Gore
and Congress said in the '80s. As Generation X, the generation
that grew up surrounded by video games, begins to fill the positions of power in society (becoming society's journalists, scientists,
and politicians), people will stop worrying about video games. In
another a decade or two, the panic over video game violence will
seem as quaint as that over Batman and Robin. When social science goes to war with pop culture, social science rarely comes out
looking better for it.

Unfortunately, many social scientists dove headfirst into this
moral panic, and so we can expect a fight to the bitter end. Make
no mistake, there is still a very active group of senior researchers,
politicians, and reporters who maintain that violent video games are
responsible for school shootings, rampage killings, and other horrific acts of real-world violence. The "evil empire" of our *Star Wars*
analogy won't explode like a Death Star, but instead will waste away,
fighting until its dying breath for every last grant dollar and news
headline.

In truth, of course, almost no one has actually examined the link
between video game violence and real-world violent acts—until now.

EASTER EGGS

1. For our more statistically minded readers, the average effect size (defined using a Pearson r) from these studies has been extremely small, ranging between r = .06 to .18.

2. The claim that the military uses violent video games to desensitize soldiers to killing is apocryphal (which is a fancy way of saying "nuts"). One of us (Ferguson) once interviewed a military psychologist about the issue. The military psychologist was perplexed by the idea, and argued that the military wants professional soldiers who think and solve problems rationally . . . not vigilantes who go shooting wildly at everything that moves. He noted that the military does use video game–like simulators (although typically these are not games like *Doom*) for skills such as decision making and team performance—but not for desensitization to violence.

LEVEL 4:

THE GRAND THEFT FALLACY

Six teenagers boldly walked down the center of a New York City street carrying baseball bats and crowbars. They had beaten and knocked the teeth out of a random bystander, broken into a storage shed, and were trying to carjack a 2008 BMW when they were arrested by police. At first, it seemed as if these youths were garden-variety thugs, or perhaps misguided teens lashing out at a world they thought had wronged them. However, as the police investigation continued, detectives came to a dramatically different conclusion—these teenagers had committed these crimes not because they were angry or incorrigible, but because of a video game.[101]

In *Grand Theft Auto IV,* players control the main character, Niko Bellic, as he freely roams the fictional Liberty City, based loosely on New York. In this computer-generated world, players can virtually commit many of the crimes the New York teenagers were accused of, including carjacking, assault, and robbery. The parallels between the behaviors of Niko in Liberty City and these teens in New York were so striking that the lead detective on the case suggested that the youths "decided they were going to go out to commit robberies and emulate the character Niko Bellic in the particularly violent video game *Grand Theft Auto*." Newspapers leapt on the story, with headlines declaring "Teens Busted in 'Grand Theft'–Style Spree" and "Video Villains Come to Life."[101, 102]

Of course, this was not the first time that *Grand Theft Auto* had been linked to serious acts of violence. This game was invoked after the arrests of William and Joshua Buckner in 2003 for homicide; Devin Moore in 2003 for first-degree murder; Cody Posey in 2004 for homicide; Ryan Chinnery in 2008 for rape and grievous bodily harm; Stephen Attard, Samuel Philip, Dylan Laird, and Jaspreet Singh in 2008 for various robberies and assaults; and in 2013, only four days after the release of *Grand Theft Auto V*, the arrest of Zachary Burgess for vehicle theft and kidnapping. Although other games, such as *Call of Duty, Mortal Kombat*, and *Doom*, have also been linked to real-world acts of violence, *Grand Theft Auto* is the game that seems to come up most often—so often, in fact, that it has made it into the lexicon of scholars. The tendency to link violent crimes to the video game habits of their perpetrators is prevalent enough to merit a catchy name: the Grand Theft Fallacy.

The Grand Theft Fallacy was on display in dramatic fashion during the murder trial of Christopher Harris. In September 2009, following a night of drinking and using cocaine, Christopher Harris and his brother, Jason, headed to the home of Rick and Ruth Gee. Christopher knew the Gee family; Rick Gee was his ex-wife's father. It is uncertain exactly why the Harris brothers initially decided to make their way to the Gee home at one o'clock in the morning. What is clear, however, is that after Christopher entered the home, something went horribly wrong. Christopher Harris beat Rick and Ruth Gee to death, along with three of their children. A three-year-old daughter, also beaten, managed to survive.[103] The Harris brothers fled, but evidence at the scene clearly linked them to the crime, and

Jason Harris soon agreed to testify against his brother, Christopher, who'd actually committed the murders.

With a mountain of evidence against their client, Christopher's defense team had few options. So they hatched a novel alternate theory of the crime. Harris, the defense claimed, hadn't killed the family at all. In fact, he'd walked in on the family's fourteen-year-old son, Dillen, killing the family, and had then been forced to kill Dillen in self-defense. The defense called upon social psychologist Dr. Craig Anderson, as mentioned earlier a longtime critic of violent games. Dr. Anderson argued that fourteen-year-old Dillen had a propensity toward violence, in part because he liked to play the violent video game *Mortal Kombat* (the best-selling American-made fighting-game series, it has sold over thirty million copies).[104] Jurors were even shown three minutes of gameplay from *Mortal Kombat* in an attempt to convince them that such games could push a child to murder his entire family. Keep in mind that Dr. Anderson's testimony was intended to sway the jury into believing that the now-deceased fourteen-year-old was guilty of murder, and that Harris was merely an innocent bystander—forced to defend himself by striking Dillen fifty-two times with a tire iron, while sustaining only a blister on the palm of his hand. This was not merely an academic researcher making an argument in the pages of some obscure journal; this is a real example of the Grand Theft Fallacy. Dr. Anderson was a respected scientist, providing testimony that might clear a defendant of the brutal killing of an entire family, simply because, in part, one of the victims enjoyed playing a fighting game. (In full disclosure, one of the authors of this book consulted for the prosecution.)

Fortunately, upon cross-examination, Anderson's testimony quickly fell apart. He was not a licensed clinical psychologist yet was speaking about risk factors for violence in a specific individual, which is usually the purview of licensed psychologists (social psychologists are not licensed clinicians). Dr. Anderson also had to acknowledge that he'd failed to interview surviving members of the family or others who had known Dillen, and that he hadn't verified the information given to him by the defense attorneys. In fact, Dillen's actual history of video game playing appeared to be slight. Although he had the violent *Mortal Kombat* game in his home, it was an outdated version, and analysis of the game console suggested he hadn't played it much. Dr. Anderson admitted that no research studies had linked playing violent video games with subsequent violent behavior, that Dr. Anderson *himself* had played *Mortal Kombat* without becoming violent, and that a majority of young boys, in fact, play violent video games without becoming aggressive. Dr. Anderson also confessed that, according to the parameters scholars like him use to define a "violent video game," even a game like *Pac-Man* would be considered "violent video." When asked about a 2011 Supreme Court decision criticizing his research, Anderson, sounding a bit like a conspiracy theorist, implied that the video game industry might have helped write it. One of the assistant district attorneys was later overheard saying that Dr. Anderson's testimony was "the most offensive testimony I've ever heard in my life." Harris was convicted. The murder trial of Christopher Harris serves as a stark reminder that anyone is susceptible to committing the Grand Theft Fallacy, and that this fallacy is not harmless. Dubious scholarly theories and the failures of logic underlying them can have far-reaching implications and affect the lives of very real, non-hypothetical people.

IMAGINARY CONNECTIONS AND THE GRAND THEFT FALLACY

The reason we humans are susceptible to the Grand Theft Fallacy is the same reason many people erroneously believe it is bad luck to walk under a ladder or break a mirror, or that bad things happen on Friday the thirteenth. Such superstitions endure because we have a bad habit of overestimating the frequency with which two events occur together. For example, if you believe bad things are more likely to happen on Friday the thirteenth, you are more likely to pay particular attention to any negative events that occur during those twenty-four hours. You get dumped by your girlfriend that afternoon—blame Friday the thirteenth. Fall off your bike and break your wrist—that stupid Friday the thirteenth. Lose all your saved data on your latest game—*argh* . . . Friday the thirteenth!

Of course, if these events had occurred on any other day, you would be unlikely to attribute them to that specific date. (Indeed, one of the authors did fall off his bike and break his wrist . . . alas, on a Sunday the eighth. Damn those Sunday the eighths!). People tend to remember examples that fit into their preexisting beliefs, and ignore those that do not. This tendency results in what is called an "illusory correlation." Illusory correlations create the false sense that events are connected, when they are, in fact, not related at all.[105]

This is exactly what happens with violent video games and violent crime. As we saw after the horrific events at Columbine and Sandy Hook, the media is quick to point out that killers played video games. In fact, almost every time a terrible act of violence is committed by an avid video game player, the media will make a connection between the violent act and the killer's interest in video games. What is missing from these accounts are the thousands of violent acts committed by perpetrators who did *not* play violent games, not to mention the millions of people who play violent video games and yet do not commit violent acts. When a crime is committed by a non-gamer, no one ever highlights the lack of a connection between violence and video games. This isn't necessarily purposeful; it's just how we work. "Mass Shooter 'Not Really Into' Video Games" isn't much of a headline. Unfortunately, this information imbalance is responsible for creating an illusionary correlation between violent video games and real-world violent crime.

Perhaps even more troubling is that illusory correlations are more likely to be created around events that are particularly distinctive and memorable.[106] Think back to when you first heard that Adam Lanza had shot twenty children and six adults at Sandy Hook Elementary School. Chances are you remember where you were, what you were doing, who you were with, what you saw, and what you heard. We remember these events so clearly because of the emotions they elicit, and also because we hear about them over and over, recalling and further cementing our memories of them. We find similar "flash-bulb" memories for other shocking events, such as the assassination of John F. Kennedy, the space shuttle Challenger disaster, and September 11th. We are confusing the ease of remembering occasions on which gamers committed severe acts of violence with the frequency at which these events actually occur together. The point is, because mass shootings carried out at schools are emotionally laden and easy for us to recall, and the media coverage of these events often mentions the game habits of the perpetrators, we overestimate how often people who play violent video games commit these crimes. This establishes the Grand Theft Fallacy even more firmly within our collective belief system, and explains why many assume that people who play games such as *Mortal Kombat* or *Grand Theft Auto* pose a significant risk to our society.

Even when they are able to recognize and overcome illusory correlations, people still commit the Grand Theft Fallacy because they do not take into account the limitations of the scientific research. As we pointed out in Level Three, virtually every study on violent video games has focused on mundane outcomes, like exposing others to irritating noises, reporting feelings of irritation, or giving hot sauce to a person who does not like spicy food. Although such outcomes might be related to being cranky or unfriendly, implying that the desire to expose someone to loud noises or hot sauce is in any way similar to a propensity to commit mass shootings is a clear example of the Grand Theft Fallacy.

Scientists who have committed the Grand Theft Fallacy themselves will often excuse their behavior through a sort of circular reasoning: *we can't design an experiment meant to examine whether violent video games cause real acts of violence*, they say, *because it would be unethical to set out to observe people hurting others as the result of exposing them to something we hypothesize might increase their violent tendencies.* This is true: no university would approve an experiment investigating whether research subjects violently assault each other after a death match in *Call of Duty.* But the implication is that, if scientists were *allowed* to examine such acts of violence, it could easily be proven that when people are exposed to violent video games, they become more violent (see Easter Egg 1). And this, of course, is demonstrably false. There have been over 100 studies in which more than 10,000 people have been randomly exposed to violent video games in a laboratory. Regardless of the fact that the scientists running these studies were constrained by ethics from examining anything more dangerous than the effects of video game violence on covert hot sauce exposure, if violent video games really did cause violence, we would expect that at least *some* of the subjects forced to play a violent video game would have attacked another subject, the researcher, or an innocent bystander. However, to date, there has not been a single instance in which a research subject lashed out and hit someone or committed any act of violence after being forced to play a violent video game in a laboratory. In short, no scientist has actually ever witnessed a person acting violently after playing a video game.

I SCREAM, YOU SCREAM, WE ALL SCREAM FOR . . . CORRELATION DOES NOT IMPLY CAUSATION

Naturally, it is possible that the reason research subjects forced to play *Grand Theft Auto* in a laboratory only refrained from viciously attacking someone with a hot sauce bottle was because the negative

effects of violent video games are simply not strong enough to overcome the social norms of how one should behave in this situation. If
this is true, it limits the usefulness of laboratory studies to examine
violence, and it means we need to move outside of the laboratory if we
want to better understand what might cause a person to become violent. This is exactly why criminologists, sociologists, psychologists,
and economists examine trends in violent crimes. For example, by
investigating criminal data, scientists have been able to demonstrate
the "heat effect": the theory that uncomfortably hot temperatures
increase violent behaviors. Consistent with this notion, FBI reports
of homicides and aggravated assaults clearly indicate that hotter cities have higher rates of violent crime than colder cities, and violent
crime tends to fluctuate along with the changing temperature.[107]

But how can we tell if heat really *causes* people to commit violent
crimes? Almost everyone is familiar with the scientific mantra "correlation does not imply causation." In other words, that just because
two things are related to each other, it doesn't necessarily follow that
one of them caused the other. For example, there is an extremely
strong relationship between ice cream sales and violent crime—as
more and more people enjoy a scoop of ice cream, there also tends
to be more and more blood being shed on the streets! However, no
one is agitating for a ban on ice cream, or arguing that it poses a
significant risk to our society. We all recognize that it is ridiculous
to presume that Ben & Jerry's Cherry Garcia might cause criminal
mayhem. Instead we understand that there is a simple explanation
for this relationship: ice cream sales are higher during the hot summer months, and acts of violence also increase when the temperature rises (ta da—the heat effect). In other words, the relationship
between more ice cream and more murder does not occur because
one causes the other, but because a third variable, heat, causes both
to increase independently. To account for such problems, researchers conduct statistical analyses that "control" for—or remove the
potential effects of—these troublesome confounding variables.[108] It

turns out that when we control for the effect of heat, the relationship between our beloved frozen treats and murder disappears. Phew!

This is what scientists do when trying to determine whether trends in violence are related to something like heat, ice cream, or video games. If we find what appears to be a relationship (correlation) between our variables—like ice cream and violence—we look for other variables, like heat, that might be underlying the relationship and affecting the particular variables we are studying, and we do our best to account for these. We control for things like the economy, the season, demographics, education levels, police presence, criminal incarceration rates, and so forth. With every variable we take into account, we become more and more confident that the relationships we uncover are real. When researchers examining the heat effect did this, they found that no other factor could account for the relationship—these results were so convincing that scientists deemed the heat effect to be authentic, concluding that high temperatures are indeed a significant cause of violence.[109]

On a larger scale, the heat effect has been invoked as a sobering warning that the slow warming of the earth caused by climate change will not only be an environmental disaster, but could result in massive increases in violence as well.[110] Although we cannot be sure that the heat effect will create a climatic dystopia on the level of *Mad Max*, it is pretty clear that you are in more danger of becoming a victim of violent crime during summer in a hot city than in the (apparently calming) chill of winter. So if you're anxious to avoid the potential dangers of the heat effect, you should probably cancel your travel plans to Libya or Iraq (both can get as hot as 130 degrees), and instead book a flight to Antarctica (and invest in an extremely heavy jacket, because the temperatures can reach 70 degrees below zero).

Just as some believe the rise in temperature of our earth will put you in danger of violence, people who fear violent video games are worried that the popularity of these games makes our world a more dangerous place to live. If you are planning to visit Japan or the

United Kingdom, you should be aware that you will be surrounded by a *ton* of gamers. Over six million dollars (USD) is spent on video games each year for every 100,000 citizens of these island empires. Before you change your mind and decide to vacation in a "safer" locale, you might want to consult the chart below, which displays the twenty countries with the world's highest rates of video game sales.[111]

VIDEO GAME SALES (PER 100,000 PEOPLE)

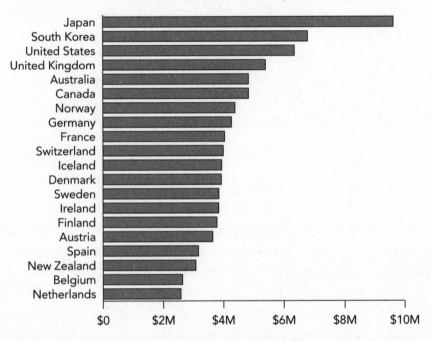

Most of the countries displayed in the chart above are fairly safe places to visit. The State Department hasn't issued advisories against travel to Tokyo or London, where the streets are teeming with gamers. According to Washington-based IntelCenter, the countries you might want to avoid are Iraq, Nigeria, Somalia, Afghanistan, Lebanon, and Yemen, as these are among the most violent in the world.[112] No one would ever suggest that the violence in these countries is due to *Grand Theft Auto* or *Call of Duty* because we recognize that it can be traced back to political instability, religious and militant extremism, ongoing civil wars, famine, and corrupt governments. In fact, almost no one in these countries is even playing video games. In Lebanon, the average citizen spends only eighty-four cents (USD) each year on video games![111] People who have argued that video games make our society less safe are forgetting about the rest of the world; the data unquestionably show that, if you are in a geographic location where lots of people are playing violent video games, you are in a much safer location than you would be if you were in a place where people do not play such games.

But, you say, perhaps such a conclusion is too simplistic. Perhaps factors like political instability or militant extremism are simply so strong that they hide any negative effects of violent video games. This is a legitimate concern, and this is why it is especially useful to examine countries that do not face such extreme dangers. For example, the twenty countries where video games are most popular do not normally face such dire conditions, but they do vary in terms of video game sales and violent crime. When we look at these countries, we find that, contrary to the fear that video games make society

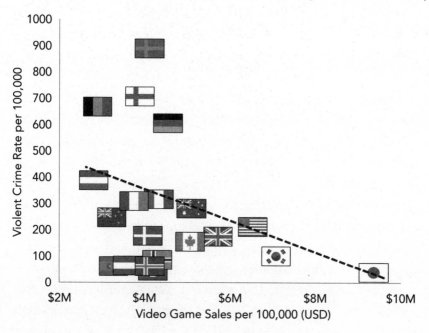

more dangerous, the opposite tends to be true. As we see in the figure below, the countries that consume the most video games are among the safest nations in the world. In fact, the three countries with the fewest game sales had a nearly 200 percent higher average violent crime rate than the three countries that sold the most games.[113]

Although the countries examined are all developed nations, they do still have important differences that might hide the effect video games have on violent behavior. In other words, just as it was important to control for other factors that may have contributed to the "heat effect," it is equally important to consider such factors here. Perhaps countries with high video game sales also tend to have fewer adolescent males (males tend to commit a disproportionate amount of violent crimes—sorry, guys), a better economy, or are simply more technologically advanced. However, just as with the heat effect, even when you take into account other potential causes, the finding still holds! Countries in which video games are extremely popular have lower levels of homicides and violent assaults than countries in which people play fewer video games.

VIDEO GAMES ARE EVERYWHERE!

Although the video game industry began in 1971 with the first commercially sold coin-operated video game, *Computer Space,* it didn't gain widespread attention until the release of the Atari 2600 game console in 1977. As we discussed in Level One, over the past forty years, the video game industry has grown to include hundreds of companies, with worldwide sales expected to grow to $82 billion by 2017.[114] This is not a surprise to gamers or anyone who has walked by a GameStop in the mall. In the United States, games are everywhere! They are in our living rooms, on our computer screens, and on our phones.

Just as our world is getting warmer, video games are hotter than they have ever been. We see the Grand Theft Fallacy at work with the belief, held by some, that the growing popularity of video games inevitably leads to more violence. The following figure displays the amount of money spent on video games between 1978 and 2011 (adjusted for inflation) and the number of violent assaults and murders that occurred during that same time period.

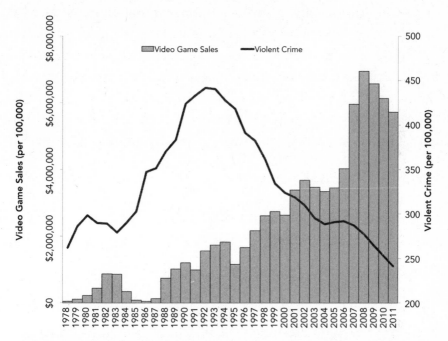

Contrary to claims that video games are related to increases in violence, we can see that in the past twenty years, violent crimes have *decreased* dramatically, even as video games have exploded in popularity. For example, since 1992, violent crime in the United States decreased by an impressive 42 percent during a time when video game sales increased by 267 percent![115] The sudden drop in violent crime came as a surprise to many researchers and media scientists who'd predicted that our country was heading toward a major crime wave, given the rising popularity of violent television and video games.

Before we get too far ahead of ourselves, allow us to say this: it is unlikely that the primary reason for such a dramatic decline in violence is that Americans prefer to commit fatalities in *Mortal*

Kombat or frag an opponent in *Call of Duty*. Instead, this general decrease in violence has been attributed to more police officers on the street, the end of the crack epidemic, and even the legalization of abortion.[116] A skeptic might conclude that these more powerful factors are the only reason video game sales are inversely related to violence. However, just as various democratic and economic factors could not account for the finding that video gaming countries are relatively more peaceful, the general decrease in violent crime in the United States does not explain the inverse relationship displayed in the figure above. When we control for the general trends in violence and in video game sales, the story remains the same—years in which video games were unusually popular were among the safest years in the United States.[115]

A STRATEGY GUIDE FOR MURDER?

Although the majority of video games contain some form of violence, it is possible that the overall sales we just examined do not provide accurate insight into when people are actually playing extremely violent video games. If these sorts of games really do make people violent, we would expect real-world violent crime to dramatically increase when people are virtually running amok through the streets of Liberty City in *Grand Theft Auto*.

Unfortunately, there is no easy way to determine exactly when people are playing violent video games in order to examine how this affects their violent tendencies. People, especially individuals who might commit murders, are not typically welcoming of psychologists entering their homes in order to record when they play *Call of Duty*.

One way around this problem is to examine other behaviors that might go along with a person playing a specific video game. For example, players often utilize "walkthroughs" or strategy guides to augment their experience. These strategy guides provide players with tips for getting through difficult levels, or even codes to alter the gaming experience. Before the omnipresence of the internet, retail sales of strategy guides for specific games frequently sold over one million copies. Back in the day, it wasn't unusual to find a dog-eared *Nintendo Player's Guide* for *Super Metroid* or *Street Fighter II* on the floor next to a Super Nintendo. These days, however, a simple Google search allows players to quickly find these guides online. Such walkthroughs and game guides are available on various websites, one of the most popular being *GameFAQs*.

Can't figure out how to best equip your character in *Call of Duty*? Google "gamefaqs Call of Duty," and you will soon be racking up virtual kills in your online death matches. Keep getting killed in the Three Leaf Clover level of *Grand Theft Auto*? Simply type the words "walkthrough Grand Theft Auto" into your handy search engine, and you will quickly learn how to survive this mission. If you do this, you are not alone. Immediately following the release of *Grand Theft Auto IV* on April 29, 2008, Google searches for "walkthrough Grand Theft Auto" increased an incredible 1,180 percent. These searches increased because millions of people were actively playing this violent video game. If playing *Grand Theft Auto* really contributes to violent crime, as people committing the Grand Theft Fallacy insist, we should find a similar spike in violent crime right around this same time period.

Using data supplied by Google, the following figure shows monthly reports of the numbers of people searching for walkthroughs of popular violent video games (e.g., *Call of Duty, Grand Theft Auto, Gears of War, Halo*, etc.) along with monthly reports of murders and assaults. Perhaps what is most obvious from this figure is that, almost every time there was a sudden surge in people searching for information about extremely violent video games, there was a similarly dramatic decrease in violent crime. In fact, it becomes clear that violent video game play and violent crime follow *opposite* seasonal patterns. More people play violent video games in the fall and winter, whereas violent crime is at its peak during the summer. One conclusion is unquestionable—any effect violent video games have on actual acts of violence is so small that it is dwarfed by whatever drives people to commit violent crimes during the summer (e.g., the heat).

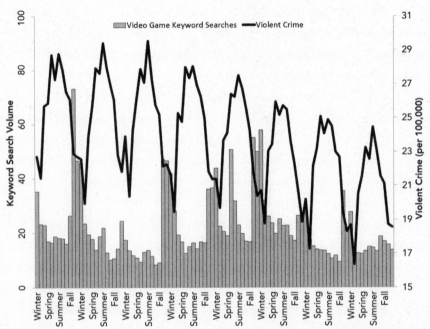

However, just as it was possible to control for social and economic variables and annual trends in violent crime, it is possible to remove these seasonal trends from the equation in order to see whether violent video gameplay is truly related to violent crime. Such a seasonal adjustment allows us to measure and remove any influence of predicable seasonal patterns (like crime tending to peak during the summer) to better reveal how violent video games are related to violent crime. At this point, you can probably guess what the data show. Even after we account for seasonal trends in violence, the months in which people played violent video games were still among the safest in the year.[115]

RELEASE DATES

Video game releases are similar to movie releases, and as with movies, the majority of the public consumes the product when it is first released. The violent first-person shooter *Call of Duty: Black Ops* earned $360 million the first day of its release, $650 million within the next four days, and had topped $1 billion in sales after forty-one days.[117] The impressive numbers for *Call of Duty: Black Ops* are not unique. For example, between 2003 and 2011, three of the most popular M-rated violent video games (*Grand Theft Auto: San Andreas, Grand Theft Auto IV,* and *Call of Duty: Black Ops*) earned over $3.5 billion in combined sales. With the popularity of such games comes the fear that their release will lead to a sudden epidemic of violence in the streets.

It was this fear that prompted critics of *Grand Theft Auto IV*, calling the game a "murder simulator,"[118] to predict that its release would constitute the "gravest assault upon children in this country since polio."[119] (Note: the most serious outbreak of polio in the United States occurred in 1952 when 57,628 people were infected, 21,269 were left paralyzed, and 3,145 died.) A newspaper put forth the grim headline "Grand Theft Auto IV: Violence Flares After Launch."[120] Rockstar, the company responsible for the Grand Theft Auto series, was forced to go to court to stop critics who were trying to prevent sales of the game through various lawsuits.

In the end, *Grand Theft Auto IV* was released in the United States as planned, on April 29, 2008. So, was this a date which will live in infamy? After 8.5 million copies of this "murder simulator" were sold in the first month, did the United States experience an epidemic of violence on par with that of polio?

Go on, guess.

One way to determine the impact that the release of *Grand Theft Auto IV* or any other game has on violence is to look at violent crime before and after the game is released. Pretty simple, right? If we see an unexpected and abrupt increase in crime when violent video games are released, it would suggest that these games might cause violent behavior. This exact same logic has been used to investigate a wide variety of important health issues.

For example, to prevent people from drinking and driving, the government often runs advertising campaigns. These campaigns typically consist of television and print ads in which people are warned that "Buzzed driving is drunk driving," "You booze, you cruise, you lose," and "Drive Hammered. Get Slammered." Beginning one spring day in March 1986, the residents of Wichita, Kansas, were exposed to a six-month-long media blitz of these colorful warnings against driving under the influence. To determine the success of this campaign, scientists examined the number of alcohol-related traffic fatalities and accidents before and after the campaign began. It was clear that these advertisements were having an impact, as the start of the campaign coincided with a sudden 22 percent drop in fatal automobile accidents.[121]

When scientists used these methods to examine violent crime following the release of extremely popular violent video games, they found—much to the surprise of video game critics—that the release of popular violent games actually coincides with a *reduction* in murders. For example, in the four months following the release of the games *Grand Theft Auto: San Andreas*, *Grand Theft Auto IV*, and *Call of Duty: Black Ops*, there were 616 fewer homicides than would have normally occurred during this same time period (see Easter Egg 2)![115]

Although *Grand Theft Auto IV* was not the game associated with the greatest decrease in homicides (that honor belongs to *Grand Theft Auto: San Andreas*, with a decrease of 269 homicides), following the release of the game, there were 123 fewer murders than would have been expected to occur in that period. Not only did the epidemic of violence that we were warned would ravage America's youth after the release of *Grand Theft Auto IV* never materialize, it seems that the game, far from being comparable to the scourge of polio, might be more aptly compared to the lifesaving polio vaccine.

In addition to the obvious good of "less murdering," the possibility that violent video games contribute to preventing violent crime has ramifications for our economy. Almost everyone is familiar with the old adage "crime doesn't pay." This may or may not be true, but one thing is certain: crime is expensive! The average home robbery ends up costing society about $6,462. This includes things like how much it will cost to increase police patrols in your neighborhood, loss of your new big-screen TV, administrative expenses, installing a new home alarm or changing the locks, lost work hours from the time you spend dealing with this situation instead of in the office, costs related to the criminal justice system, and so forth. Other crimes are even more expensive. Motor vehicle theft runs about $10,722, arson $21,103, violent assaults $107,020, rape $240,776, and each murder ends up costing society a staggering $8,982,907.[122] That means that *Grand Theft Auto: San Andreas, Call of Duty: Black Ops,* and *Grand Theft Auto IV* potentially saved not only 616 lives, but also a staggering 5.5 billion dollars.

WHY VIRTUAL VIOLENCE CAN MAKE YOU SAFE

As we've seen, despite the widespread notion that violent video games are related to increases in violent crime, the exact opposite seems to be true. Countries that consume more video games have lower levels of violent crime than those devoid of this media. Likewise, as video games have become more popular over time, homicides and violent assaults have decreased; even the release of extremely popular violent video games tends to be followed by dramatic downturns in the murder rate.

What is perhaps most striking about these findings is that they are not unique to video games—other forms of violent media have also been linked to decreases in violent crime. Contrary to the fear that violent television poses a threat to our society, assaults, rapes, and murders all decrease when people are watching extremely violent television shows.[123] Violent movies have been linked to similar decreases: as with video games, years in which the most violent movies were released coincide with lowered rates of violent crime[124] and decreases are also observed in the days immediately following the release of popular violent films. During the opening weekend of the gory film *Hannibal,* for example, assaults decreased 5.2 percent![125] It is remarkable that, regardless of the medium—games, movies, or television shows—the story is the same. When society is exposed to violent media, there is a consistent reduction in real-world violence. So, how is it that violent video games might make the world a safer place?

CATHARSIS?

Games are like sports and make us less violent and aggressive by giving us an outlet for our natural animal behavior. We love aggression and there needs [sic] to be mediums for us to use it or else it'll come out somewhere else. It's like having sex or going to the bathroom. You need to do it somewhere or else you'll go crazy. It's better to have it happen on a TV screen than in front of your wife and kids when you're drunk at a dinner party.
—Online forum comment

The sentiment expressed in the comment above is shared by many who believe that violent video games reduce our anger by giving us a way to vent our stress—allowing us to go on virtual rampages instead of real ones. In fact, gamers often explicitly indicate that they play violent video games in order to "feel relaxed" and to "help get my anger out."[126] The notion that the best way to find relief when you are upset or angry is to express these feelings seems, on the surface, like common sense. Feeling frustrated? Punch a pillow. Bad day at work? Go to the gym and assault a punching bag. Trouble with your spouse? Get some head shots in the latest first-person shooter.

While the idea behind this logic has been around for centuries, it was popularized by Sigmund Freud, who believed that people's minds are filled with unresolved conflicts, anger, stress, and anxiety, and that the only way to cleanse our minds is to let these negative emotions out. This is the basis of "catharsis theory," which posits that releasing one's anger reduces feelings of aggression. In this conception of human nature, our emotions are analogous to steam in a teapot. Imagine a teapot filled with water on a hot stove top. Normally, the steam in the teapot would safely vent through the spout. However, what happens if we put a cork in the spout and leave the water boiling? Eventually, if we don't remove the cork to let some steam out, the teapot might explode! In much the same way, catharsis suggests that if we keep our emotions bottled up and do not allow ourselves to safely "blow off some steam," we run the risk of these emotions building up until they erupt in an unpredictable and dangerous manner.[127]

The belief in the salubrious effects of expressing our anger can be found all over the world. Search for "stress ball" on Amazon and you will be presented with hundreds of squishy balls you can violently squeeze whenever you are upset. A personal favorite is a gigantic thirty-one-pound blue ball that is advertised as being able to soothe not only your soul, but also the pain associated with calcium problems—its price is $1,995. In Tokyo, stressed-out residents are invited to vent their anger by yelling as loud as possible in the city's annual screaming contest. A recent winner of this event hit a decibel level of 111.6 (about as loud as a turbofan aircraft at takeoff) as she let out her frustration about a politician.[128] Websites like rantrampage.com invite users to "Get your complaints off your chest and get a real good night's sleep" by posting anonymous rants to an online forum. At the turn of the century, one therapist even recommended regularly attending boxing matches or bullfights as a way to vent sadistic impulses.[129] But does releasing our aggression really work to reduce it?

As with most questions related to human behavior, the answer is a complex one. As we'll discuss in Level Eight, there's good evidence to suggest that playing video games, including violent games, can indeed reduce stress. Bottling up stress probably *isn't* a great idea, and finding positive ways to relieve tension and anxiety is generally healthy. Playing an action game may not be much different from going for a jog, working on your car, or any other hobby you enjoy—the benefit comes more from engaging in a pleasant, distracting activity than from venting anger per se. The social aspect of gaming may also help, in that being around others who enjoy your company tends to be stress relieving. So, for the most part, gamers are probably right when they say that gaming reduces their stress.

As for venting anger specifically, studies have had decidedly mixed results. In the early 1960s, one of the earliest studies to examine catharsis was carried out by asking nine-year-old children to build structures out of blocks—each working collaboratively with another child. The children were tasked with building five different structures; best of all, for each one they successfully created, the researcher promised them a shiny nickel (keep in mind, this was the 1960s, and these were nine-year-old children). It seemed like a pretty sweet deal, as the structures weren't particularly tricky. However, unbeknownst to the child subjects, the other kid in the experiment—their supposed partner—was really working for the researcher! This patsy's job was to do everything in his power to prevent the child from earning his nickel. He'd "accidentally" knock over the blocks, and mock the poor kid by saying, "Ha! You really need the money. Let's see how you can get it now." Who knew researchers were such trolls in the '60s? After the children failed at the building-block tasks (none of them earned any money, thanks to that little schmuck), some were allowed to shoot a toy gun at targets shaped like little boys and girls. The idea is that these children were being given the chance to vent their anger. According to catharsis theory, this "venting" should have made the kids feel better and calmer—paralleling the belief expressed by some gamers that taking their anger out on virtual enemies makes them less likely to blow up in the real world.

But back at the block experiment, as each child was leaving the laboratory, he saw the kid who'd kept him from his nickel sitting at a table with electric wires attached to his hands, leading to a shock apparatus. (This got dark pretty quickly!) The children were told that they could "get even" by pushing a button and administering electric shocks to the interfering tot who'd wronged them earlier. Fortunately, the kid attached to the electrodes did not really get shocked—researchers just wanted to see how many times the child would try to shock him. Contrary to the idea that letting our anger out makes us more peaceful, the children who were allowed to "blow off steam" by shooting at human-shaped targets tried to zap the kid in the chair just as often as those children who did not shoot the play gun.[130]

On the other hand, another study from about the same period did find evidence supporting catharsis.[131] This study was especially interesting because it examined boys living in a residential home, making the conditions a bit closer to "real life" than those of many laboratory studies. Some of the boys watched aggressive TV shows—like the great early *Batman* series starring Adam West (KA-POW!)—while the rest watched only nonaggressive programming. Interestingly, over time, the boys who watched the caped crusader battle the diabolical Joker actually became less aggressive! Some folks criticize this study, noting that the boys who were only allowed to watch nonaggressive TV became frustrated. They wanted their Batman! However, this is more or less what we'd expect if catharsis is helpful—that being deprived of opportunities to vent might sometimes make things worse.

Since these early studies, dozens more have been conducted, coming to a wide range of conclusions on the possible benefits of catharsis. It probably won't surprise readers that the a priori position researchers hold regarding media violence seems to be a pretty good predictor for what results they achieve. Those researchers who think media violence is bad just can't seem to find a catharsis effect in their studies,[132, 133] whereas more skeptical researchers often do![134, 135, 136, 137] Along with potential researcher bias, laboratory studies of catharsis suffer from the usual limitations of laboratory studies of human behavior—they are artificial, and often not very realistic approximations of the real-world situations they hope to illuminate. But even ignoring this for the moment, catharsis studies have a particular weakness: they assume that any given activity ought to be equally cathartic for everyone. Rather than annoying people and then letting them pick a cathartic activity (which is what happens in real life), everyone is assigned a set activity (punch a pillow, shoot a toy gun, watch *Batman*) that is assumed to be generally cathartic. But this is a dangerous assumption. If you annoy people and then assign them an activity that they also find annoying, this may indeed increase aggression. But if so, it's not because catharsis didn't work.

For example, you, personally, might find needlepoint to be incredibly soothing. But for the authors of this book, for whom an encounter with needle and thread usually ends in a visit to the emergency room, trying to engage in sewing crafts merely increases stress. If one were to conduct a study on the cathartic effects of needlepoint and happened to include non-needlepointers like us as subjects, one might conclude that needlepoint is agitating rather than cathartic. Draw the subjects from a local sewing circle and you'd get different results entirely. Catharsis works as a match between an individual and a task that they choose, and a given task cannot be assumed to work for everyone. Too often, social science makes "one size fits all" assumptions! Violent video games may, in fact, be very cathartic for some people. Others, particularly those not experienced in gameplay, may find them frustrating and become angrier, at least in the short term. In either case, it has less to do with the presence or absence of violence and more to do with whether people are engaging in an activity that they enjoy and that pleasantly distracts them.

So, if you feel that playing a violent game makes you less stressed, are you right? Probably. Does it then also make you less aggressive? That answer is more complicated, and, given the pool of largely low-quality research out there, the best we can do is shrug and say, "Who knows?" Perhaps the best way to think of gameplay is as a short-term stress reducer, but one with relatively little impact on longer-term aggression, either to increase or decrease it.

So, if violent video games are indeed associated with reduced societal violence, perhaps there's a better explanation than catharsis.

KEEPING TROUBLEMAKERS OFF THE STREETS

Weekdays at 3 PM: this is when young people are most likely to commit violent acts.[138] Weekdays before 3 PM are the safest times, when you are least likely to be murdered or assaulted by a rogue teen. The reason for this period of safety is obvious—school. By keeping youths contained in a fairly well-supervised location, we greatly reduce the amount of mayhem and destruction they can visit upon us. However, once the bell rings at three o'clock, schools around the nation send kids out onto the streets, and youth-related violence increases. We might recall high school mostly as a heady mishmash of angst, pep rallies, proms, and silly fashion (seriously, what were we thinking with parachute pants?) but schools have another, important function—in addition to their stated purpose of, you know, teaching kids things—they make our world a safer place.

Students who complain that their schools feel like prisons might be on to something. The logic behind the theory that keeping kids in school helps reduce violence is the same offered by various criminologists and economists who have concluded that physically incarcerating criminals in prisons reduces violence. It is estimated that for every person kept in prison, there are fifteen fewer crimes each year.[139] The reason both schools and prisons reduce crime is an obvious one: if you remove a potential perpetrator from the streets, he or she cannot commit a crime there. In order for a violent crime to take place, a perpetrator must be in the same location as a victim, and this location must usually be relatively free of those who would be likely to prevent the crime. Criminologists call this simple and powerful insight "routine activity theory," and have used it to explain the occurrence of all types of criminal activities—from corporate crime, copyright infringement via peer-to-peer sharing, work violence, and cyberbullying to standard criminal fare like robbery and violent attacks.[140] Essentially, if you can affect the presence of the perpetrator (e.g., place him in school), the victim (e.g., prevent him from walking down that dark alley), or those who might prevent the crime (e.g., increase the number of police officers), the crime is unlikely to occur.

Schools, therefore, reduce violence in three ways that work in tandem: First, they remove potentially violent youths from the streets. Second, schools also protect potential victims by placing *them* in classrooms—male teens are among those most likely to be victims of violent crimes. Finally, once in school, these potential criminals and victims are supervised—by teachers, administrators, and security personnel. Now, obviously, not every student in school is violent or destined to be the victim of violence. Not all violent youths even go to school. The point is, by removing a large percentage of the population from the streets and putting them behind desks, schools—like anything that prevents criminals and victims from meeting in an unsupervised and dangerous environment—reduce violence.

It is estimated that the average gamer spends about twenty-four hours a month playing games.[141] This level of gaming might be disappointing to parents and significant others who do not enjoy blasting virtual aliens. Perhaps they feel this time could have been spent more productively, for instance by playing basketball at a park, seeing a movie with friends, or going on a date. Instead, gamers are confining themselves to their homes for these hours, playing *Grand Theft Auto* or *Call of Duty*—which, in effect, removes them from the outside world. Sure, they may play socially, online or with friends, but they're not out roaming the streets. If any of these gamers happen to be violent, society will be protected from these individuals for each hour they spend playing. Even if none of these gamers are violent, by being in the relative safety of their homes, they are much less likely to be victims of violence.

The additional benefit of video games, especially violent ones, is that they target the exact people most likely to commit crimes and to be the victims of crime. The profile of a typical gamer, a guy between the ages of fifteen and twenty-nine, is almost an exact match for the profile of both the typical violent criminal and the typical crime victim![142] Now consider for how many hours video games keep these potential criminals and victims entertained and off the streets. Male gamers within this target age in the United States spend a total of 468 million hours each month playing video games. In a way, video games are the ultimate crime-reduction program, one that naturally targets those individuals at the highest risk for committing, or being victims of, violence. No taxpayer money required.

By now it should be clear that video games do far more to reduce violent street crime than to cause it. But despite the overwhelming evidence that the world is not made more dangerous by *Grand Theft Auto*, many still believe violent video games are a primary cause of one horrific form of violence in particular—school shootings.

EASTER EGGS

1. Of course, if a video game researcher truly believes this statement, it raises the question of whether he or she should be carrying out *any* experimental research on violent video games. Just as it would be unethical for a researcher to intentionally expose children to the dangers of cigarettes for a research study, a researcher who truly believes video games are this dangerous should have serious ethical reservations about exposing children to this media in the name of science.

2. Interrupted time-series analyses from Markey, Markey, and French (2014)[115] and annual population rates of the United States for the years each game was released were used to estimate the reduction in homicides. It is worth noting that other scholars in different areas have also found that violent video games are related to decreases in violent crime.[143, 144, 145]

LEVEL 5:

THE BIG LIE ABOUT SCHOOL SHOOTINGS

I t was a cool December morning when a nondescript Honda Civic stopped in the No Parking zone outside of Sandy Hook Elementary School in Newtown, Connecticut. Classes had just begun when a man in a hat and sunglasses exited the car carrying a rifle, a Glock 20, two pistols, and a large supply of ammunition. In less than ten minutes, the shooter—Adam Lanza—had killed twenty first-graders and six adults before turning the gun on himself.

The aftermath of the Sandy Hook shooting left everyone stunned. We both recall the sense of dread we felt the next school day when our own elementary-aged children set out for school. While school shootings were not new, they were a phenomenon most people associated with high schools. So, as with Columbine, it felt like a fresh horror, taking one of the locations we'd trusted as safe for our children and making it a place to fear. As a society, we wanted answers as to why this tragedy had occurred, and what could be done to prevent such a thing from happening again. What followed were debates about gun control, placing armed guards or security systems in schools, and mental health resources. However, when it was discovered that Adam Lanza had played violent video games, a substantial share of the public's concern shifted from real to virtual firearms.

Following the shooting, many media outlets reported that Lanza was not only obsessed with the first-person shooter game *Call of Duty*, but that this fascination was partially responsible for the murders. One veteran law enforcement officer, who was not even involved with the investigation, went so far as to suggest that Adam Lanza had transformed his desire to achieve a high score in a video game into a craving to score the greatest number of "points" (i.e., kills) in a real-life mass shooting. To obtain this high score, the officer reasoned, Adam Lanza selected an elementary school because it offered easy targets.[146] The officer also asserted that Adam Lanza learned many of the techniques he used in the attack from the video games he played. There was no evidence to support either of these dramatic conclusions, but this did not stop the media from covering them.

In response to the tragedy at Sandy Hook, Vice President Joe Biden convened a meeting focusing on violent video games, inviting a number of scholars—including one of the authors of this book (Ferguson)—and video game industry executives to participate. Surprisingly, during the meeting, the vice president stated that he did not actually believe video games were a serious concern or an important cause of mass shootings. Instead, he suggested that the video game industry's main problem was one of image, and also suggested that they do more to reach out to older adults and inform them about the existing ratings system. (See Easter Egg 1.)

In a press conference on gun violence held less than a week after the meeting, President Barack Obama called for the Centers for Disease Control and Prevention to investigate the effects of violent video games, saying that "Congress should fund research into the effects that violent video games have on young minds." You might well wonder, if the vice president was so dubious about video game violence being connected to mass shootings, why the White House called for more research on the topic in the wake of the Newtown tragedy. We can only speculate, of course, but it seems the White House may have included video games in order to appear that they were going after a wide range of cultural issues, rather than focusing solely on the hot-button issue of gun control. In the same press conference, for instance, Obama said, "While year after year those who oppose even modest gun safety measures have threatened to defund scientific or medical research into the causes of gun violence, I will direct the Centers for Disease Control to go ahead and study the best ways to reduce it."

Whatever members of the White House believed behind closed doors, President Obama's press conference forever linked violent video games to the Sandy Hook shooting. Various legislators soon joined this chorus of concern, with Senator Lamar Alexander even arguing that "video games is [sic] a bigger problem than guns, because video games affect people."[147] What followed was the introduction of numerous state and federal bills, including the federal "video games enforcement act," all aimed at protecting our children from the harmful effects of violent video games.

Throughout this book, we've seen how the media, politicians, and researchers have attempted to connect this medium to real acts of violence—for instance, as vividly illustrated by a 2013 Fox News story with the headline "Mass killers often share obsession with violent video games."[148] A recent report by the National Science Foundation even identifies exposure to violent media as one of three primary risk factors contributing to school shootings (the other two are access to guns and lack of mental health resources). The report concludes that reducing children's exposure to violent video games may be one solution to the epidemic of rampage shootings.[149] In response to reports like this one, schoolteachers and administrators around the country have been provided with "checklists" identifying the warning signs of students at risk of becoming the next

Adam Lanza. Educators in Michigan received the report "Checklist: Preventing and responding to school shootings," which provided a twenty-six-item list they could use to identify students who might become violent.[150] Parents in Colorado were given checklists in order to evaluate whether their own children were at risk for committing acts of violence at school.[151]

Once potential perpetrators are identified by these checklists, school officials or parents are instructed to refer them to counselors, mental health services, or law enforcement. As seen in the example checklist below, some of the items are obvious red flags, like "Has brought a weapon to school," "Is abusive towards animals," and "Consistently makes violent threats when angry." However, amidst these more sinister items is "Plays a lot of violent video games." Michigan and Colorado are certainly not unique in issuing such guidelines; numerous states, professional associations, and concerned groups have similarly noted that interest in violent video games is a potential "warning sign" of a school shooter.

EXAMPLE ITEMS USED TO IDENTIFY POTENTIAL SCHOOL SHOOTERS[150, 151]

- Has engaged in violent behavior in the past
- Is abusive toward animals
- Has brought a weapon to school
- Has a substance abuse problem
- Has been a victim of abuse or been neglected by parents/guardians
- Expresses sadistic, violent, prejudicial, or intolerant attitudes
- Has actually attempted suicide or acts of unfashionable self-mutilation

- Has repeatedly witnessed domestic abuse or other forms of violence
- Pays no attention to the feelings or rights of others
- Reacts to disappointments with extreme and intense anger or revenge
- Is involved in a gang or antisocial group
- **Plays a lot of video games**
- Consistently makes violent threats when angry
- Has inappropriate access to firearms
- Has uncontrollable outbursts abnormal for someone that age
- Seems preoccupied with weapons or violence, especially associated with killing humans

THE PROBLEM WITH WARNING SIGNS

We intervene early if we think a youngster has reading problems. We intervene early if we think a youngster has adjustment problems and matters of that type. So why shouldn't we intervene early if we think a youngster may be prone to violence?
—Joseph Cirasuolo, Superintendent of Schools, Wallingford, CT (1999)[152]

As evidenced by the quote above, school bigwigs who employ checklists to identify potential threats do so with the best of intentions. There is little doubt that these individuals are motivated by a genuine desire to keep the children in their schools as safe as possible. However, these checklists can have harmful consequences for the very children they are designed to protect. In 2013, a thirteen-year-old autistic student was suspended from school after he drew a picture

of the '90s video game character Bomberman. Based on this cartoonish drawing—Bomberman's level of violence is roughly akin to
that of Wile E. Coyote—the administration decided that it was best
to remove the student from school to "ensure everyone's safety while
the incident and intent were assessed."[153] School administrators run
the risk of unfairly labeling nonviolent students as potential threats
because of misunderstandings, or simply because the child does not
reflect the desired image of a typical student.

One might be tempted to conclude that if such checklists can
identify a future Adam Lanza, Eric Harris, or Dylan Klebold, it
might be worth incorrectly labeling a few innocent kids as violent
in order to save others from murderous rampages. We have to admit
that there is something appealing in this logic. However, this reasoning only works if the items on these checklists actually are effective
indicators of school violence. If not, then not only will such checklists wrongly label some innocent children as violent, but they may
also fail to detect those who pose a real threat.

Dr. Peter Langman is a clinical psychologist and an expert in
evaluating youth at risk of committing school shootings; he is the
author of the books *Why Kids Kill: Inside the Minds of School Shooters* and *School Shooters: Understanding High School, College, and
Adult Perpetrators*. Contrary to the checklists used to identify potential offenders, Dr. Langman warns that most of the valid warning
signs of school shooters are fairly explicit.[154] Look for a child who
is stockpiling weapons, writing up plans of attack, and even directly
telling others about a murderous plan. This is exactly what Andrew
Golden did: days before killing four students and one teacher at
Westside Middle School in Jonesboro, Arkansas, Andrew Golden
stood on a cafeteria table and announced: "You're all going to die."
His accomplice in this rampage, Mitchell Johnson, told others that
he had "a lot of killing to do" and even warned that "tomorrow you
will find out if you live or die."[155] Unfortunately, such obvious warning signs are often ignored, and instead, checklists, the media, and

others focus on whether or not perpetrators played video games, wore trench coats, or listened to Marilyn Manson.

Not only is "Plays a lot of violent video games" a poor predictor of future school violence, many of the cases responsible for creating the myth that school shooters play these games have since been disproven. In the days following the Sandy Hook Elementary School shooting, it was widely reported that Adam Lanza spent hours in his basement obsessively playing gory video games. This speculation resulted in headlines such as "Sandy Hook Shooter Motivated by Violent Video Games," "Killer's Basement His Eerie Lair of Violent Video Games," and "Adam Lanza Copied Video Game Scenario." However, the state of Connecticut's comprehensive final report on the shooting, released in 2013, revealed that if Adam Lanza did have a video game obsession, it was not with blasting virtual enemies, but rather with moving his body to the rhythms of upbeat pop music.[156] Data recovered from his car's GPS device led to the discovery that Lanza played the game *Dance Dance Revolution* at the local movie theater for anywhere from four to ten hours a week. Acquaintances interviewed by investigators confirmed that Lanza mostly played nonviolent games, his favorite being the ultra-cute and beloved classic *Super Mario Brothers*.

The Sandy Hook shooting was not the only such event to be linked to violent video games, only to have that link turn out to be nonexistent. Following the shootings at Virginia Tech University in 2007, countless media outlets suggested that the killer, Seung-Hui Cho, was influenced by the violent first-person shooter game *Counter-Strike*. However, a governmental panel created to investigate the shootings found no evidence that Cho had ever played or even owned the game *Counter-Strike—or any other violent video game*.[157] Even the popular notion that Columbine shooters Eric Harris and Dylan Klebold had created levels in *Doom* resembling parts of their high school is a myth. These killers did indeed play *Doom* and, like many players, they created custom levels—but these levels occurred in fictional worlds (one level asked players to kill demons on the fictional planet of Phobos). There is no evidence to suggest that they ever modified *Doom* to simulate the physical layout of Columbine High School, or that they played it over and over in order to "train themselves for the massacre."[158]

VIDEO GAME ABSTINENCE AND VIOLENCE

The desire to protect children from terrible acts of violence is understandable, but unfortunately, there is no evidence that checklists correctly identify potential perpetrators, much less that they have ever prevented a single school shooting. And it's more than the fact that not all kids who enjoy violent games are at risk of becoming violent. Actually, data from the United States Secret Service finds that the opposite might be true—*abstinence* from playing violent video games is a better predictor of future school violence than *interest* in this medium.

It might seem odd that the Secret Service is involved in preventing school violence. After all, their mission is to protect the president and vice president of the United States; we usually think of Secret Service agents as the people who run alongside armored limousines in dark suits and sunglasses, identifiable by their stern expressions and the curled wire of their earpieces. However, the Secret Service also employs less visible strategies to protect the members of the White House. These covert operations fall under the broad heading of "Threat Assessment," and focus on identifying individuals who might be dangers to the president or other high-ranking protectees.

It turns out that real-life assassins are nothing like the cunning fictional masterminds depicted in movies and books. Instead, these killers tend to lead fairly boring, pedestrian lives before they attack public officials. Most are socially isolated and view the assassination as the best means of improving their lives and achieving some level of fame or notoriety.[159] The would-be assassin of Ronald Reagan, John Hinckley Jr., was a former busboy and college dropout. In high school he'd had few friends and spent hours alone in his room. He eventually became obsessed with the actress Jodie Foster, and decided that killing the president of the United States would elevate his status sufficiently to garner her attention. In a letter he wrote to the actress immediately before his attempt on Reagan's life, he declared his intent to shoot the president because "I cannot wait any longer to impress you." By examining the cases of John Hinckley Jr. and other assassins, the Secret Service was able to create a prototype, or "profile," to be used to identify individuals who pose threats to public officials.

This approach proved so useful that, in 1998, the Secret Service established the National Threat Assessment Center in order to prevent violent behavior among the general public. Following several well-publicized school shootings, including the tragic events at Columbine High, the researchers at the Secret Service used the profiles of known school shooters to adapt their system for identifying political assassins into one meant to detect perpetrators of school violence. (See Easter Egg 2 for more information.) They found the following:

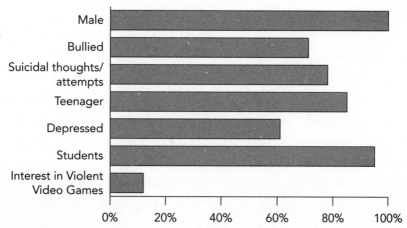

THE CHARACTERISTICS OF A TYPICAL
SCHOOL SHOOTER

As you can see in the previous figure, the school shooters tended to be male, were bullied by their peers, had previously attempted suicide or experienced suicidal thoughts, had a history of feeling depressed or desperate, and were students at the school where the violent act was carried out. This is consistent with the stereotype often presented of a school shooter, although such characteristics are too broad to be very useful in identifying future perpetrators. One trait, however, occurred much more rarely than most people suspect: only a small minority of school shooters played violent video games. Contrary to the claims of the media, politicians, and researchers, only 12 percent of school shooters exhibited an "interest in violent video games."[160] (See Easter Egg 3.)

The average perpetrator examined in the Secret Service study was born after 1981 and committed his crime around 1995. Most of these attackers grew up during what is referred to as the "golden age of video games." During this period, rapid technological innovation prompted the popularity of both home and arcade video games to skyrocket, with annual US home video game sales soaring from $250 million to an amazing $4.7 billion.[161] As preteens, these attackers saw the introduction of the Sega Genesis and Super Nintendo; while visiting friends or family it's likely they'd have seen games like *Streets of Rage*, *Ghosts 'n Ghouls*, *Castlevania*, and *Contra*. In arcades they watched others play *Street Fighter II* and the ultraviolent *Mortal Kombat*. These future killers witnessed the arrival of online "death matches"—gamers virtually shooting each other in games of *Doom* and *Duke Nukem 3D*. In short, there is little doubt that these school shooters grew up in a world where violent video games were not only available but overwhelmingly popular. Yet even with the widespread availability of virtual blood and gore, only 12 percent were attracted to this media.

A lack of interest in violent video games continues to be a common feature of shooters in more recent attacks. For this book, we asked Dr. Peter Langman to provide an assessment of the media habits of the perpetrators of the ten most violent mass shootings on school campuses since the release of the Secret Service report. Among these are such infamous individuals as Seung-Hui Cho (Virginia Tech, 2007), Jeffrey Weise (Red Lake Senior High School, 2005), and Adam Lanza (Sandy Hook Elementary School, 2012). All told, the ten mass murderers were responsible for the deaths of over 100 people between 2005 and 2012. Contrary to the media image of these shooters as obsessed with virtual violence, Dr. Langman's analyses of their habits found that only 20 percent played violent video games with any amount of regularity. Not only is interest in violent video games rare among school shooters, these perpetrators actually express significantly *less* interest in this violent medium than most of their peers. If you were to enter any high school in America, you'd find that about 70 percent of the male students habitually play violent video games.[162, 163] To put this into perspective, the figure below displays the video game habits of school shooters and those of the typical high school student. (See Easter Egg 4 for more detail.)

Who is more interested in violent video games?

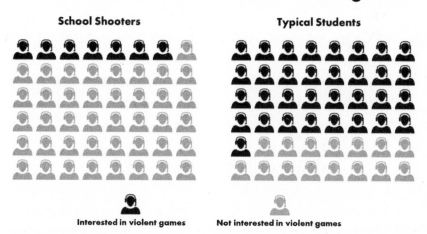

School Shooters   Typical Students

Interested in violent games   Not interested in violent games

Persistent beliefs in a link between mass shootings and video games also rely on a psychological concept called *confirmation bias*. When we believe in something very strongly, we tend to pay closer attention to events that confirm our beliefs, and ignore or dismiss events that would challenge them. We've created an illusionary correlation between perpetrators of a particular kind—generally young, middle-class guys—and violent video game play. Thus, when a young male commits a horrible crime, we pay a lot of attention to the issue of video games. In a way, of course, this is "cheating." Almost all young men and boys have played violent video games, so it's very likely that our hypothetical shooter has as well, at least at some point. As we've seen from examples like Sandy Hook and Virginia Tech, even those shooters who were infrequent players of violent games are sometimes mistakenly used to support this mythical link. By the time early speculation is discredited, it is too late to make much of a difference—we are far more likely to remember news coverage we saw at the time of the event than a follow-up report published months after the fact.

But consider the following example. On one Friday in February of 2012, a horrible shooting rocked the University of Alabama in Huntsville. An ordinary meeting of the biology department was suddenly interrupted by a disturbed individual with a history of erratic and even violent behavior. This person methodically shot several professors in the head at close range, execution style, only stopping when the gun jammed. Three professors died and three others were wounded. The shooter was apprehended minutes later upon leaving the building.

Deranged violent video gamer? Well, no. The shooter in this case was forty-four-year-old Amy Bishop, another professor in the biology department, apparently distraught over not receiving tenure. Not only did she have a history of volatile and threatening behavior, but Bishop is now thought to have killed her younger brother over twenty years ago in a shooting incident ruled an accident at the time. No one has speculated that this middle-aged neurobiologist and mother of four was influenced by violent video games. In fact, in media coverage of the case, no one mentioned video games at all, not even to observe that Bishop *did not* play them. Bishop is only one such example of a tragedy involving an older adult shooter, in which the topic of video games is simply avoided. When the shooter is a young male, we talk video games; when the shooter is an older man or a woman, we don't. And so the impression that mass shooters always play violent video games is maintained by simply ignoring cases that do not support this false belief.

WHAT'S NORMAL IS NORMAL

The video game habits of killer Seung-Hui Cho are notable not because he reveled in virtual gore, but because he was a twenty-three-year-old Virginia Tech student who did *not* conform to the social norm of playing violent video games. His roommate and many of his classmates found him "strange," and the fact that Seung-Hui Cho never played video games—most other students did—was one of the oddities they cited.[157] It is not always clear why we feel unease around others whose behavior deviates from the expected; we may be especially alert around people like Seung-Hui Cho because displays of nonconforming behavior can be a sign of deeper underlying psychological issues.

To demonstrate the power of conformity, we're going to show off our psychic skills. We have never met you, but allow us to tell you a few things about yourself:

You bathe regularly. When on an elevator, you face toward the door. You attended (or are attending) high school. It is unlikely that you would show up to a church service in a bathing suit. You say "hello" when answering the phone. Although you might talk aloud to yourself when you're alone, you are unlikely to do so in public.

So, are you amazed by our psychic abilities? We're (psychically) guessing not—you were probably underwhelmed by this demonstration because you figured out we were simply listing traits that apply to almost everyone.

We like to think of ourselves and our children as distinctive individuals. We are independent thinkers and our desires are not dictated by others; we are unique. However, as our psychic abilities demonstrated, there are many behaviors we express that are not particularly distinctive. This is because we all change our behaviors in order to fit in with our friends, families, and peers. We wear appropriate clothes, face the front in an elevator, and don't talk to ourselves in public in order to avoid inviting the scorn and distrust of others. Go ahead: we dare you to have an animated conversation with yourself about economic equality while wearing a pink tutu and a cowboy hat as you ride in a full elevator, facing the back wall. Obviously this is a bit extreme, but you need only step outside and observe how others dress and interact with one another to understand the power of social norms.

Conforming to the expectations of our social group is not only a basic feature of human behavior, it is a sign of psychological health. The link between conformity and health was demonstrated to dramatic effect in pioneering research conducted over thirty-five years ago in Berkeley, California. Imagine you are a teenager in the 1970s, growing up in the birthplace of the hippie movement, which rebelled against the conservative ideals of the previous generation and embraced the sexual revolution, psychedelic music, and recreational drug use. You just bought the newest Pink Floyd album, *Dark Side of the Moon*; you set aside time each week to watch *M*A*S*H* and *Good Times* on TV; and almost everyone you know is smoking pot. This scenario is not so far removed from reality, as, at the time, a clear majority of young people in the area were experimenting with marijuana.[164]

So, hypothetical Berkeley teen, when your friends pass around a joint, what do you do? Much to your parents' dismay, if you are psychologically healthy, you probably take it. This is what the Berkeley researchers found—those youths who were well-adjusted, inquisitive, and sociable were also the most likely to experiment with pot.

In contrast, teens who abstained from the drug were more likely to be anxious, unable to enjoy experiences, prone to avoiding close relationships, and not well liked by others. However, it was not the lack of pot smoking that caused the abstainers to exhibit these qualities. The study followed a group of children from preschool through adolescence. At the age of seven, years before they had the opportunity to experiment with marijuana, the future abstainers expressed these same unhealthy characteristics. These children were described by their parents as fearful, anxious, not curious, not energetic, not responsive to humor, and not cheerful.[164] In short, the young people in 1970s Berkeley who avoided drugs mostly did so not out of moral fortitude, but because they were uptight social outcasts.

This research does not imply that drug experimentation and psychological health go hand in hand—context is everything. In Berkeley during this specific time period, youth marijuana use was a normative activity, and not engaging in such a normative behavior was, by definition, deviant. Consistent with this reasoning, in contexts where drug use is *not* a normative activity for teens, abstainers do not display the same psychological issues seen in abstainers in the Berkeley study.[165] The principle extends beyond drug use, of course. In general, children who are deviant—who do not share the same interests as their peers—often have trouble finding acceptance. Many are rejected, forced to entertain themselves because no other children seem to understand them.[166] Simply put, it is developmentally appropriate for youths to seek out experiences that are the norm for their peer group. This doesn't mean that these experiences are always good ones, or that they don't have potential consequences of their own. But it does mean that while, as parents, we might worry about some of these popular activities (playing video games, for instance), it is important for us to remember that children who fail to engage in them often suffer from maladaptive characteristics and experience rejection as a result.

We are not advocating mindless conformity, of course. Neither of your authors could exactly be described as exemplars of the mainstream. (Markey has the unusual hobby of collecting vintage computers, and Ferguson is a huge fan of *Dungeons & Dragons*, both sure paths to geek-cred, but not necessarily prom-king status.) Rather, the point is this: if your goal is to identify troubled kids, or compile a list of "warning signs," note that it is *unusual* behavior that functions best as a risk factor, not behavior that is normal. And at the moment, playing video games—even violent ones—is the norm.

REJECTION, SOCIAL SKILLS, AND VIDEO GAME PLAY

We like to be liked. Everyone gets upset when they feel ignored, unappreciated, or as if others do not want them around. For most of us, this sense of rejection results in some hurt feelings, which—after a few tears, perhaps—we get over. However, for some, a sense of rejection can be so intense that it leads a person to commit extreme acts of violence. Following the 1999 Columbine shootings, Dr. Dewey Cornell testified before the House Judiciary Committee that most school shooters feel "lonely and isolated."[167] Consistent with this conclusion, researchers have found that in almost every school shooting, the perpetrator felt that others had rejected him. These shooters felt bullied and ostracized by their peers, and they acted violently in order to maintain their self-esteem by demonstrating their power and showing others they were not to be trifled with.[168]

The unfortunate motivational power of rejection was vividly demonstrated in 1997 when sixteen-year-old Luke Woodham stabbed his mother, killed two students, and injured seven others at his high school before being stopped by an assistant principal. Before the shooting, Woodham handed a message to one of his friends:

"I am not insane, I am angry. I killed because people like me are mistreated every day. I did this to show society, 'push us and we will push back' . . . All throughout my life I was ridiculed, always beaten, always hated . . . It was a scream in sheer agony saying that if you can't pry your eyes open, if I can't do it through pacifism, if I can't show you through the displaying of intelligence, then I will do it with a bullet."[169]

The rejection experienced by many school shooters appears to be, in part, related to the difficulty they had interacting with others.[168] Early news coverage of the Sandy Hook shooting reported that shooter Adam Lanza was "weird," "different," and a "socially awkward" person with very few friends. It was later discovered that Lanza had been diagnosed with Asperger syndrome, a disorder not related to violent behavior, but one that often causes difficulties in social interactions.

Although some people are born with better social skills than others, there is little doubt that interacting with other people increases our social competence. Every activity we engage in with other humans provides us with an opportunity to learn how to better initiate, build, and maintain social relationships. This is why one of the most popular techniques used by psychologists to teach social skills to children (or adults) is simply to have them interact with other people![170] In short, just like golfing, driving, and playing the piano, the best way to improve your social skills is practice, practice, practice.[171] To practice golf you might go to a driving range. To practice social skills, you join others in activities in which you share a common interest—you do things you like together. Video games are even more popular with the youth of today than marijuana was with those long-haired kids in the Berkeley of the 1970s. A child who grows up in the world of Nintendo, Sega, Xbox, and PlayStation and abstains from video games will miss out on numerous social interactions related to this medium. Even children recognize the social importance of video games—many characterize gaming as a way to interact with current friends and even make new ones.

Adults often overlook the value of simply playing games—any game, whether it is hide-and-seek, Monopoly, or a video game. It is easy to dismiss any of these activities as a waste of time that does little other than temporarily improve our mood. However, psychologists have long stressed the benefits of play for both children and adults.[172, 173] Play lets children improvise, try out imaginary identities, and construct narratives. Children take fictional journeys with their friends: they rescue princesses, put on plays, form families, and skulk around as secret agents. Ferguson's son, Roman, tells elaborate stories using Legos. However, at twelve, Roman often worries that playing with Legos will make him look childish to his peers, showing how adult social pressures can impede play instincts (which is a little surprising, considering his ostensibly "adult" father currently has the Lego *Star Wars* X-Wing, Gandalf, and *Doctor Who*'s TARDIS sitting on his desk). But playing encourages children to problem solve and to collaborate. Kids playing together come up with techniques for dealing with conflict—working out various resolutions, learning how to interact with their peers, and experiencing different emotions. These interpersonal skills—learned by "just playing"—are likely why children who engage in fantasy play tend to have better social skills and generally positive social interactions, are more popular, and possess greater empathy.[174, 175]

The benefits afforded by playing with friends are just as strong in the virtual world as they are in the real one. Contrary to the stereotype of video gamers as introverts who isolate themselves in their parents' basements, more than 70 percent of gamers play with friends. Depending on your age, you might even recall planning your next virtual move while sitting on the floor with your own friends in front of your Atari, Nintendo, or PlayStation. And along with the actual play of video games, there is an active gaming subculture. In this world, kids have conversations about games, share games, have gaming "meet ups," and strategize with one another. For example, as the sons of both authors can attest, the popular game *Minecraft* has become central to much of the social interaction among the elementary and middle school crowd (see Easter Egg 5). This game allows players to set their own goals, collect resources, battle enemies, craft items like tools and furniture, and freely create a three-dimensional world. When our sons and their friends get together to play *Minecraft*, they communicate with each other about the game world, deal with disputes, and come to agreements as to what will occur in their virtual realm. Even when the game itself is off, they make plans about what to build next, how to defeat an enemy, or how to craft a certain item. Parents often express concern that their kids are "obsessing" about a video game, but video game play is not so different from play in the real world, and provides the same opportunities to practice interacting with others, dealing with conflict, and working out collaborative solutions to problems.

These days, many friends who play video games together are doing so not on living room floors but in the virtual world. *World of Warcraft* has over twelve million players who regularly socialize online. They form "clans" and work together to battle giants, the undead, wolves, and dragons while searching for treasure. Even casual gamers connect with friends and family in social media games like *FarmVille* and *Restaurant City*. Any game that rewards players for working together to achieve a common goal will teach social skills that generalize to relationships in the real world.[176] These real-life skills help gamers not only socially but emotionally—research shows that young people who play video games tend to be more satisfied with their lives and experience fewer conduct problems, peer problems, and emotional issues than those who do not.[177]

And playing with others is just as good for us whether we are working together to build a virtual community in *FarmVille* or plotting to infiltrate a bank using pistols, knives, and machine guns in *Grand Theft Auto*. Although the images presented in such a game are violent, researchers have found that youths who play violent video games cooperatively tend to express helping behaviors in the "real world."[178, 179] Such cooperative gameplay even fosters feelings of camaraderie and altruistic behaviors between people who might not normally get along. One of us (Markey) lives just outside of Philadelphia. He is well aware that a person wearing a Philadelphia Eagles jersey will probably not be moved to shower someone wearing a New York Giants jersey with brotherly love. However, if these two sports fans were made to work together in a violent game like *Grand Theft Auto,* they would subsequently be less aggressive and more supportive toward each other in the real world.[180]

To sum up, unlike most school shooters, young people who play violent video games are not maladjusted social outcasts. Instead, playing video games, like engaging in any popular activity, is an indicator of underlying psychological health. Enjoying the same activities as one's peers is not only normal, it provides a sense of acceptance and belonging—feelings most school shooters lack. As we've seen, video games build social skills: by playing with friends, gamers learn how to compromise, follow rules, take turns, resolve conflicts, and solve problems. Given this link between video games and social skills, it shouldn't be surprising that children who play video games every day also interact with their friends in the "real world" just as frequently as other kids.[163] Contrary to their stereotype as antisocial loners, people who enjoy violent first-person shooter games like *Call of Duty* or fighting games like *Mortal Kombat* are also more sociable, outgoing, and talkative than those who do not enjoy these games.[181] And as the data collected by researchers and the Secret Service has shown, school shooters, contrary to their own stereotype, play violent video games *less* than the average youth.

The link between violent video games and school shootings is a myth. There is no evidence that video games cause people like Luke Woodman, Adam Lanza, and Seung-Hui Cho to pick up real guns and murder their families, peers, and teachers. These violent perpetrators lashed out at the world not because they'd practiced killing invading demons in *Doom* or performed gruesome "fatalities" in *Mortal Kombat,* but because they lacked social skills, experienced intense peer rejection, and were unstable and psychotic.

If you've read this far, you've seen that the crusade against violent video games is as much about culture as it is about actual danger, that the research supporting this crusade is seriously flawed, and that there is no connection between video game violence and school shootings or, indeed, any other acts of real violence. However, saying that it doesn't result in bloodshed isn't the same as saying this uniquely interactive media has no negative effects. The next two chapters of this book focus on some of these additional concerns—beginning with video game addiction.

EASTER EGGS

1. One other amusing anecdote emerged from this meeting. In the midst of it, Vice President Biden stated that he understood that youth violence was going up, particularly among very young children. As you learned in a previous chapter, this was absolutely not true. Youth violence, among all ages, has been declining for decades. There is no way to parse the data to come to any other conclusion. So, Ferguson raised his trembling hand to inform the vice president of the United States that he was wrong. Your brave author then proceeded to pass around a graph using the government's own data, depicting the massive decline in youth violence even as video game sales soared. To this day, Ferguson nervously awaits his IRS audit.

2. In order to develop this profile, scientists at the Secret Service identified thirty-seven incidents of school violence perpetrated by forty-one individuals. By examining police reports, school reports, court records, and mental health information, as well as interviewing surviving perpetrators, the researchers were able to create the profile of a typical school shooter.

3. One potential limitation of the Secret Service report is that it included several cases that occurred before violent video games were widely available. For example, the Atari 2600 had been out for only a year on October 15, 1978, when a thirteen-year-old in Lanett, Alabama, shot his principal with a .22 caliber handgun. However, even when these cases are removed from the Secret Service analysis, the percentage of school shooters with some amount of interest in violent video games increases only to 14 percent.[160]

4. Although the differences in video game habits between school shooters and typical high school students are dramatic, scientists recognize the importance of conducting statistical tests to get a sense of whether these differences are "real" and meaningful or

just a result of chance. The math behind these statistical analyses is sometimes complex, but the basic logic is fairly easy to understand. Imagine you flipped a coin fifty times. Say out of these fifty flips the coin came up heads ten times. Everyone knows the coin should come up heads about 50 percent of the time. So what are the odds of a coin coming up heads ten out of fifty times (20 percent) when probability tells us to expect heads 50 percent of the time? It turns out this is pretty unlikely to happen—the odds of getting so few heads by chance are only one in 100,000. Based on this result, you would be correct to suspect something fishy is going on with your coin! You might not know exactly why it is different, but it is safe to assume that there is something about your coin that makes it produce significantly fewer "heads" flips than a typical coin.

5. Much like computing the probability of a coin flip, it is possible to determine whether the popularity of violent video games among school shooters is statistically less than that of typical students. Out of the forty-eight school shooters examined by the Secret Service and Dr. Langman, only seven were interested in violent video games—15 percent. It seems safe to assume, given the data, that 70 percent of typical students have an interest in violent video games.[163] Just as we did with a given series of coin-flip results, it is possible to compute the odds that only seven out of forty-eight school shooters (15 percent) would have had an interest in violent video games, given that 70 percent of youths typically express such an interest. It turns out the odds of such a finding occurring due to chance is one in thirty-six trillion (that's a thirty-six with twelve zeros after it)! In fact, the probability that this result is just a statistical fluke is less than the chance of flipping a coin forty times in a row and having it come up heads each time, or of getting hit by a falling meteorite, or of being struck by lightning *twice* in a single year. This not only discredits the belief that interest in violent video games is a valid indicator

of children who might be dangerous, but demonstrates that this notion is entirely backward.

6. We are tempted to jokingly point out that *Minecraft* is sometimes called "Mine-Crack" because of its overwhelming popularity.[182] Alas, as you will learn in the next chapter, many people take this comparison a little too literally and believe video games really *are* as addictive and damaging as illicit drugs. We can already see the headline if we included a "Mine-Crack" joke: "Video Games Are Like Crack Cocaine, Say Book's Authors."

LEVEL 6:

VIDEO GAME ADDICTION

One evening in 2012, tragedy befell a young man at an internet café. Chen Rong-yu entered the establishment in Taipei, Taiwan, at about 10 PM and paid for twenty-three hours—almost a full day—of computer access. Rong-yu was a regular customer, and this wasn't particularly unusual. He was there to play *League of Legends*, a popular online game often featured in professional video game tournaments. *League of Legends* is fast paced and requires intense concentration—it is not uncommon for players to remain at their computers for long periods, completely absorbed. That night, however, about halfway through his time, Rong-yu slumped over. The waitress attending to the café's customers figured he was sleeping. For the next nine hours, people in the café continued to come and go around him without noticing anything amiss. Only when Rong-yu's twenty-three hours were up and the waitress tried to rouse him did she learn the horrible truth: his face was blackened, and his rigid hands remained outstretched toward the mouse and keyboard. He had died hours earlier.[183]

It would later be determined that twenty-three-year-old Chen Rong-yu had a preexisting heart condition. This, combined with the cool temperatures of the café and long hours spent in sedentary activity, led to the formation of a blood clot, which traveled to his heart and killed him. The game hadn't killed Rong-yu directly, of course, and were it not for his preexisting condition, even his obsessive twenty-three-hour gaming binges would likely have been physically harmless. But the case of Chen Rong-yu is just one of a number that have popped up in news headlines linking a death to the overuse of video games. Sometimes these stories involve players neglecting their own health because they were unable to tear themselves away from the controller, other times the players neglected children or loved ones. Do these cases represent a new epidemic? Like many issues related to video games, the question of whether they have the addictive potential of alcohol, methamphetamine, or gambling is one that has produced its fair share of controversy and confusion. Of course some people use video games in ways that are not healthy—that's true for just about anything pleasurable. But is there something unique about video games that makes them more addictive than other activities that people enjoy?

WHAT IS VIDEO GAME ADDICTION?

We often hear parents complain that their children are "addicted" to video games. Usually these complaints come in mildly exasperated tones—in most of these cases, Junior's parents do not really think he is *addicted* to video games. Parents would not roll their eyes and wag their fingers in annoyance if they thought their child were addicted to cocaine! These parents feel that Junior's time would be better spent doing homework or mowing the lawn—not that we adults were much more enthusiastic about these tasks when we were kids. When our children spend a lot of time on an activity we don't personally value, we tend to call it an addiction, but, clearly, we know this is different from an addiction to alcohol or pills. In many ways, saying our kids are addicted to video games is like saying that we are addicted to chocolate or Netflix. We don't mean it in a clinical sense. In fact, at present, only one behavioral addiction—gambling—is recognized by the American Psychiatric Association as a mental illness.[184] Other things we hear called addictions, like sex or food or work, are not officially recognized as such.

So what makes something an addiction? After all, many people play poker without becoming addicted to gambling, or toss back a martini without becoming alcoholics. The key when it comes to addiction is the interfering nature of the behavior. That is to say, a behavior may have become addictive if it is interfering with a person's other life responsibilities. While it may not be recognized as a separate and diagnosable mental illness, video game playing, just like gambling (or sex, food, exercise, etc.) *can* be addictive, and we evaluate this by examining whether it interferes with our ability to do schoolwork, get to work on time, or maintain our relationships. Consider the following two examples:

- Jose is a twelve-year-old boy who loves video games. Left to his own devices, he could easily spend four to five hours a day playing games, more on weekends. Jose sometimes tussles with his parents over this, because they would like him to have more varied interests. He has maintained good grades in school: mainly As and Bs. He frequently plays video games online with a wide circle of friends.
- Amanda is a thirteen-year-old girl who enjoys playing video games on her iPad. She plays for roughly two to three hours each day. She is also active in dance and an engineering club at school. When she comes home, she has difficulty focusing on schoolwork, and gravitates

instead to her iPad. Her parents haven't had much luck getting her to finish her homework. As a result, her grades have been slipping, and she is at risk of failing eighth grade. Amanda is aware of the problem but has difficulty reducing her gameplay.

Which of these two preteens is more likely to be addicted to video games? If you answered "Amanda," you are absolutely right. Her grades are slipping as a direct consequence of her time spent on video games rather than homework, and she has difficulty changing her behavior despite being aware of the problem. Note: time spent on an activity isn't the best predictor of addictive behavior. This is the first of the great myths of video game addiction. Jose actually spends more time on video games than Amanda does, but he is still engaged with his schoolwork and his friends. He doesn't always agree with his parents about how much he should play, but these types of disagreements are normal. His parents may not approve of or understand his hobby, but being intensely involved with a single hobby is not necessarily a sign of addiction.

Consider the case of Rebecca Colleen Christie. In 2006, Christie was playing the online game *World of Warcraft* for up to fifteen hours a day, neglecting her three-year-old daughter. Christie completely abandoned her parental duties, and, eventually, her small daughter starved to death. At the time of her death, the girl weighed only twenty-three pounds. Christie was sentenced to twenty-five years in prison.[185]

For Rebecca Christie, playing *World of Warcraft* was an addiction because it diminished her ability to take care of her daughter. Of course, this is an extreme example; most cases of video game addiction are, thankfully, not remotely as severe. Because outcomes like those of Christie and Chen Rong-yu are so unusual, they make the news, which gives the public a mistaken impression about what video game addiction is really like. The effects are more commonly mundane, such as being late for work, neglecting schoolwork, or for-getting important dates.

Just as common as the myth that video game addiction is a func-tion of how much a person plays is the myth that video game addiction is "just like" addiction to illicit substances such as alcohol, metham-phetamine, or heroin. These claims make for great headlines, but they are not based on reality. It is important to remember that even when a person is truly addicted to video games, the consequences—while often distressing—are typically nothing like the problems expe-rienced by people who are addicted to drugs and alcohol, or even gambling. The table on the next page provides some fairly standard examples, based on real cases of alcohol addiction, heroin addiction, and video game addiction, to provide some perspective.

We certainly acknowledge that addictions can vary in magnitude—on the one hand we have "functional alcoholics," on the other, those who have let their babies starve in order to play video games. Nonetheless, the examples in the table are pretty good repre-sentations of typical cases and nicely illustrate that not all addictions are equally harmful.

One of the leading researchers in this field—Dr. Mark Griffiths, director of the International Gaming Research Unit at Nottingham Trent University—has firsthand experience with the media and oth-ers wrongly conflating video game addiction with other, more severe types of addiction. In July 2014, British newspaper *The Sun* ran a checklist Dr. Griffiths had created to identify symptoms of video game addiction alongside an article proclaiming video games to be "as addictive as heroin."[186] As Dr. Griffiths explained in a follow-up article of his own, *The Sun* piece had sensationalized and exag-gerated a complex issue.[187] Substance addictions typically involve intense biochemical reactions that result in physiological tolerance (the need to consume more and more of a substance to get the same effect) and withdrawal (unpleasant and sometimes potentially fatal medical symptoms resulting from discontinuation of the substance).

PROTOTYPICAL CASE OF **ALCOHOL** ADDICTION

Ted is a forty-five-year-old white male who has been drinking daily for over twenty years. He has difficulty maintaining a job, his wife has left him, and he has poor relationships with his kids. His doctor has told him that he is starting to show signs of Karsakoff syndrome, a neurological degeneration typical of long-term alcoholics, as well as liver disease. Nonetheless, alcohol is Ted's main stress reliever, so he continues to drink.

PROTOTYPICAL CASE OF **HEROIN** ADDICTION

Amy is a forty-four-year-old Hispanic female who has been using heroin regularly for about twenty years. Without heroin, she has difficulty functioning at all—her body is in pain, and her mind is unable to focus on anything other than getting more heroin. When she's on the drug she's calmer, but she has missed out on having a real career or family, instead bouncing between odd jobs and occasional prostitution.

PROTOTYPICAL CASE OF **VIDEO GAME** ADDICTION

Nigel is a forty-one-year-old black male from the United Kingdom who has been an avid gamer for nearly thirty years. He loves online games like *World of Warcraft* and, by his own admission, plays them too much, sometimes passing on real-life social opportunities to game. He holds a job in the tech industry and is sometimes late due to his gaming. This has led to a few reprimands, which make him feel bad. His kids are well adjusted, but he sometimes worries that he doesn't spend enough time with them.

Behavioral addictions, like video games, don't tend to involve these types of reactions because the addict is not taking in a foreign substance. The effects of the addictive behavior are created entirely within the body and involve only the amounts of "addictive" chemicals our bodies produce themselves.

Part of the reason some, like *The Sun* newspaper, have equated video games with drugs is that they have a basic misunderstanding of the role of dopamine. Dopamine is a chemical in our brains involved in feelings of reward and pleasure, among other things. If you are enjoying this book (and we hope you are), dopamine is being released in your brain right now! Basically, anything fun results in the release of dopamine. This is essentially how your brain tells you that you're having fun. Now, some illicit drugs, like methamphetamine, cause *massive* releases of dopamine. Such an immense overstimulation of the brain's reward centers fosters psychological addiction to the drug. Because video games are fun, they also result in the release of dopamine, and this observation has tempted some journalists (and even some scholars, who should know better) to make direct comparisons between video games and illicit drugs.

This bracing combination of scientific illiteracy and Puritanism is nothing new. For example, in addition to announcing that video games are like heroin, *The Sun* has also compared cupcakes to cocaine.[188] Basically, whenever journalists (or some scientists) want to suggest that something enjoyable is dangerous or bad, they point out that it releases dopamine and imply that it may be just as addictive as drugs. What is never mentioned in these sensationalistic comparisons between video games, heroin, cupcakes, and cocaine is the *amount* of dopamine released by these activities and substances. As seen in the following figure, the effect on dopamine levels of playing video games is not even remotely comparable to that of dangerous drugs.[189, 190] So, while it is true that playing *Grand Theft Auto* causes dopamine levels to rise, the quantity of dopamine released while roaming the streets of Liberty City is much closer to that triggered by eating a slice of pepperoni pizza than by consuming methamphetamine.[191]

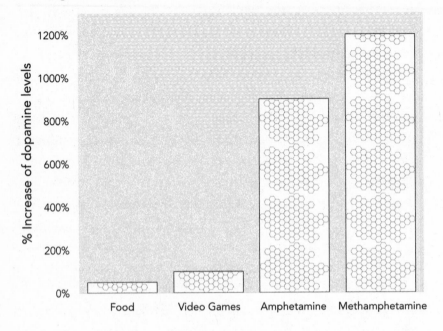

HOW COMMON IS VIDEO GAME ADDICTION?

In psychology or medicine, we use the term *prevalence* to describe how common a disorder is. For instance, in 2014, the World Health Organization estimated that about 4 percent of the world's population experienced alcohol addiction. That is its prevalence. Remember, at this point, video game play is common among almost all children and young adults. If video games really were as addictive as alcohol or methamphetamines, we ought to be battling a massive epidemic of dysfunctional youth! But, if you look in most classrooms, you will find that most kids seem to be doing pretty well.

Part of what makes determining the prevalence of video game addiction tricky is that researchers don't entirely agree about what constitutes its symptoms. Psychiatrists like to have clear lists of symptoms to identify and tally to make a diagnosis. In the American Psychiatric Association's *Diagnostic and Statistical Manual of Mental Disorders*[184] (DSM-5), psychiatric conditions are basically boiled down to symptom checklists. For the DSM-5 diagnosis of multiple personality disorder, for instance (technically called dissociative identity disorder), a practitioner is told to look for symptoms such as the presence of two or more personality states within an individual's mind, the tendency for these personality states to take control of the person's behavior at different points in time, and memory loss for events occurring while other personalities are in control. This can be a controversial way of defining and understanding mental illness, but it does work to keep clinical practitioners more or less on the same page.

Exactly what this checklist should look like for video game addiction is still unclear. One major reason for the current difficulty is that many of the people defining the symptoms of video game addiction are older psychiatrists who tend not to be gamers themselves. These scholars typically do not understand what healthy engagement with video games looks like, which leaves them ill equipped to distinguish it from addiction. For example: Do you get excited when you play your favorite video game? Well, according to some scholars, this is one indication that you may be a video game addict.[192] The potential result of such classification schemes is what we call a *false positive*. A false positive occurs when someone is identified as having a mental disorder—like video game addiction—when, in fact, they are perfectly fine. Such misdiagnosis is often the result of people who don't understand a behavior and so assume that it's nuts. A person who has rarely played video games might simply be unable to see how someone could be more excited by controlling a virtual character than by playing outside, watching football, or completing their homework, leading them to inappropriately label this excitement as maladaptive. Of course, the use of psychiatry to discriminate against people by labeling their behavior "mentally ill" is nothing new. For decades homosexuality was considered a mental illness, and women were often slapped with a diagnosis of "hysteria" (which translates to "wandering uterus"). Even today, diagnoses such as ADHD are controversial because of the perception that their symptom criteria are so broad as to include many "normal" kids and adults. The lines between normal and disordered behavior are often complex, and where money is involved, the incentives to overdo it, even in good faith, are considerable.

Because the checklists of symptoms used by past scholars to diagnose video game addiction have varied quite a bit, prevalence estimates have also varied, coming in anywhere from basically zero to near 20 percent. Can you imagine if 20 percent of the population were really addicted to *anything*? Society would cease to function! Most of the best studies, however, seem to suggest that somewhere around 1 to 3 percent of people who play video games may develop symptoms of addiction.[193, 194, 195] Although this prevalence rate is similar to that of alcohol addiction, it is important to remember what we discussed earlier—the majority of individuals addicted to gaming have relatively mild symptoms compared to those with other addictive disorders. People dependent on alcohol are at an increased risk of engaging in dangerous behaviors due to impaired judgment, emotional control problems, heart issues, liver problems, brain damage, high blood pressure, ulcers, sexual dysfunction, and death. In contrast, people addicted to video games most often face issues like doing poorly on homework or having trouble getting to work on time because they cannot tear themselves away from the computer.

Recently, the American Psychiatric Association provided a checklist of symptoms that may eventually become the standard for diagnosing video game addiction (see the following box). In the DSM-5, "internet gaming disorder" is presented as a "condition for further study." These are conditions the psychiatric community has decided merit additional research. Depending on the outcomes of these studies, Internet Gaming Disorder may or may not become an officially recognized disorder in future editions of the DSM.

PROPOSED CHECKLIST OF SYMPTOMS FOR INTERNET GAMING DISORDER

✓ Preoccupation: Do you spend a lot of time thinking about games?

✓ Withdrawal: Do you feel restless when you are unable to play games?

✓ Tolerance: Do you feel the need to play more or use more powerful equipment to get the same excitement as before?

✓ Reduce: Do you feel you should play less, but you are unable to?

✓ Give up other activities: Do you reduce participation in other recreational activities?

✓ Continue despite problems: Do you continue to play games despite knowing they have a negative impact on your life?

✓ Deceive: Do you lie about how much you game?

✓ Escape mood: Do you play games to reduce anxiety or stress?

✓ Risk: Do you risk loss of significant relationships or employment because of games?

According to the proponents of this checklist, if you have experienced at least five of these symptoms in the past year, you are addicted to video games.

While some of the items in the checklist make sense, others are a little bizarre. For example, if your spouse is going to leave you, and you are about to lose your job because you can't stop playing *Grand Theft Auto*, you probably do have a problem. But what's wrong with playing a game of *Tetris* or *Super Mario Brothers* because you had a stressful day at work? Sure, if you use heroin or even gambling as your go-to stress reducer, this is a bad thing—these are high-risk behaviors with serious consequences. But isn't altering our moods and making us feel happier and less stressed more or less what all hobbies are for? What if you unwind by reading books or exercising or watching sports on TV? Are those warning signs of addiction, too? This is a good example of older non-gamers assuming that a normal behavior is indicative of a problem. Many healthy people play video games to reduce stress, just as the checklist developers themselves might use other, less newfangled and thus better-understood activities, like playing chess or listening to records on the Victrola.

Another unusual item on the DSM checklist is whether subjects have reduced their participation in other activities because of their video game playing. But we often jettison old hobbies when we take on new ones; this is not unusual. Again, if a formerly avid knitter stops knitting in order to devote more time to cocaine or gambling, this is obviously not good. But, if she stops knitting because she wants to play *Assassin's Creed* instead, what's the big deal? Older adults assume that changing hobbies is bad when the hobby you switch to is gaming, because they don't typically see value in gaming.

Many of the symptoms on the APA's proposed checklist are relatively normal behaviors that could cause a person to be identified as an addict when game playing isn't actually causing them any problems. Unsurprisingly, scholars continue to debate the symptoms used to diagnose Internet Gaming Disorder.[196, 197]

A real danger of focusing on video game addiction is that it may cause us to overlook whatever underlying issues are driving obsessive gameplay. To illustrate this, a Danish scholar, Dr. Rune Nielsen, described to us the case of Maria, a fourteen-year-old girl (details are changed for anonymity) who stopped going to school. Instead, Maria sat at home all day, playing internet games like *World of Warcraft*. When her parents spoke to a school counselor, the counselor decided that the issue was video game addiction. So Maria's parents took away her computer. Did Maria go back to school? Nope. She sat around the house all day, bored. Maria didn't even seem too upset about losing access to her games. Nonetheless, it took months before anyone realized that video games weren't the issue. It turned out that Maria was *afraid* to go to school—she felt like she was being bullied by one of her teachers. No one had bothered to ask her, and she was reluctant to bring it up herself. Luckily for Maria, once she was switched to a different class, she felt better and willingly returned to school. This story is not meant to suggest that video games are never the culprit, of course, only that obsessive video gameplay is often a symptom of another underlying problem.

HOW TO KNOW IF SOMEONE IS ADDICTED TO VIDEO GAMES

Perhaps your child or someone you care about is playing a lot of video games. How do you know when to worry? Given the issues with the DSM checklist for video game addiction, it is not always easy to tell.

First, ask yourself if the reason you're concerned is because the person is playing more than *you* would if you were in her place. This isn't compelling evidence of addiction. If a person's life is going well—that is to say, her school, work, and social responsibilities are all being met—there is little reason to suspect a video game addiction. The person in question may be highly engaged with video games but, as mentioned earlier, the amount of time spent playing is not always a good indicator of whether a person is addicted.[198] As we saw with Maria, we can sometimes rush to judgment when it comes to new technology. We also have to be wary about assuming that behaviors that are normal for a younger age group are a sign of mental illness. Old folks always think teenagers are batty (the feeling is mutual)!

What's more, even if gaming does seem to be interfering with a person's responsibilities, it still might not be a case of video game addiction. Human behavior is complex. If a person plays video games a lot and is also having problems in their life, these two things may or may not be connected—in other words, it does not mean their gaming is the cause of those problems. In truth, even when video games *are* an issue, they are usually only one piece of a larger puzzle. Video games do not have the chemical power of crack cocaine—a person rarely picks up a video game and transforms from someone perfectly functional and well adjusted into an out-of-control addict. The development of a video addiction is usually a sign of an underlying issue.

If you are still worried about video game addiction, Dr. Griffiths,[199] the researcher mentioned earlier in this chapter, has provided an excellent model to help us understand this phenomenon. According to Dr. Griffiths, here are some things to look for when evaluating whether someone might have a problem.

SALIENCE

Salience refers to the degree to which an addiction takes over a person's mental life. Is the person thinking about video games all the time, even when he's not playing? Is he unhappy unless he's playing video games? When not playing, does he spend all of his time obsessing over when he will play next to the point that he can't concentrate on other tasks? To be clear, looking forward to playing a new game, chatting about video games with friends, and thinking about video games from time to time is not a sign of addiction. Lots of people get a little bit obsessive about their hobbies. Think of all the golfers or hunters or sports enthusiasts who can't stop yakking about their chosen pastimes. But by salience, we mean that thoughts about gaming become so overwhelming that it is difficult for the person to think about anything else.

MOOD MODIFICATION

As we discussed earlier, using video games to relax or improve one's mood is not necessarily a bad thing. This is something we all do with hobbies. However, if video gaming is the *only* way a person is able to achieve happiness, that is a problem. Is the person unable to get going in the morning without playing video games? Is the person unable to unwind from stress in any way other than by gaming? Are video games the only thing that improves the person's mood? If a person's mood becomes *entirely* dependent upon video games, this can be a sign of addiction.

TOLERANCE

Tolerance is a classic symptom of substance abuse, wherein a person must take in more and more of a substance to get the same effect. For instance, some alcoholics may brag about how much they can drink without getting drunk, drinking nonalcoholics under the table. With behavioral addictions, this issue is trickier. For video games, tolerance may be demonstrated when people become less and less satisfied with the types of games they once enjoyed playing. Each individual session of gaming produces less and less joy. They may feel the need to play longer, more intense sessions, without ever feeling satisfied. They may buy more and more games and more and more equipment, without satisfaction or even pleasure.

Again, merely enjoying a lot of gaming is not necessarily tolerance, particularly if the person seems satisfied and is having fun. Some dedicated gamers may also enjoy buying top-of-the-line equipment. For example, Oculus Rift virtual reality equipment and computer hardware powerful enough to run it can easily cost in excess of $2,000 (at least as of this writing). This might seem outrageous to non-gamers, but it is not so different from the expensive equipment people buy for other hobbies like sailing, biking, scuba diving, collecting sports memorabilia, skiing, stamp collecting, mountain climbing, or even competitive ballroom dancing (seriously, some people spend over $10,000 a year on competition fees, dresses, and dance lessons). The point is, as long as people can afford their hobbies and they're having fun, spending a lot of money isn't a sign of addiction—if a gamer can afford the elaborate setup for Oculus Rift and enjoys using it, there's little reason for concern. But if, instead, someone seems continually driven to buy more than they can afford, or is never happy with what they have, that's another matter.

WITHDRAWAL

Like tolerance, withdrawal is a common aspect of substance addictions. If you are addicted to the caffeine in coffee and you try to go a couple of days without drinking a cup, you may notice yourself getting headaches and feeling tired and crabby. These are withdrawal symptoms, courtesy of your caffeine addiction. Granted, withdrawal from substances like heroin or alcohol is much worse—but it's still withdrawal!

Withdrawal from a behavioral addiction, for instance to video games, is likely to cause psychological symptoms. If the person stops playing, does she become stressed, irritable, or depressed? Does she experience physiological symptoms like an upset stomach, headaches, insomnia, or loss of appetite? Withdrawal is more than simple annoyance at not being able to play. A teenager becoming sullen when her video game use is restricted is normal. Becoming stressed to the point of not being able to enjoy the rest of her life at all, or having stomachaches and trouble sleeping, is not.

CONFLICT

Conflict is the element of Dr. Griffiths' model that most closely resembles the issue of "interference" we discussed earlier in this chapter. Conflict occurs when the person's gaming needs lead him to stop meeting his responsibilities, which puts him into conflict with others. Does the person disregard the negative consequences of spending too much time on games, even though these consequences are obvious? Is the person in conflict with friends, family, bosses, or teachers over a failure to meet expectations? Is the person in conflict with himself because he knows he games too much, but can't seem to stop?

RELAPSE

Relapse occurs when a person reverts to problematic behaviors despite efforts to change. A smoker who quits but then goes back to smoking has relapsed. With video games, relapse occurs when a person tries to cut back on her gaming but can't do it. So, has the person tried to game less but found that she couldn't manage it despite a sincere effort?

It's important to note that if someone expresses only one or two of these issues, he or she is not addicted to video games. Just thinking about video games a lot (salience) or wanting to play them more and more (tolerance) does not make a person a video game addict. However, if a person experiences *most* of these issues, he or she might have a problem. Another way of putting it is that people who healthily engage with video games will find that the hobby adds value to their lives. In contrast, individuals who have an unhealthy or addictive relationship with video games will inevitably discover these games detract value from their lives. For people who are not familiar with gaming, it can sometimes be difficult to tell the difference: they can't imagine what it could possibly add to a person's life, and they might think the gamer is "missing out" and should be outside or doing something more constructive. But being unable to see the appeal of an activity is not a sign that the activity is harmful.

VIDEO GAMES: KINDA-SORTA ADDICTIVE?

The good news is that for almost all kids and young adults, playing video games is simply a normal part of their development. The overwhelming majority of people who play video games do so while also balancing a productive work or school schedule and an active social life. But a few may struggle with that balance. Parents and loved ones can help by implementing clear and consistent rules and some sensible interventions we'll discuss in the final chapter. For some people, video gaming can become addictive, but in most of those cases, as with many behavioral addictions, video games are only one part of a larger, complex set of problems. Poor gaming habits are usually symptomatic of underlying issues, not the cause.

While video game addiction may be a real thing, it is hardly the looming epidemic some make it out to be. People who develop this problem tend to have relatively mild symptoms, and an addiction to video games is not comparable to an addiction to alcohol, methamphetamine, or even gambling. But in an era of moral panic, headlines such as "Video games are like heroin," tend to get a lot more attention than the mundane truth.

The truth is, like anything fun, games can be overdone. Moderation is everything! This is just as true with video games as it is with fast food, candy, potato chips, and exercise. Surprisingly, as you will learn in the next chapter, video games might be the key to helping you master moderation, get that fit body you always wanted, and maybe even fine-tune your moral compass.

LEVEL 7:

STRONG MORALS AND FIT BODIES

On my honor, I will do my best, to do my duty, to God and my country, and to obey the Scout Law, to help other people at all times, to keep myself physically strong, mentally awake, and morally straight.
—The Scout Oath, Boy Scouts of America

The Boy Scouts began in 1910 with the intention of teaching young men to make moral choices by instilling in them a sense of self-reliance and physical efficacy. After its creation, former president Theodore Roosevelt, who was often worried about the "manliness" of American boys, quickly threw his support behind the fledgling organization and was eventually made its honorary vice president. The Boy Scouts were a perfect match with Roosevelt's long-held belief that physical activity builds moral character. To help build his character, Roosevelt played tennis and polo, rowed, rode horseback, boxed, practiced jujitsu, hunted white rhinos, and regularly skinny-dipped in the Potomac River during the dead of winter. Soon children all over the United States were following Roosevelt's lead (well, except for the white rhino and winter skinny-dipping parts)—joining the Boy Scouts, getting active, and thus becoming morally as well as physically fit. This definitely makes one of the authors (Markey) question his own character, considering he frequently orders delivery from the pizza place across from his home in order to avoid the insupportably strenuous task of crossing a street (shame often prevents eye contact with the delivery guy).

One method the Boy Scouts employ to encourage moral and physical development is to award merit badges to those who achieve certain goals. Demonstrate that you can cross the wake of a boat four times while water-skiing. Get a merit badge in water sports. Climb three different routes on a rock face and rappel down, get a merit badge in climbing. Currently, there are more than 100 such badges, recognizing achievement in activities like rowing, archery, kayaking, and horsemanship. And, in 2013, the Boy Scouts added a new item to this long list of badge-worthy pursuits—video games!

Considering the emphasis the Boy Scouts place on moral fiber and physical fitness, it isn't too surprising that some people were upset by the creation of this badge. Parents envision video-gaming teens as slovenly and indifferent, hands in a bag of potato chips, and homework undone. Along with the specific concerns about violent games we've discussed previously, educators and policymakers worry that these games contribute to a lack of morality, and that video games in general make us lazy and fat. Newspaper headlines have certainly reinforced these concerns, accusing video games of causing both the perceived slackening of morals among today's youth and the obesity epidemic.[200, 201] One prominent game researcher has gone so far as to quip that playing violent video games causes us to "cheat more" and "eat more."[202]

These negative beliefs about the impact of video games on our morality and our bodies seem to spread like wildfire. Obviously, if these assumptions about video games are correct, the Boy Scouts should probably not be giving out merit badges for this morally corrupt and health-compromising activity. But what does the science say? Does playing video games—especially violent ones—lead players to become less morally sensitive? Does this digital media reduce physical activity and/or actually cause obesity?

REAL AND VIRTUAL MORALITY

The summer of 1961 was unusually warm at Yale University in New Haven, Connecticut. Temperatures in June were nearing ninety degrees as students shifted their attention from their studies to the trial of Nazi Adolf Eichmann in Jerusalem. Israeli agents had captured Eichmann, the officer who'd organized Adolf Hitler's "final solution," the year before in Argentina, and he was now facing war crimes charges. Eichmann's only attempt to justify his horrific actions was to say he was simply "following orders." The three-judge panel trying his case did not find this to be a satisfactory excuse; they found him responsible for millions of deaths, and he was eventually hanged. During the trial, Stanley Milgram, a recent PhD graduate, started his position as a research psychologist at Yale. Eichmann's defense sparked the young professor's curiosity, and he wondered exactly to what extent people could be controlled by authority figures and made to "follow orders."[203] To investigate this question, Milgram went on to perform one of the most influential and controversial experiments ever conducted.

Milgram placed an ad in a local paper with the headline "We will pay you $4.00 for one hour of your time" (a fair price back then, and still more than we typically give undergraduate participants today) to find men between the ages of twenty and fifty willing to participate in a study. Each volunteer soon found himself in a plain basement laboratory with concrete floors, under the watchful eye of a stern researcher in a white lab coat. After the volunteer was seated, the researcher presented him with a very large and intimidating electric-shock machine with switches labeled from 15 to 450 volts. The researcher then taught the volunteer how to use this sinister-looking machine to test the memory of an unfortunate "student." The volunteer had seen the student led into an adjoining room, to be hooked up to the electric-shock machine, but could only hear, not see, the student during the experiment.

The volunteer would test the student's memory by reading him a few words, which the student would repeat back. At some point, the student goofed, and the volunteer was told to push the first button labeled 15 volts. The student cried out in pain. The lesson continued. As the student made more errors, the shocks to be delivered by the volunteer became progressively more intense. At 150 volts, the student screamed, "Ugh! Get me out of here! I told you I had heart trouble! My heart is starting to bother me now! Get me out of here, please!" When the student was shocked with 300 volts, he said, "I absolutely refuse to answer any more. Get me out of here! You can't hold me here! Get me out of here!" After 330 volts were delivered, the volunteer heard a prolonged, agonized screech, followed by, "Let me out of here! My heart's bothering me. Let me out! Let me out! Let me out! Let me out! Let me out!" If the volunteer told the lab-coated supervisor that he wanted to stop shocking the student, the supervisor said that it was essential that they continue—all the way up to 450 volts.

Was this volunteer a psychopath? Immoral? If so, he was in good company: most volunteers submitted to the researcher's authority and continued shocking the student. The good news for the student was that he wasn't really getting shocked. He was in on the experiment the whole time, and the screams of pain the volunteer heard were audio recordings. Milgram wasn't interested in hurting people;

he just wanted to see if the volunteers would follow orders from the lab-coated authority figure, which they typically did. The good news for the volunteer was that his actions, however horrible they might seem, weren't evidence of psychopathy or immorality—just human nature.

The volunteers did not zap their fellow man without emotion. During the study, all of the volunteers became distraught, agitated, and even angry about what the experimenter was asking them to do. They sweated, cried, trembled, laughed hysterically, and dug their fingernails into their flesh; several even had uncontrollable seizures.[204] Because of the extreme emotional distress experienced by these volunteers, Milgram's study raised serious questions about the ethics of putting people in such stressful situations in the name of science. Ultimately, future researchers would never again be allowed to conduct this type of experiment on humans.

But while pretending to electrocute real people may be off-limits, there is nothing stopping researchers from shocking virtual humans. This is exactly what they did not long ago at the Immersive Virtual Environments Laboratory at University College London, where Milgram's study was replicated with a virtual-reality character receiving electric shocks in lieu of a human subject.[205] Just as the volunteers in Milgram's study heard the "students" scream each time they were shocked, the volunteers in this recent study witnessed the computerized victim express great distress when virtually zapped. She screamed, protested that she had "never agreed to this," begged for it to stop, and eventually, the volunteers watched as she slumped over in her virtual chair and stopped responding. The whole time, the human participants were aware that the character was not real. What makes *this* study interesting isn't that most of the volunteers followed orders and shocked the virtual subject up to 450 volts, but that they found it greatly upsetting to do so. The volunteers exhibited the same signs of physical stress when shocking a computer character as those in the Milgram study had when they thought they were shocking a real person. Several volunteers even withdrew from the study because they were so upset! Although it was obvious that no one was really getting hurt, they experienced a strong emotional reaction to the virtual character's virtual suffering.

The poor virtual student receiving "shocks" during the study

The idea that we experience emotions in response to the perils of fictional characters is certainly nothing new. Fictional movies, books, and television shows evoke feelings of sadness, joy, and fear, even though we realize that the characters are not real. Even video games elicit these emotional responses, especially now, when advances in graphics have enabled more cinematic narrative games and the widespread inclusion of "cut scenes"—essentially movie-like scenes that play at set places to advance the story. In the PlayStation game *The Last of Us,* many players found themselves heartbroken when (spoiler alert!) the main protagonist's daughter, Sarah, was shot by security forces. In this heart-wrenching scene, players witness a father's emotional breakdown as he holds his dying daughter in his arms. Numerous other games—like *Red Dead Redemption, BioShock 3, Final*

Fantasy VII, Call of Duty: Modern Warfare 2, Journey, The Walking Dead, and *Shadow of the Colossus*—also contain scenes guaranteed to wring emotion from even the most jaded gamer.

Gamers often maintain publicly that they are well aware that video games are "not real," and thus they remain unaffected by the violence and suffering visited on virtual characters.[206] However, as demonstrated by the extreme distress felt by the volunteers shocking a computerized character in the virtual Milgram experience, knowing that the characters in games are fictional doesn't keep us from fostering emotional bonds with them. Perhaps it was different in the early days of video games—we probably didn't fret over the morality of directing Pac-Man to gobble up poor Blinky, Inky, Pinky, and Clyde. Nor did we lose any sleep over our role in an Italian plumber's squishing rampage, which claimed the lives of countless Goombas and Koopa Troopas in the Mushroom Kingdom of *Super Mario Brothers.* But today, thanks to virtual characters who look and move like real humans and have compelling stories to tell, what constitutes ethical and decent behavior in a video game is far murkier than it was when we were controlling a yellow circle eating dots and pixelated ghosts.

In *Grand Theft Auto V,* the mission "By the Book" requires players to torture an alleged terrorist for information. The player gets to select a preferred torture device: a sledgehammer, electric cables, or even waterboarding. Many gamers felt that this scene was inappropriate, immoral, disgusting; various human rights groups (including Freedom from Torture and Amnesty International) publicly denounced the violence depicted in this scenario.[207] A similar moral dilemma faces gamers in *Call of Duty: Modern Warfare 2,* when the player is put in the role of an undercover operative who has infiltrated a terrorist cell. While undercover, the player finds that he has little choice but to participate in the massacre of hundreds of civilians at an airport. Politicians and the media quickly criticized the morality of the scenario, labeling this game the most controversial of the year and even comparing it to the Nazi propaganda created by Joseph Goebbels.[208] Of course, many of the complaints came from people who had only heard about the game, not actually played it, and didn't know the context of the scene (the player is an undercover antiterrorist operative, and is not forced to shoot any civilians himself), just that players participate in an airport shooting as part of a terrorist cell.

While such extreme concerns about the moral content of video games may be overblown, these examples make it clear that the games of today often involve both our emotions and our morality.

MORAL KOMBAT!

We may judge games for the morality of their stories, but the virtual behaviors we express inside these games often reflect our own "real-world" moral sensitivity. Take BioWare's hugely popular series *Mass Effect,* in which players are presented with numerous moral decisions while they attempt to save the universe. In a mission called "Project Overlord," players come across a gruesomely restrained man who is being used to power a bizarre experiment. A player can choose either to free the man or to simply continue, turning a blind eye to the suffering of this human guinea pig. Based on a player's behavior in these types of situations throughout the game, he or she is given either "Paragon points" (for acting morally) or "Renegade points" (for acting immorally). At the end of the game, these points are tallied, and they give insight into the level of morality the player displayed overall. Most players (about 65 percent) choose the moral Paragon path, but the remaining 35 percent elect to follow the path of the Renegade.[209] Some evidence suggests that whether a person chooses to play as a righteous hero or a nefarious scoundrel is not random, but instead is largely determined by his or her moral sensitivity to the real-world suffering of others. That's right: people who are less concerned with the well-being of others in the real world are more likely to play *Mass Effect* as a morally depraved Renegade.[210] (See Easter Egg 1.) Of course, some people may purposefully play a game in an "immoral" way in order to explore a role that differs remarkably from their real self. However, the fact is that—whether we mean to or not—we tend to carry our own beliefs into ambiguous video games like *Grand Theft Auto* or *Mass Effect*, and act according to them when we are given the freedom to do so.

In addition to reflecting our real-world ethical principles, our actions in video games can themselves affect our morality. Maybe this doesn't surprise you—after all, the media is always warning us about the negative impact that violent video games have on moral development. The basic reasoning behind this concern is that game participants may detach from the outside world, instead immersing themselves in a virtual world where violence is prevalent, and often portrayed as the solution to conflict. In this way, so the theory goes, video games prevent gamers from learning the difference between what is right and what is wrong.[211] However, the latest research examining morality and video games has found that not only is this fear unjustified, it is actually backwards! Violent video games *can* affect our morality—but for the better.

Even more surprising: the games that have the greatest positive impact on our moral sensitivity are those that contain graphic, antisocial violence, for instance games like *Grand Theft Auto, Manhunt,* and even *Postal.* In one recent study, all participants played a first-person shooter, but half played as a terrorist shooting innocent bystanders (antisocial violence), and the other half played as a UN soldier shooting terrorists (justifiable violence). Although these games involved the exact same violent acts, the gamers who played as terrorists experienced far more guilt over their virtual behavior, and this led to greater subsequent moral reflection.[212] In other words, virtually engaging in violent antisocial behaviors caused players to become more morally sensitive to the suffering of others.

The guilt experienced by these players may seem surprising, but as we learned from the virtual Milgram study, even when we are aware that we aren't hurting real people, we experience real emotion when we perpetrate virtual violence.

The guilt we feel when we do anything we recognize as wrong, whether in a video game or in the real world, is a moral emotion.[213] Ever cheat on a test? Hurt someone's feelings? Lie? If so, chances are you felt guilty. Nothing makes you more aware that you've done something wrong than the emotional tidal wave that hits you upon realizing that you forgot to call your mom on her birthday. (Still sorry about that, Mom!)

Guilt is a powerful tool that provides us with quick feedback on the acceptability of our actions. Furthermore, feeling this uncomfortable emotion serves to motivate us to avoid making this mistake again. You may respond by writing your mom's birthday into your day planner years in advance, thinking of her birthday whenever you hear your friends talking about their parents' birthdays, or being hyperalert to any signs that the special day is approaching. When we feel guilt, we ruminate and reflect on what we did (or forgot to do), and become sensitive to whatever circumstances evoked that feeling.[213] The guilt evoked by committing unjustified acts of violence in a video game allows us to become more morally sensitive to harming others.[212]

On the surface, it seems counterintuitive that engaging in unjustified virtual violence would lead to greater moral acuity, but this conclusion is consistent with years of research examining violent films and television. Scholars in the 1990s completed a landmark investigation, called the National Television Violence Study, which explored this very issue. By examining and coding over 10,000 hours of television programming and more than 1,600 participants, it was found that watching television shows or movies in which "violence is undeserved or purely malicious *decreases* the risk of imitation or learning of aggression."[214] However, the public still expresses great distress in response to this kind of media. Take the 2005 horror film *Hostel*, which tells the story of travelers kidnapped by a powerful group that pays to torture them to death. After watching this movie, essentially a ceaseless barrage of horrific acts of violence perpetrated on a group of innocent travelers, it is easy to see why *Hostel* is often referred to as "torture porn." Many responded with both moral outrage and fear about what effects films like this might have on the people who watch them. The film critic for the *Daily Mail* called *Hostel* "the most revoltingly violent pornography ever to have polluted mainstream cinema" and decried it as "disgusting, degrading, and dangerous."[215] Contrary to these fears, however, movies like *Hostel* are exactly the types most likely to make us more sensitive to the suffering of others.

Although all media portraying acts of unjustified violence have the potential to make us more morally sensitive, the degree to which we are connected to the characters in video games supercharges this effect. While watching *Hostel,* viewers likely responded with anger, fear, and disgust when they saw a man torture one of the travelers by drilling holes into his chest and legs. Although these emotional responses are powerful, the viewers would have been unlikely to experience guilt during this scene because they were not the ones inflicting the suffering. However, many players who participated in the extremely realistic-looking airport massacre of hundreds of civilians in *Call of Duty: Modern Warfare 2* likely did experience guilt—their virtual character was the one responsible for the deaths of these innocent, albeit virtual, people. With video games, players experience emotions in response to their *own* actions, which is why games are the medium with the greatest potential to positively affect a person's moral acuity.[212]

DESENSITIZATION

The idea that violent video games—especially those containing unjustified violence—can increase our moral sensitivity is in stark contrast to many people's fears that such media desensitizes us to violence. The core of this fear is the belief that repeatedly viewing virtual violence will cause people—especially children—to become detached and emotionless in the face of violence in the real world. This notion seems to draw on the observation that, in combat, soldiers often become numb to the brutality, chaos, and death that surround them on the battlefield. According to this argument, by normalizing violence, people who play *Grand Theft Auto*, like soldiers in wartime, become desensitized to the real-life consequences of violence and less empathetic toward the victims of such violence.[216]

Desensitization is a real psychological phenomenon. In fact, systematic desensitization is one of the most powerful therapeutic techniques we have to help people with phobias.[217] Imagine that you suffer from an extreme fear of flying, but you really want to vacation in Hawaii. Probably the most terrifying—and ineffective—action you could take in this situation would be to just toss your flowered shirt in a suitcase and hop on a plane bound for the Aloha State. A much better technique would be to slowly expose yourself to the thing you're afraid of: maybe you'd start by simply reading a book about airplanes. After successfully conquering this first step, you could move on, perhaps driving to the airport and watching the planes take off and land. If you start to feel anxious, you might employ a relaxation technique, like deep breathing, until you are comfortable enough to go on to the next stage. Next you might go inside the airport, then sit on a plane for a while, then go on a short flight, and finally, eventually, take that dream trip to Hawaii! What you've been doing here is normalizing the idea of flying in order to desensitize yourself to the fear of plummeting to your death in a metal cylinder with wings!

Scholars have examined whether exposing people to violent media might numb them to violence, in much the same way as people can become desensitized to their fear of flying. Consistent with this reasoning, one researcher found that the more people watch violent movies, such as *A Clockwork Orange*, *Vigilante*, and even

Soylent Green, the less empathy they feel for the characters portrayed in these films.[218] Similarly, other scholars have found that the more frequently people are exposed to violent media, the less they respond emotionally to that type of media in the future.[219] There seems little doubt that, as we consume more and more violent media, we do in fact become desensitized to violence depicted in such media.

However, as you may have spotted, this research only examines how violent media desensitizes us to other *violent media*, not how it affects our sensitivity to *real-life* acts of violence. This is a pretty important distinction, as most people worry that violent media makes us numb to the suffering of real people, not that it makes us less upset when we see more violent films or play more violent games. It turns out that when we see real acts of violence, such as scenes from a war or the deaths of real people, we find it upsetting, regardless of how much violent media we have consumed.[220] It doesn't matter how many head shots players have taken in *Call of Duty* or how many hours they've spent causing virtual bloodshed in *Grand Theft Auto*: everyone is disturbed when they witness a real-life homicide or see violence perpetrated on someone else. When we see a real person hurt or killed, those who watch violent media and those who watch nonviolent media get equally upset.

So, despite public fears and the fact that video games have become more violent over the past forty years, gamers themselves have not become numb to the suffering of real people. In fact, as we have learned, the unjustified video game violence that is most decried can actually lead gamers to become more morally sensitive toward the pain of others.

OBESITY AND GAMES

In the preceding sections, we learned that many common beliefs about video games are not merely wrong: they are backward. Video games are not linked to school shootings—in fact, school shooters are less likely to play violent video games than their average peers. Violent video games *are* connected to real-world violent acts, but they are related to a decrease in violence, not an increase. Playing violent video games doesn't make us cold-blooded; it can actually heighten our moral sensitivity.

Of course, even if video games aren't dangerous for our minds, it is exceedingly common for people to fear that this media might be unhealthy for our bodies. Parents and others find it concerning that gamers seem content to sit on a couch directing a speedy blue hedgehog to run and jump, rather than running and jumping themselves. One recent poll found that over 75 percent of parents believe that video games and television are the primary causes of obesity among children and teens, ranking games above other causes such as junk food, fast-food marketing, and lack of exercise.[221]

The truth is, adults and children *are* getting fat! As seen in the following figure from the Centers for Disease Control, every state in the US has an obesity prevalence rate above 20 percent, and almost half have obesity rates over 30 percent.[222] There is little doubt that obesity is one of the most significant health issues in modern society. Obesity has been linked to diabetes, heart disease, stroke, and even some forms of cancer. Around the world, nearly three million people die each year from diseases brought on or worsened by being overweight or obese.[223] Obesity is of such great concern that, in June 2013, the American Medical Association officially declared it a disease in and of itself.[224]

The primary reason for the obesity epidemic is straightforward —we've decreased how much we move around and increased how much we eat. Unfortunately, modern society encourages both of these trends. In our daily lives, most of us are not very physically active. We drive to work, walk from our cars to our offices, sit behind our desks until 5 PM, walk back to our cars, and drive back home. Then we eat a big meal and sit on the couch, watching hours

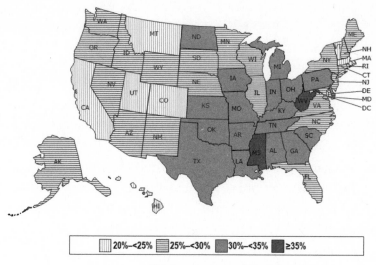

20%–<25%   25%–<30%   30%–<35%   ≥35%

Obesity rates among US adults

of television. Of course, we could compensate for this sedentary lifestyle by exercising, but studies show that 80 percent of us don't bother.[225] All of the delicious, processed, easily accessible food we consume makes this problem even worse. Because fast food is cheap and easy to get our hands on, the proportion of youths who eat regular meals at McDonald's, Burger King, or other similar restaurants has increased by nearly 300 percent since 1977.[226] High-calorie soft drinks like Coca-Cola and Mountain Dew are now so popular that they have become the greatest source of calories in the average teen's diet.[227] Sadly, your authors note that age does not seem to help. We were once able to consume all the donuts we liked without worry. Now, approaching middle age, we seem close to resembling donuts ourselves.

In short, the reason Americans have gained so much weight is that our society has made it easy to engage in unhealthy consumption and makes sedentary lifestyles the norm. But while modern society as a whole has certainly been criticized by the public and the media for contributing to weight gain, somehow video games in particular are often singled out for an extra share of the blame.

CHUNKY PIXELS

As we've mentioned before, the image of a gamer, for many, is one of an overweight teenager who sits alone for hours in a dark room, a bottle of Mountain Dew within reach, and Doritos crumbs clinging to his protruding stomach. Many parents work to minimize their children's gaming out of the fear that their kids will turn into overweight video game zombies. Perhaps they choose not to allow televisions in their children's rooms, or designate specific times for gameplay. Parents who are unable to enforce rules like these may use time-management devices that connect directly to the game console or television and automatically turn the device off when the child's allotted time is up. When your authors were younger, our parents took a more direct approach—they hid our game controllers (we are still a little bitter about that effective tactic). While at first this indeed reduced our play, the ultimate result was that we developed savant-like abilities to find hidden controllers. Our parents might not have succeeded in instilling self-control in us with their strategy, but we are both now really good at finding lost keys and phones around the house!

Of course, all these strategies are implemented by parents with the best of intentions, in the hopes of encouraging their kids to stop playing video games, get off the couch, and avoid weight problems. It seems like common sense that the more time a person spends watching TV or playing video games, the more weight he or she will gain due to inactivity. However, this is one area in which common sense fails us. Based on a massive study that examined the screen habits of over 44,000 children, watching television does not seem to have any meaningful impact on weight. In fact, the amount of time spent watching television accounts for only about 1 percent of a child's total weight! Perhaps most surprisingly, there was no relationship at all between how much time children spent playing video games and their body size.[228] In other words, the stereotypical image of an overweight gamer is simply not accurate. Gamers, just like everyone else, come in all shapes and sizes!

Given that screen time seems to have only a small impact on our waistlines, it probably isn't too surprising that limiting a child's screen time typically has no effect on his or her weight. This was demonstrated dramatically in 1996, when a school in California tested a program designed to fight childhood obesity by decreasing the amount of television students watched.[229] The kids attended multiple fifty-minute lessons on the importance of reducing screen time and learned tricks for motivating themselves to turn off the tube. Newsletters were sent to the students' parents to encourage them to get involved, and parents were even given television time-management devices to help them limit their kids' screen time. By the end of the school year, the program had been a success, sort of. The students' screen time had been reduced by an amazing 43 percent! However, this dramatic change in media consumption did not have much impact on the children's weight. The average child lost only about one pound (see Easter Egg 2). Although losing one pound is better than losing zero pounds, this was a trivial result given the intensive effort and striking change in the children's media habits. Had the students just made the minor switch from drinking soda and juice to drinking water, they would have lost about fifteen pounds within the same time period.[230] This is a stark illustration of the fact that changing other habits—for instance the food we consume—is about 1400 percent more effective for weight loss than reducing screen time.

GETTING ACTIVE

The reason that reducing screen time has little to no effect on a person's weight is pretty straightforward: just removing a video game from someone's hand doesn't guarantee that he or she will start exercising. Numerous studies have found that there is absolutely no relation between how much time people spend in front of a television and how much physical activity they exert over a typical day.[231] In short, people generally spend the same amount of time sitting around whether they're watching TV (or playing video games) or not. Even when parents have banned television from their homes, their children do not then spend more time running around outside.[229, 232] Unfortunately, there is no evidence to suggest that sedentary youths suddenly become active when media is limited or removed. Indeed, the authors often find that when our children are admonished to do something other than play *Minecraft* or *Madden NFL*, they typically just pick other sedentary activities, like Legos or board games. Cajoling and/or demanding that they go outside results in complaints ranging from unreasonable bees, bright sunlight, mud, the need to put on shoes/shirts/pants, to the grass being too green (seriously, when one of our kids was two, this was her concern), and that it is simply far too hot "out there" during the summer. We begin to wonder whether central air might not be one of the main culprits of our country's obesity epidemic.

However, while it's true that limiting people's screen time does not increase their physical activity or decrease their weight, this doesn't mean that video games can't have an impact on obesity. A more effective way to encourage physical activity may be to supplement regular video gaming with what is called "exergaming." Exergaming combines video games with physical activity, allowing participants to work out while they play. The idea of melding games and exercise can be traced back to 1982, when Atari released the Joyboard. By connecting this simple balance board to an Atari 2600, players could virtually ski, moving their bodies as if they were really slaloming down a mountain. In the mid-1980s, various companies expanded on this idea by offering products that allowed gamers to connect exercise bicycles to their favorite game system and compete in virtual bike races. And in 1988, Nintendo released the Power Pad, a floor-mat controller with twelve large sensors that players stepped on in games like *World Class Track Meet* and *Dance Aerobics*.

All of these products had some level of success, but due to their high cost (Nintendo's exercise bike sold for an astounding $3,500) and generally unengaging gameplay, they never really caught on with the public. This all changed with the 2006 release of the Nintendo Wii. The Wii's runaway popularity with casual gamers, and the more widespread inclusion of motion controllers and cameras in gaming systems, *a la* Xbox Kinect, have led to an avalanche of exergames in recent years. Walking down the aisles of a local video game store, you'll see hundreds of games designed to help you stay active and lose weight while having fun. On the next page are some of the most popular exergames, along with the estimated number of calories you'd burn if you played the game for thirty minutes.

The first thing that stands out in this list is the variability in the number of calories these games burn. Hitting the back nine on *Wii Sports Golf* only burns about 98 calories, but if you take it up a notch with *Zumba Fitness*, you can work off about 250. To put these numbers into perspective, let's look at how they compare to more traditional forms of exercise. While knocking a virtual tennis ball back and forth for half an hour in *Wii Sports Tennis* burns about 159 calories, going on a moderate jog in the real world for the same amount of time burns twice as many. Other real-world exercises, like biking (239 calories), using a ski machine (353 calories), using a rowing machine (316 calories), or doing aerobics (270 calories) also typically burn more calories than exergames.

There is little doubt that, all things being equal, traditional exercise is a more efficient way to lose weight than bopping around to Fatboy Slim in *Just Dance*.[233] However, if you aren't motivated enough to actually go to the gym or run around your block, the effectiveness of traditional exercise is irrelevant. After all, the most effective exercise is not necessarily the one that burns the most calories, it's the one that you'll actually do! Most exercise programs ultimately fail

Game		Description	Calories Burned in 30 Minutes
Dance Dance Revoution		Early rhythm game in which players stomp their feet to match the rhythm of a song	243
Wii Sports: Golf		Gamers can swing a virtual club as they try to sink the golf ball in as few strokes as possible	98
Wii Sports: Bowling		Players try to knock down as many pins as they can in this virtual bowling game	117
Wii Sports: Baseball		Players hit and pitch baseballs over the plate	125
Wii Sports: Tennis		Singles or doubles, players virtually hit a tennis ball back and forth	159
Wii Sports: Boxing		Gamers box against their friends or computer opponents by moving both arms	216
Zumba Fitness		Game based on the Zumba fitness program	250
Just Dance!		Rhythm game in which the players mimic the dance moves of onscreen characters	200

because people don't enjoy the activity in the first place and aren't motivated enough to continue, especially once they become bored. This lack of motivation and enjoyment in exercise comes to prominence during adolescence, when kids commonly stop engaging in physical activities due to waning or changing interests and increased demands on their time.[234] Luckily, because video games are so inherently enjoyable, it is much easier to motivate people to engage in exergaming than in traditional exercise.

Not only are these games fun, they provide a low-stress path to fitness for people who are too intimidated to work out. Many people, especially the young, report that they don't exercise because they are worried about being teased or criticized by their more fit peers.[235] No one likes to be the last kid picked to play baseball or the first to be hit in the face with a dodgeball (trust us . . . as nerds we were always the last kids picked, and we still flinch at the sight of a dodgeball). Exergames provide players with a nonjudgmental environment in which to work out, often within the safe confines of their own homes, and even the most self-conscious players will discover that they can direct their attention toward the action on the screen instead of worrying about their body or physical prowess.[236] What's more, exergames supply rewards for accomplishment that are far more immediate than the sometimes nebulous goals of health and svelteness—you get points, you win, you are treated to the cheers of a virtual crowd. By giving us a medium that is interactive, challenging, and rewarding, exergames provide the same intrinsic motivation as traditional video games, but with the added benefit of burning calories.

The secret to successful and sustained weight loss is to consistently engage in healthy activities.[230] Let's say you run one 5K race. You've burned 400 calories—that's great! But you would have burned almost three times as many playing thirty minutes of *Wii Fit*'s running game every day for a week. Basic math tells us that consistently engaging in exergaming activities, even for brief amounts of time, could help people lose significant amounts of weight over the long term. The following figure illustrates how many pounds the average person could drop playing an exergame that burns about 150 calories (e.g., thirty minutes of *Just Dance*, *Wii Sports Tennis*, *Dance Dance Revolution*, or *Wii Sports Boxing*) each day. You may not lose anything the first week, but in a month you could be a little over a pound thinner. This may not seem like much, but in a year, you could be down more than fifteen pounds—not bad for playing a video game! Of course, these estimates assume you don't suddenly start eating extra doughnuts every morning or stop engaging in the physical activities you did before. The point is, exergames can have a dramatic effect on your body, as long as you use them consistently. And face it, you may have better luck convincing your kids to play *Dance Dance Revolution* than to brave the bees and too-green grass outside.

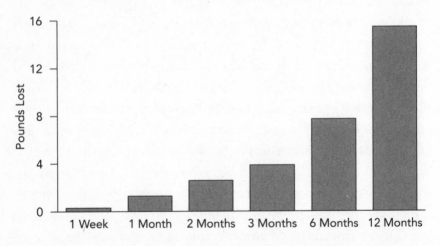

Estimated weight loss for a person who plays exergames for 30 minutes a day

LESSONS FROM THE BOY SCOUTS AND THEODORE ROOSEVELT

It's right there in the Boy Scout Oath. Two of the goals of a Boy Scout are to keep "physically strong" and "morally straight"—video games have the potential to help us do both. So while, on the surface, a merit badge for video games might seem incompatible with the out-doorsy, do-gooding spirit of the Boy Scouts, in fact it is quite the opposite. As we have seen, the science behind video games is often similarly at odds with what many people believe about them. So go ahead—get that merit badge and show off your moral and physical superiority! There is no reason to fear that playing video games will turn us all into fat, immoral slobs. In fact, as you are about to see, they may have a host of other benefits—from improving hand-eye coordination to fighting depression.

EASTER EGGS

1. On his second play-through of *Mass Effect*, Markey completely maxed out his Renegade points by doing everything evil and underhanded he could think of. For the sake of his character, he might want to start crossing the street to pick up his own pizzas.

2. This weight change was computed taking into account the changes that occurred in a control group and the fact that children naturally get taller. Consistent with this study's finding, a recent review published in *Pediatrics* concluded that programs designed to reduce screen time have no effect on body size.[237]

LEVEL 8:

ACHIEVEMENT UNLOCKED

Nineteenth-century America was not a good place to be sick. There were few doctors around, and those there were tended to be extremely expensive—no great loss, as most had only limited medical knowledge in the first place! Heck, the idea that people got sick from germs wasn't even popularized until 1861, when Louis Pasteur took it up.

As an alternative to doctors, people often turned to various unproven remedies sold in local markets or via mail order. Most of these "medicines" were marketed not as cures for one illness, but as miracle drugs that could treat almost every problem imaginable. Take, for example, Parker's Tonic, which was advertised as help for dyspepsia, neuralgia, sour stomach, wakefulness, rising of the food, yellow skin, "pain," stomachaches, liver disease, coughs, consumption, asthma, colds, bronchitis, indigestion, diarrhea, dysentery, rheumatism, chills, malaria, colic, cramps, and liver disease—all while also giving beauty to graying hair. Pretty amazing stuff, especially for only fifty cents a bottle (about eleven dollars today). Not surprisingly, like most "cure-alls," Parker's Tonic actually cured nothing. In fact, the secret ingredient was alcohol: a lot of it! Each wonder bottle of Parker's Tonic contained a whopping 41.6 percent alcohol. That's about the same as vodka or whisky. Taken in sufficient quantities, it probably *was* a cure for "wakefulness," in that you'd eventually pass right out.

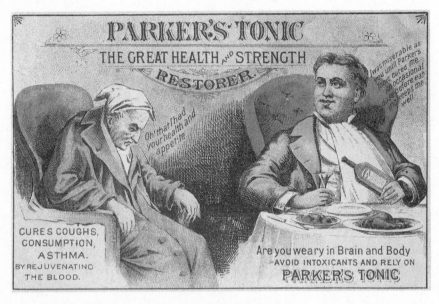

Today, most people are suspicious of products that claim to address multiple problems. Of course, this doesn't mean such amazing products do not exist. Penicillin technically does just one thing—dispenses with bacteria—but this means it can treat pneumonia, urinary tract infections, bronchitis, gonorrhea, syphilis, tonsillitis, gangrene, and a host of other illnesses. Recently, some scholars and technology advocates have suggested that video games might also have a wide variety of benefits, improving numerous aspects of our lives: giving us better mood control, social skills, hand-eye coordination, and sharpening our minds in general. With a skeptical eye toward such claims, in this chapter we'll try to figure out if video games are really a multitasking electronic penicillin, or whether they are more like the modern equivalent of Parker's Tonic, doing little to help us with our problems, except perhaps to make us temporarily forget they exist.

MAKING US FEEL BETTER

High school sophomore Jett was going through one of the darkest times of his young life. At school, he was incessantly bullied by his peers. At home, he was becoming increasingly estranged from his alcoholic father. Jett was sinking into a dangerous depression and had even begun to seriously consider suicide. Fortunately, he ultimately found solace in what may seem an unlikely place: the violent video game *Fallout 3*. In this role-playing game, players control a character in a world destroyed by nuclear war, where they must make numerous choices about how to rebuild civilization as they fight to stay alive. Jett found himself immersed in the story, but, more critically, *Fallout 3* gave him the sense that he was able to accomplish things, influence others, and change the world—even if the world was a virtual one. The game was an escape, sure, but it was more than that, too. As Jett writes on a blog detailing his experience: "I was saving people, changing lives, and vanquishing evil—I felt like someone worth living as, and this translated to my real life and gave me a more optimistic outlook on the future."[238] *Fallout 3* elevated Jett's mood and gave him sense of purpose when he most needed it, allowing him to pull through a difficult period and hold on until things got better in his "real life."

Jett is not alone: many teens and adults have found that video games help them get through rough times. We're not saying that every time someone whips out *Plants Versus Zombies* the world becomes a slightly happier place (although, as we learned in Level Four, it may become a safer one!), but lots of people turn to video games, even violent ones, to relieve stress or put themselves in a better mood. Does this work? Does blasting other characters or players make people feel better? The short answer is yes, but, as ever, with a few caveats. As we discussed earlier in the book, video games work more or less like any other hobby. As long as it's an activity you enjoy, it will relieve stress and make you feel better. If you *don't* enjoy it . . . well, obviously it won't do these things. If you don't like crocheting, it isn't going to relax you or make you feel any better after a hard day. If making doilies, shawls, blankets, thong underwear, or god knows what else via yarn and hook sounds appealing to you, then crocheting is a great way to unwind! As we noted in Level Four, for the authors of this book, efforts involving needle and thread usually end with an emergency room visit. The hobby has to match the individual.

A variety of theories have been developed to explain how people use video games to improve their moods, including mood management theory,[239] uses and gratifications theory,[240] and self-determination theory.[241] One element emphasized by all of these theories is that people seek out specific media that they believe will help them reach positive mood states. So, for example, when one of the authors of this book (Markey) is feeling sad or down, he turns to a show he enjoyed in his younger days: *Full House.* Watching the hijinks of Danny, Jesse, and Joey as they raise D.J., Stephanie, and Michelle simply makes him feel better about life. In contrast, the other author of this book (Ferguson) becomes irate when he sees *Full House.* To him, this is the worst show on the planet. Because *Full House* affects our moods very differently, it should come as no surprise that one of us is the proud owner of the entire series on DVD, whereas the other would rather eat those DVDs, cases and all, than watch them. Media use is an active process of selecting media and interpreting it, not a thing done *to* us. Selection is an especially important part of the process, because, like other hobbies, media works to elevate mood only as long as it matches your interests and intent. It's this *match*, more than content, that is important. This is why playing a violent video game lifts the moods of some, while others might find such a game stressful. However, not all types of media are equally effective at stress reduction and mood repair (that is, making us feel better). Passive media, like sitting on the couch and watching your favorite television show, can certainly make you a bit happier or calmer. But because video games are actively engaging and require our full concentration, playing Xbox or PlayStation is generally more effective at repairing our moods than bingeing on Netflix.[242]

Of course, any hobby can become frustrating when something goes wrong. Even if you love crocheting, you will not find it particularly soothing if that blanket you have been working on for months unravels, or you find your sweater has three sleeves. This isn't much different from getting mad when your favorite team blows the play-offs or you lose at cards. You might enjoy blasting virtual aliens in a video game, but only if you don't find the game itself frustrating. Games are supposed to be challenging, but sometimes a game presents challenges that seem so unfair that it's as if the game's developers were out to get you. One of the most intriguing studies on video games in recent years is one we referenced in Level Three, by Oxford psychologist Dr. Andrew Przybylski. Some previous studies had found that a session of playing a violent video game caused an increase in mild aggression—sometimes, as you'll recall, in the form of unrequested hot sauce. In his series of experiments, Dr. Przybylski systematically varied the frustration level and violent content of video games played by laboratory subjects.[241] He found that it was frustration, *not* violent content, that caused mild aggressive feelings. It didn't matter if a game was violent or not; if the game's goal was near impossible to achieve, people became upset when playing it.

But when not overly frustrating, video games are particularly good at relieving acute stress. In some studies, participants are purposefully stressed using a task called the Paced Auditory Serial Addition Task (or the PASAT—psychologists love acronyms; it makes us feel like we're doing smart stuff). This task was originally designed to test for neurological impairments, but it is so unpleasant that it makes a great stress inducer for research purposes. Basically, in the

PASAT, participants hear a series of single-digit numbers and are asked to add each number to the previous number and type in their answer—if you hear "4" and then "8" you would quickly enter "12." Sounds easy, but the numbers keep coming, and you must add each new number only to the one before it. So, while you're keying in "12," the next number is already being read, let's say "3." Now you must quickly add three to the preceding number, which was eight. But, your poor brain is still thinking twelve, because that's what you are typing into the computer. Argh! Everybody hates the PASAT . . . except laboratory psychologists. This task quickly becomes stressful, even for people with normal functioning. It's not the kind of stress that people face when they lose their job or have an argument with a spouse, but it's a good way to irritate people and replicate the low-level stress we all experience. Researchers have found that one way people can recover from the stress produced by tasks like the PASAT is to play video games. That's right, simply playing a video game, whether violent or nonviolent, reduces stress, hostility, and improves mood.[243, 244, 245] Again, it probably does this just as any hobby a person naturally enjoys would. Score one for the gamers!

MAKING FRIENDS IN A VIRTUAL WORLD

For many who play them, perhaps the greatest appeal of video games lies in the opportunity they provide to hang out with friends. The belief that gaming detracts from time spent with peers and on other social activities is still one of the most common gripes among oldsters. Of course, not all games need be played socially, but there's a considerable discrepancy between the stereotype of the gamer as an antisocial loner and the reality that most games are played in very functional social networks and are in fact social outlets for the people who play them.[246] Increasingly, many games are being released in multiplayer formats only, which means they cannot be played alone at all. For example, to coincide with the blockbuster movie *Star Wars: The Force Awakens,* Electronic Arts released the multiplayer game *Star Wars: Battlefront.* Instead of a single-player mission, this game offered players a chance to battle the evil Empire with the help of friends around the world or with a buddy on a couch. Underscoring how much people enjoy playing video games with others, *Star Wars: Battlefront* went on to sell over twelve million copies in its first two months. Of course, social video gameplay isn't new: even the Atari 2600 came with two controllers, and video games got their start, you'll remember, in crowded arcades.

Researchers have known for some time that people, particularly young people, use video games to develop and maintain friendships.[247] This is probably most evident to those who play massively multiplayer online role-playing games, like *World of Warcraft, EVE Online,* or *Star Wars: The Old Republic.* In these games, players often form "guilds" or "clans" composed of people who might be located anywhere in the world and regularly play together online. Some of these groups last just a couple of weeks, but others persist for decades. Many come to think of their fellow guild members as close friends, no different from the friends they might have in the real world. These members regularly interact with one another, and not just about battle strategy: they talk about their personal lives and share their secrets, fears, hopes, and dreams. Some of these friendships even blossom into romantic relationships and marriage—in the real world![248] Indeed, given the number of subscribers to these games (current estimates are over twelve million), there are more potential romantic partners in the *World of Warcraft*'s world of Azeroth than there are on Match.com and OKCupid combined!

The anonymity of the internet has often been rued due to its potential for rude emails or nasty comments. However, this same anonymity makes it possible for people who are uncomfortable with social interactions in the real world to form social connections in a less threatening digital one. The virtual world provided by video games has real potential to help those who have difficulty in offline relationships. A German study[249] found that shy teens often use games to form social connections that they are unable to form in real-life contexts. For these shy youths, games provide an obvious life-enhancing social outlet. Other studies have replicated these results, finding that introverts experience much less anxiety when interacting in a virtual world than during interactions at school, work, or in other social situations.[250] It probably isn't too surprising, then, that shy individuals often turn to virtual connections as a way to fulfill their desire for social interactions[251] and that, frequently, the connections formed through games or other online interactions blossom into real friendships just as meaningful as those developed offline.

Not only can video games help shy kids—and adults—make friends, they can also aid children with developmental disabilities such as autism spectrum disorders. Scottish psychologist Dr. Kevin Durkin has been studying kids with developmental disorders for years, and has found that games provide these children with a less-threatening environment in which to form relationships and practice their social skills.[252] If things don't work out, it is easier to move on and try again in a virtual world than it is in a classroom or work environment, where the pool of individuals is smaller and you'll still have to be around those who've rejected you.

BRAIN EXERCISES

David Cathers came of age during the Great Depression and lived through World War II and the communism scares of the twentieth century. He worked hard as a laundry pickup/deliveryman, married the love of his life, and raised a family. A beloved grandfather, he retired in his sixties and settled down to spend his twilight years in his native Rhode Island. However, in his early seventies, he experienced a series of transient ischemic attacks (ministrokes). These caused a sudden cognitive decline, and David was hospitalized for several weeks. He recovered and returned to normal life, but in his late seventies it happened again, and this time the cognitive decline was permanent. As often happens with dementia, David began engaging in odd behaviors: he became paranoid about strangers in his apartment's basement laundry and once stopped his car in the road and stood in front of it for no apparent reason.

One day, while visiting his daughter's home, David, appearing confused, flew out the door and began walking randomly around the neighborhood until a neighbor called the police. When they arrived, David, who had no prior history of criminal behavior or violence, assaulted a female police officer. The police brought him to a psychiatric hospital, where he was diagnosed with brain atrophy, potentially due to another series of ministrokes. His dementia rendered him incapable of caring for himself or even recognizing family members.

It is a sad story, but not as uncommon as you might think: dementia is the leading cause of disability in the elderly, and the proportion suffering from it jumps to 20 percent after age 75 and climbs from there. Even normal aging comes with some loss of memory and mental acuity.

But there is evidence to suggest that we might be able to forestall cognitive decline by playing video games. One recent study found that playing three-dimensional driving simulations improved memory and attention in older adults, and that these gains persisted for at least six months.[253] Other studies have found that computer games enhance cognitive performance among the elderly, improve decision making, and even help prevent Alzheimer's disease.[254, 255, 256] Recognizing a potential untapped market in the affluent crossword-and-Sudoku set, some game manufacturers have implied that video games can actually make us smarter in the same way exercise makes us stronger. Nintendo's *Brain Age: Train Your Brain in Minutes a Day!* claims that the game will "flex" your mental muscle and "keep your brain in shape." Although Nintendo is very careful not to offer any scientific validation for these assertions (they promote the game as an "entertainment product"), consumers are clearly led to believe that playing the game will help keep them mentally sharp.

The implicit promise that *Brain Age* would improve cognitive skills was an effective one—the game went on to sell more than four million copies worldwide and spawned several sequels. Its popularity was so immense that several companies quickly cashed in on the *Brain Age* excitement, releasing similar games (*Big Brain Academy, Brain Challenge, Brain Exercise,* etc.), creating a new genre known as "brain games." However, not all scholars are confident about the effectiveness of brain-training games. One group of about seventy-five scholars even got together to write a statement objecting to the "claim that brain games offer consumers a scientifically grounded avenue to reduce or reverse cognitive decline when there is no compelling scientific evidence to date that they do."[257] These researchers acknowledge that, while some studies have found that brain-training games may be effective, many other studies have failed to find any evidence of this. In short, these scholars were concerned that the positive effects of brain games had been exaggerated by other scientists, the media, and the video game industry (see Easter Egg 1).

As we've seen with video game violence, it's not uncommon for the influence of games to be exaggerated by both scientists and the media. And we certainly don't doubt that the game industry is inclined to selectively tout studies that support their products (good luck finding an industry that *doesn't* do this). But the scholars who signed the statement on brain games did more than simply suggest these products were ineffective at preventing cognitive decline; the statement also warned that brain games might actually cause harm! For example: "Time spent playing the games is time not spent reading, socializing, gardening, exercising, or engaging in many other activities that may benefit cognitive and physical health of older adults." We've discussed the fact that video games are typically played as a social activity, but here again they are portrayed as anti-social. And who says video games are less cognitively demanding than reading? And what the heck is so great about gardening, any-way? These scholars imply that brain games may hurt the very thing they were developed to help, our cognitive skills, but what evidence do they offer to support this conclusion? None, nothing, nada! This statement is revealing in its narrow concept of appropriate activities for the elderly (only those you might see in a Boniva commercial, apparently), a generationally naïve judgment made by older adults who simply don't understand games. Exactly to what extent brain training might benefit a person is still unclear, but there is *no* evidence to suggest playing these games causes any cognitive harm, even if it's true they convey little cognitive benefit.[258]

This is not the first time scholars have scolded an industry for exaggerating the benefits of a product only to immediately fail to learn their own lesson and exaggerate the product's potential harms. In the late '90s, parents across the United States discovered the joys of baby videos like *Baby Einstein.* Parents of restless infants quickly learned that they could plop their children in front of one of these videos for twenty minutes, giving themselves a window of peace in which to brush their teeth or read a newspaper. As with brain training games, some of the companies that made these videos implied that their products could increase babies' intelligence. Such claims were not based on any sound scientific evidence, and several researchers quickly took these companies to task for exaggerating the benefits of their videos. However, in 2007, several pediatricians made headlines when they claimed their research had shown that not only do baby videos not make babies smarter, they actually make them dumber![259] Trouble was, these pediatricians, like the baby video industry itself, wanted people to take their word for it—without see-ing the data. The University of Washington, where the pediatricians were employed, even went to court to prevent the release of the study data after some producers of baby videos requested it.[260] When the data was finally made public and reanalyzed by independent scholars (including one of the authors of this book), it became pretty clear that the pediatricians had bungled their analysis.[261] Basically, the videos neither boosted nor dulled the intelligence of babies. Subsequent studies from Harvard University and Boston Children's Hospital have confirmed this reanalysis, finding that television viewing has no effect—good or bad—on children's cognitive and language development.[262] Like with brain games, researchers were correct to call into question the claims that baby videos had a cognitive benefit. However, also like with brain games, these researchers turned right around and committed the same sin by exaggerating the potential harmful effects of this media.

Just as baby videos are not going to make your kid smarter, it seems pretty safe to conclude that brain games, while fun, will not help you qualify for a Mensa membership. However, for older adults, playing video games does appear to slow some cognitive decline—in much the same way as other activities with high cognitive loads, like crosswords, reading, or yapping about politics with friends. Most importantly, there is no evidence that these games are harmful or that if *Brain Age* takes grandma away from reading or even, god forbid, *gardening*, it will be particularly tragic.[263] So, if you or your grandma are not big fans of digging around in the dirt, but you *do* enjoy brain games, go for it! Just don't expect it to hold your Alzheimer's at bay.

IMPROVING HAND-EYE COORDINATION

One of the largest and most interesting areas of research into the benefits of video gameplay concerns what most people call hand-eye coordination, and what scholars call "visuospatial cognition."

Basically, this research examines whether games (especially certain types of action games) can be used for training: to improve particular abilities that would be useful in real life. Can playing *Halo 4* repeatedly make someone a better engineer or surgeon? If so, the next time you need surgery, perhaps you should be just as concerned with whether your surgeon enjoys *Call of Duty* death matches as you are about where she went to medical school.

Studies in this area work similarly to those we discussed in Level Three. Specifically, people (usually college students) are brought into a lab, where they perform a task and then play an action game for a short amount of time. Once they are done blasting aliens in *Halo* or shooting enemy soldiers in *Call of Duty,* researchers have the subjects repeat the task they performed before gaming to determine whether certain skills show any improvement. Usually, the skills examined involve hand-eye coordination or the ability to scan for and identify various items on a computer screen. For example, one common task involves a kind of shell game on steroids: participants see three or four of a particular shape, perhaps a triangle, surrounded by a larger number of other shapes, such as circles. They are then asked to keep track of the triangles. But, halfway through the task, all the triangles become circles, and participants have to continue tracking them. It's fun but becomes increasingly difficult as more shapes appear on the screen with each iteration or level of the task. Using tasks like this, researchers have found that people who play action games are better at switching quickly between one task and the next.[264] In other words, games improve our multitasking skills.

And though the image of a gamer is often of a geek in glasses, playing games actually seems to improve vision. Specifically, people who play action video games can see smaller type on a computer screen and have greater contrast sensitivity than those who do not play these games.[265, 266] Action games also appear to increase our spatial cognition, that is, our ability to acquire and use information about our environment. The reason why is likely obvious to anyone who has ever played a first-person shooter. In these games, players must be constantly aware of their entire virtual environment, not just what is right in front of their guns. To be successful in *Halo*, for instance, a gamer must repetitively scan his or her surroundings in order to detect any grunts, jackals, or brutes that might be lying in wait. All of this "practice" scanning virtual worlds seems to benefit our spatial skills in the real world. Some research even suggests that, for women, playing action games actually erases traditional gender gaps in spatial cognition, an area in which men usually perform better.[267]

One surprising finding from this type of research is that many of the games you might expect to benefit visuospatial cognition actually don't. Most notably, *Tetris*. If you haven't played or seen it, *Tetris* involves rotating differently shaped blocks as they descend so that they fit together to form solid rows. When you succeed in creating a row, it disappears. If the blocks begin to pile up and eventually reach the top of the screen, the game ends. Because this game involves mentally rotating objects in your mind, and having to do so quickly, we would expect this to be an obvious visuospatial trainer, right? Wrong![268] It turns out that playing *Tetris* will make you a better *Tetris* player, but not much else. Two observations follow from this. First, common sense doesn't always translate into fact. Second, when studying the effects of video games, it's important to consider and evaluate a phenomenon called "transfer of learning."

Transfer of learning is the idea that learning in one context can transfer to a different, but similar, context. The likelihood of transfer is dependent upon the similarity of the tasks. Learning how to tie one shoe easily transfers to other shoes because the task involved is almost identical from one shoe to another. Learning how to play floor hockey may make you intuitively good at soccer, but it probably won't help your swimming skills much. In most learning contexts, the goal is to learn a skill in one situation that will then transfer to a different situation. Sometimes the situations are a lot alike—when we learn math skills, we expect that the ability to add and subtract will transfer from the classroom to making change and adding up prices in the real world. Other times, the transfer of learning is more complicated. For instance, we might instruct a group of children on gun safety. In a classroom, the children can be taught important gun safety rules, like not picking up a gun they find, telling an adult if they ever run across a gun, and never pointing a gun at others. Kids who've taken such a class will easily repeat the rules back to you when prompted, so we know that they've definitely learned something. But what happens when these kids leave the classroom and go home, or to a friend's house? You probably already know the terrifying answer. If these children happen to stumble across a real handgun and a box of bullets when no adults are present, they will suddenly forget all about the rules they just learned! Research shows that even after learning the rules of gun safety in a classroom, children will happily play with real guns, try to load them with bullets, and even point the guns at each other.[269] What the children learned in the classroom clearly did not transfer to a new environment. Of course kids are, well, kids, but the same principle holds true for adults. Learning just doesn't transfer all that easily between varied circumstances. Therefore, visuospatial skills learned in a video game will best transfer to real-world situations that are somewhat similar to the environment of a video game.

The importance of environment for transference of skills from video games to the real world is probably most evident in the realm of surgery. It turns out that surgeons who warm up by playing action games are better at performing certain types of operations. Given how transfer of learning works, it is not surprising that these types are those that use computers, such as laparoscopic surgery. This finding has been reliably demonstrated across multiple studies,[270] and, as the following figure indicates, surgeons who play video games tend to make fewer mistakes, perform these surgeries more quickly, and have better surgical skills than those who do not play video games.[271]

Some studies even suggest that action video games are better than simulators specifically designed to be used in training for laparo-scopic surgery.[272]

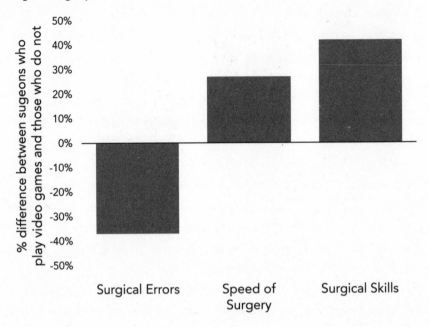

In fairness, not all scholars are convinced of these results regarding the training of visual attention.[273] Wally Boot, a psychologist at Florida State University, has noted that some of these studies have serious limitations (small and selective samples, poor matching between video game conditions, etc.) and more research is needed before we should start requiring future surgeons to play *Halo* in medical school.[274] Indeed, some scholars have found that the benefits of video gameplay do not seem to extend to traditional surgical skills (like using a scalpel).[275] Thus, learning in action game playing transfers to laparoscopic surgery because, by happy coincidence, the kinds of tasks and skills required are relatively similar. Even though traditional surgery is also visuospatial in nature, it isn't similar enough that playing video games can help. Still, this limited benefit is a compelling one, and as a result of this research, some hospitals have begun setting up video game lounges for their surgeons.[276] Pretty cool, right? Oft-maligned first-person shooter games, now coming to save people's lives!

IS IT A "VIOLENT" GAME OR AN "ACTION" GAME?

As we have learned throughout this book, society is interested in both the degree to which certain games can instigate violent or aggressive behavior and the degree to which games can confer positive benefits such as improved visuospatial cognition. Curiously, a lot of research into both the "good" and the "bad" focuses on the same genre—first- and third-person shooter games, like *Call of Duty* and *Grand Theft Auto*. More curiously still, the language researchers use when describing such games often changes depending upon whether the effects they are investigating are good (like visuospatial skills) or bad (like violent crime). In this chapter, we used the same terminology employed by researchers who examine visuospatial skills: "action video games." And, in earlier chapters, we used the same terminology employed by scholars who examine violence and aggression: "violent video games." It is telling that, when studying the alleged negative effects, they are "violent video games," meriting comparisons to the mechanisms of mass shootings.[277] Yet, when looking at the impact of these same first- and third-person shooters on hand-eye coordination, suddenly they become "action games." Sometimes, the *same* researcher will refer to a "violent video game" in an article focused on aggression, and call the identical game an "action game" in an article about visuospatial skills. Scholars themselves are changing their descriptions depending upon what aspect of the game they want their readers to focus on. If you want people to like the game, call it an "action game." If you want them to dislike it, call it a "violent video game." This would be like scientists studying a particular concoction, calling it "Death Potion!" when researching its dangerous side effects, but "Transcendent Elixir!" when examining its health benefits. This is obviously marketing . . . and who knew scholars were so good at branding their products.

This is not a minor issue; rather, it points to both the sloppiness and the emotionally overwrought nature of the field of video game scholarship. Perhaps the biggest mistake made by scientists in this field was ever using the term "violent video game" in the first place. This label is simply too laden with emotion—what's more, it is conceptually meaningless. What exactly makes a game "violent"? Some scholars have argued that any game that depicts "characters intentionally harming other characters who presumably wish to avoid being harmed" is a violent video game.[278] By this definition, almost *all* video games, from *Pac-Man* to *Grand Theft Auto,* are "violent video games." It is a bit like lumping comic books, the Bible, Stephen King, Shakespeare, and a how-to book on fishing together as "violent literature" and pretending such a category makes sense at all.

IF VIDEO GAMES TEACH POSITIVE SKILLS, WHY DON'T THEY ALSO TEACH NEGATIVE ONES?

So the brutal, merciless, savage mass murder of first-graders in Connecticut was another in a long line of avid video game players who turned their sick fantasy into our tragic reality. Surprised? . . . violent video games are "murder simulators" that train kids to kill.
—Lt. Col. (Ret.) Dave Grossman[279]

If health video games can successfully teach health behaviors, and flight-simulator video games can teach people how to fly, then what should we expect violent, murder-simulating games to teach?
—Drs. Douglas Gentile and Craig Anderson[280]

One of the questions about video games we see most often is something along the lines of this: "If video games can help teach, say, laparoscopic surgery, why can't they also be teaching kids how to shoot and/or kill people?" This type of question sounds sensible on the surface but has basic logical fallacies built into it. The fact that video games can affect learning in one area does not mean that they can affect learning in every area! It is ridiculous to think that just because something has one kind of effect on one thing (for instance, action games or flight simulators enhancing surgical or flying skills), it is suddenly expected to have the power to affect everything else as well. (We also note that, personally, we'd prefer not to fly on a commercial jet where the pilot had been trained solely on Microsoft's *Flight Simulator*.)

To illustrate the problem with this logic, imagine we asked this question: "If penicillin can successfully cure infections, then why shouldn't it cure cancer?" Starting from the beginning, a point where perhaps you don't know much about the mechanisms of penicillin or cancer, this is a reasonable question, maybe worth looking into. But, once you start to gather information and conduct research, if the evidence reveals that penicillin *does* cure bacterial infections and yet has no effect on cancer, the question is moot. By all means, test for both effects, but, ultimately, if the evidence supports one kind of effect and not the other, the reasonableness of the original question no longer really matters. That's kind of where we are at with video game research. There is good evidence to suggest that action/violent video games can improve some very specific visuospatial skills, but a lack of evidence suggesting these games can lead to violence.

The reason video games do not teach kids how to kill is what we discovered earlier in our discussion of *transfer of learning*: we are much more likely to be able to transfer what we learned in one situation to another if these situations are similar. For example, a computer game that requires quick and precise hand movements can improve a person's ability to perform computer-aided surgery, which also requires quick and precise hand movements. In contrast, kids who master the game *Street Fighter*, in which karate moves are performed by pressing a series of buttons, do not develop actual karate skills. Even the most skilled player in *Street Fighter* will not have learned how to pull off Ryu's hurricane kick, E. Honda's hundred hand slap, or Ken's rising dragon fist—no matter how much he practices playing the game. Nor is manipulating a *PlayStation* or *Xbox* controller while playing *Call of Duty* going to teach someone how to shoot a gun at another person. As seen in the box on the next page, the skills learned in a typical first-person game about how to shoot a virtual handgun have almost no relationship to the skills involved in shooting an actual handgun.

To review, playing games—even violent . . . er, *action* games—may be associated with some notable benefits. The evidence for emotional benefits seems strongest: video games, like most hobbies, can reduce stress, increase positive mood, teach social skills, and even foster friendships with like-minded people. Of course, sometimes, even leisure activities can become stressful, and video games won't work as a stress reducer for everyone—it may seem obvious to say so, but you have to *enjoy* video games to get the emotional benefits, just as with any hobby. And that's probably the best way to think of games, as a hobby neither more beneficial nor more harmful than any other. Overall, those playing games to calm themselves and become happier are probably doing just fine.

The evidence for cognitive benefits is less clear. If you are hoping games will make you smarter or cure grandpa's Alzheimer's, you're probably out of luck. But they may be useful tools for developing some narrow, specific visuospatial skills. And they may also help keep older brains active, which could play a small role in staving off age-related cognitive decline. Here again, the benefits are probably similar to other cognitively engaging hobbies like reading or puzzles—no more, no less.

The available scientific evidence seems to suggest that video games are neither Parker's Tonic (which had no benefits—aside from

HOW TO FIRE A HANDGUN . . .

. . . IN THE REAL-WORLD:

1. A two-handed grip is best.
2. Four fingers of your nondominant hand should be under the trigger guard.
3. Point the thumb of your dominant hand forward while placing this hand as high as possible on the grip.
4. Make sure your fingers are clear of the slide or hammer (that thing on the back of the gun).
5. You should stand with your feet and hips shoulder width apart.
6. Slightly bend your knees.
7. Bring the gun up to your target.
8. Using your dominant eye, align the sights on your gun.
9. Develop your sight picture by focusing on the target after you have leveled the gun.
10. Control your breathing—keep your body calm.
11. Do not pull the trigger—instead you want to press it by applying constant pressure.
12. After shooting, you want to "follow through," just as a golfer might after striking a ball.

. . . IN A TYPICAL FIRST-PERSON SHOOTER:

1. Pull the left trigger to aim the gun.
2. Pull the right trigger to fire the gun.

the martini-like level of alcohol) nor are they penicillin; instead, they're something in between. Video games are not going to save the world, but they might address some specific problems. If you are feeling stressed, lonely, or even looking for love, go hang out online with your *World of Warcraft* clan. If grandpa is worried that he isn't getting enough mental stimulation, hand him your Nintendo DS. If you want to be a better surgeon, go ahead, blast some aliens! Best-case scenario, these activities will actually help—worst case, you get to have a little fun.

At this point in the book, if you're a gamer, you are probably convinced that despite the dire warnings of politicians and others, games like *Mortal Kombat* are not going to destroy civilization as we know it. Let's be honest—you likely held this belief before reading the first page! If you are a non-gamer, or a concerned parent, you may still feel somewhat uneasy about this interactive medium. Hopefully, we have been able to provide you with a more balanced view of video games to counteract all the unsupported doom and gloom you've heard from politicians and the media. But it is perfectly understandable that parents, even those who aren't reflexively anti-game, might be worried about how much time their children dedicate to video games and what exactly these games contain. With rapid advances in technology and the near-daily release of new titles, the video game world can quickly become overwhelming for parents trying to keep up.

One thing we can tell you now: if your goal, as a parent, is to act as a wall between your child and advancing technology . . . you will not succeed. You may even do more harm than good along the way. Instead, the goal of parents should be to better understand new technology and media themselves, making it easier to identify and create a balance that works for their families. What parents need is guidance—a strategy guide to help them navigate the pixelated video game minefield . . .

EASTER EGG

1. It is worth pointing out that there is a counterstatement taking the first statement to task for claiming there was a consensus.[281] This second statement was signed by even more scholars than the first (curiously, a couple of scholars appear to have signed both) suggesting no consensus ever existed.

LEVEL 9:

A STRATEGY GUIDE FOR PARENTS

Veronica is a fifteen-year-old girl who is very shy, has never had many friends, and has few hobbies or interests. Recently, she started to play the online game *World of Warcraft* . . . a lot! Her grades, which were never great in the first place, began to slip. She began to ignore what few outside hobbies she had to spend all her time gaming. On the other hand, the game has brought her happiness in a way nothing has before. She has made new friends through *World of Warcraft* and now even has a boyfriend she met playing online. Unsure of what to do and concerned about Veronica's gaming habits, her mother reached out to us for advice.

According to Veronica's mother, the two of them sometimes argued over video games, both about what content was appropriate and how much time Veronica should spend playing. Like just about every other child on the planet, Veronica found video games more interesting than homework. However, none of these problems were major: Veronica was an OK student and did not have any serious behavior issues. Mother and daughter actually got along pretty well, with no more than the usual arguments for Veronica's age. The main predicament seemed to be that Veronica preferred gaming to focusing on academics, and, of course, her mother had other priorities for her daughter! Further, Veronica's mother couldn't understand the appeal of video games—particularly not the bloody role-playing and action games Veronica liked—and worried these games might be desensitizing her daughter to cruelty in real life.

Veronica's mother's concerns are those experienced by almost every parent trying to raise a child in a world rich with interactive media.

1. **TIME:** Is Veronica addicted to video games? Can (and should) anything be done to limit the amount of time she plays?
2. **FRIENDS:** Even if Veronica's mother sets limits on gameplay in her own home, what about when Veronica visits friends who own video games?
3. **INFORMATION:** How can Veronica's mother better understand her child's interest in video games? Are there trustworthy resources she can turn to for information about the games and their content?
4. **VIOLENCE:** Is it OK for Veronica to play these violent role-playing and action games? Will they influence her to become violent or desensitize her to violence in the real world?

TIME: SCALING BACK VIDEO GAMES

Veronica's mother believes that gaming is causing problems for her daughter, but she also recognizes that *World of Warcraft* has become an important outlet for Veronica, and that removing it entirely could come with its own risks. As we learned in Level Six, true video game addiction is extremely rare[282, 283, 284] and if she is tempted to seek out professional treatment, Veronica's mother should exercise extreme caution. Like anything else that has gotten a lot of public attention, people have tried to capitalize on parents' fears of video game addiction. Many centers offer treatments that have absolutely no evidence supporting them. Some of these treatment facilities are more like prisons, where video game "addicts" are essentially locked away in order to undergo intensive daily therapy. Other centers send children into the desert or the woods to live for a couple of months, at a cost upwards of $30,000! Granted, this wilderness adventure will certainly prevent these children from playing video games—not only is there no electricity, but the necessity of keeping warm, fed, and uneaten by bears keeps them plenty occupied. Unfortunately, there is very little evidence to suggest this has a lasting effect once the kids return to civilization (and their computers). In general, parents should be wary of any treatment center that uses scaremongering as a recruitment tool. The more a clinic emphasizes that your child is doomed without their therapy, the less reputable said clinic is likely to be.

Don't get us wrong, there are some very good clinicians out there, genuinely trying to help those who struggle with this problem. A very small number of kids and adults truly do need the intervention of clinicians to help regain control of their gaming. Yet in many cases—including Veronica's—the video game issue might best be addressed by parents themselves. With this in mind, we offer a few insights for both Veronica's mother and other parents who are concerned about their children's video game habits.

NEED FULFILLMENT

First, it helps to understand why a child has chosen to spend time playing video games as opposed to engaging in other activities. Self-determination theory[285] suggests that people are often attracted to video games because they help them fulfill psychological needs that they've been unable to meet in real life. Consider the case of Veronica. Her attraction to *World of Warcraft* was not an accident. She was having difficulty fitting in socially—online, she felt more comfortable and was able to make friends and even establish a romantic relationship. She might have been overdoing it, but playing this video game was serving a very real and meaningful purpose for her.

Related to this, excessive video gameplay often arises from an underlying problem.[286] In Veronica's case, the underlying issue was her shyness. The virtual world of the video game helped her overcome this and opened a whole new social setting for her. It's not surprising, then, that she had difficulty regulating her play: the game gave her social outlets that simply had never existed for her before. Understanding the underlying problem can help put video game use in perspective. Because these games are often used to meet psychological needs, suddenly restricting access can have its own—sometimes dire—consequences. Cutting a child off from her entire social support network, whether it is in the real world or a virtual one, is a risky proposition, even if she is abusing the technology used to access that support network. This is not to say that Veronica doesn't need to learn to find balance in her video game use, only that any interventions need to be sensible and compassionate toward what motivates that use in the first place.

SHOOTING THE BREEZE

Unfortunately, when it comes to technology, parents and children often see things very differently and have difficulty understanding one another's point of view. If a child is struggling to balance her gaming with other responsibilities, then parents have a valid concern. However, the child may have a valid perspective on her media use as well—one that parents are unaware of. A parent, especially one who is unfamiliar with video games, is going to have trouble understanding what amount of gaming is normal, or even why a child might be interested in video games in the first place.

Thus, struggles over technology often become a battle of wills. In order to have the best chance of getting to the heart of the issues involved and addressing them successfully, parents must explain their concerns (and the reasoning behind them) calmly, and also take the time to listen to their child's concerns. Every kid is different, of course, but, if parent and child have an established, loving relationship, most kids will work with their parents—as long as they feel their parents are listening to them. The key point here is the importance of communication: both parent and child should take the time to be sure that they understand each other's perspectives. Indeed, previous research has found that parents who understand their kids not only have better relationships with their children, but these children also tend to be better adjusted, psychologically, than those of parents who just don't "get" their kids.[287]

SETTING LIMITS

This one probably seems obvious—but it can be tricky. Problems can arise both when parents fail to set appropriate limits and when they become draconian and overdo it. For instance, Veronica's mother may be tempted to simply close her daughter's *World of Warcraft* gaming account. But, because Veronica seems to depend on this game to satisfy her social needs, this would likely cause at least as many problems as it solves.

Instead of completely removing Veronica's access to her game, a better tactic might be to set up a program in which her access is contingent upon satisfying certain requirements. For instance, an hour's worth of homework might be rewarded with a half hour of video game time—the same for an hour of household chores. Most kids don't want to do homework and chores. But the less enjoyable activities come first, then the games. Parents should clearly delineate the rules and enforce them *reliably*. This might sound very basic—and it is!—but setting clear expectations for what needs to be done in order to play video games has been found to be very effective in helping families balance media use with other responsibilities.[288]

Longer term, parents can set daily limits on game time tied to certain benchmarks. Exactly where parents initially set these daily limits will depend on how much their child currently plays. Veronica's mother decided to start with sixty minutes of game time on school days. If Veronica does well on her next report card, her game time will be extended to ninety minutes, and so on. That way, time spent gaming can be gradually increased while remaining contingent upon meeting other requirements. And if things begin to slip, gaming time can be reduced once more. If Veronica doesn't complete her chores, her game time might be reduced to thirty minutes. Again, it is most important that the behaviors parents wish to target have clear consequences, good and bad. And when determining these consequences, it is always best to leave the child an avenue toward the return of his or her game time. A total ban without a clear path to restoring privileges merely instills hopelessness and resentment. Remember, whatever a parent's personal feelings about gaming, the goal is to balance gaming with other activities, not to quash it altogether.

THE GIFT OF TIME

Perhaps you remember the great joy you felt when your parent tossed a baseball around with you in the backyard, or sat down to attend your imaginary tea party or real, if tuneless, musical revue. Today, video games provide an opportunity for children to create real memories with their parents in a virtual world. A father and son might work together to defeat Bowser in the latest installment of *Mario Brothers*, while in the next room mother and daughter help each other build an enormous virtual compound in the world of *Minecraft*. Mothers and sons may meet up online to conduct raids in *World of Warcraft*. Ferguson's son Roman is rarely seen in such fits of hysterics as those that result from blasting his father going head-to-head in *Lego: Marvel Superheroes* (at which Roman is, alas, quite adept). Even though these memories are being created in an electronic playground, they are just as real, and just as important, as any memory created in the real world. Even parents who don't want to play video games themselves can foster connection by putting forth the effort to watch their child play. The warm thrill we might recall from seeing our parents in the stands of our Little League games is the same felt by a child who loves video games when a parent takes the time to watch and express interest in the activity they value. Not only is playing with our kids fun, but research has found that children, especially girls, who play video games with their parents are less likely to internalize problems or express aggressive behaviors.[289] Positive emotions associated with video gameplay are also thought to be behind the links between video games and creativity, increases in self-efficacy (the belief in our ability to achieve goals and work through problems), and even the satisfaction of basic psychological needs.[290, 291, 292]

S.O.S.

If a parent has tried addressing concerns about their child's gameplay through communication and understanding, and implementing a clear and consistent system of consequences does not seem to work, it may be time to seek help from outside experts. School counselors are often a good place to start, and can connect parents with additional resources. However, as we mentioned earlier, it is important to make sure that any experts are truly interested in the welfare of the child and not simply looking to make a buck by capitalizing on the latest moral panic.

FRIENDS: KEEPING UP WITH THE JONESES

Veronica's mother worried that even if she forbade her daughter from playing games with content she found objectionable, Veronica might well still have access to these games at a friend's house. Obviously, Veronica's mother is not alone in being worried about what her child is doing when away from home. One of the problems many parents face when attempting to set boundaries on media for their children is their children's friends—and those friends' parents. Parents who rigidly restrict their children's media often become upset at other parents who do not share their opinions or enforce the same limits. Parents at both extremes—those who allow their children to watch whatever they like and those who reflexively restrict anything that could possibly raise an eyebrow—are abdicating their responsibility to make informed decisions about their children's media consumption. But even parents who carefully consider whether a certain type of media is appropriate for their children will inevitably encounter similarly thoughtful, engaged parents who have nevertheless made a completely different decision. And this is OK!

If a parent is well versed in the content of a particular R-rated movie or M-rated video game, and decides to allow his or her children to access this media before age seventeen, ultimately that's the parent's right—and no one else's business. When friends from families with different values are playing or hanging out together, it gets more complicated. What if family X allows M-rated video games, but a child from family Y—which doesn't allow such games—wants to play with a child from family X? Get ready for the old "But Jimmy's family lets him play *Call of Duty*! I'm the only kid who doesn't have

Call of Duty!" argument. We get it, this is obnoxious, but kids have been doing it since the dawn of time. ("Grom's family has the wheel, and we don't. What gives?") Parents will have to make their own judgments: Is the media in question so bad that they must protect their child from it at all costs? The reality is, neither giving in nor refusing to give in will ruin a child's life. Well-informed parents need to go with their gut and be confident in their decision. If they run into resistance, they should be respectful of their child, explain their reasoning, and give their kid a little space to be annoyed.

If parents discover that their child has been exposed to media they find objectionable, one option is to use the situation as an opportunity for discussion. A few years back, one of your authors was listening to Pandora radio in the car with his then nine-year-old son, Roman (the aforementioned master of *Lego: Marvel Superheroes*), when the Ice Cube song "Gangsta Rap Made Me Do It" came on. For those who don't know it, this particular song drops the N-word about a thousand times. This is a dilemma familiar to many parents: Scramble for the controls and try to shut off the radio before the damage is done? Or let the song play out and talk about the content? In this case, Ferguson decided that the best tactic would be to let it play. When the song was over, Roman and his father had a long talk about the N-word, its racist and hateful origins, and that it is never to be uttered. This objectionable song proved an unexpectedly useful platform for discussing racism, as well as the family rules about offensive and/or explicit language.

In some situations, scrambling for the controls may be the right response (pornographic images, torture-porn violence, any country music, etc.). But while we're not suggesting that a copy of *2Pacalypse Now* is an indispensable parenting tool, reflexively shielding children from anything we find offensive can be counterproductive. By acting as if they're made of spun glass until they turn eighteen, we not only unfairly patronize our children, we deprive them of opportunities to have serious conversations with us about things that really matter. It is certainly understandable that a parent might think it important to prevent children from encountering "problematic" media. However, research suggests that such "helicopter" parenting styles are linked to children who lack self-efficacy, have higher levels of narcissism, are alienated from friends, possess ineffective coping skills, and experience greater levels of stress.[293, 294]

Granted, not all kids are the same, and it is important to make parenting decisions based on your actual child, not a hypothetical one—and to graduate your approach based on age. Using *Grand Theft Auto* as an opportunity to discuss misogyny and violence toward women might not be appropriate or effective with a five-year-old, but it may with a fifteen-year-old. You should use your best instincts, with an eye toward education rather than keeping your children bubble-wrapped until they are thrust onto the stage of adulthood without having had serious conversations with you about sex, communication, racism, aggression, and so on. Don't forget, these are also opportunities to talk to your children about the ways in which what they see in media may not be representative of real life. In the end, conversations are almost always more productive than restrictions.

INFORMATION: BE INFORMED . . . BUT BE MINDFUL OF THE SOURCE

Throughout this book, we've seen that information about video games, whether it comes from the video game industry itself or anti-game advocates, is often filtered through various agendas. Being aware of those agendas can help parents process the value of various pieces of information. Veronica's mother was aware of this issue and asked us whether there were any scientists, government entities, or professional advocacy organizations that could provide objective information on media. The answer, of course, is that a source of purely objective information simply doesn't exist. Information is filtered by politics, money, moral crusades, personal egos, and hosts of tangled biases and assumptions. What comes out on the other end of the process is rarely objective, verifiable fact. But that's simply a function of human nature, and certainly not unique to the topic of video games.

That being said, parents interested in information about the content of a particular game should look to the Entertainment Software Rating Board (ESRB). As we discussed in Level One, the ESRB system rates games from EC-Early Childhood (content is intended for young children) to AO-Adults Only (content is suitable only for adults eighteen and up). These ratings are displayed on the lower left-hand corner of the front of each game box and repeated on the lower left or right corner of the back of the box. Research has found that people overwhelmingly agree with the ratings the ESRB gives to games, that these ratings tend to be strongly enforced by retailers, and that over 90 percent of parents report finding it a useful rating system.[295, 296, 297] In addition to game ratings, the ESRB also provides "content descriptors" describing content within the game that may be of interest to parents. These can be found on the box with the rating, and are meant to help inform consumers about the reasoning behind that rating. For example, the ultra-cutesy *Mario Kart 8* was given an E (Everyone) rating and the sole content descriptor of "comic mischief." *Grand Theft Auto V* was rated M (Mature 17+) and given the following descriptors: "blood and gore," "intense violence," "mature humor," "nudity," "strong language," "strong sexual content," and "use of drugs and alcohol." Checking these descriptors allows parents to assess game content far more accurately and completely than by simply relying on a broad ESRB rating like T or M. Worried about virtual violence? Avoid games with the content descriptors "blood and gore" or "intense violence." Losing sleep over junior being exposed to indecency? Stay away from games with the content descriptors "sexual themes" or "nudity." Whatever a parent's concern, there is probably a content descriptor addressing it—as can be seen in the box below.

ESRB CONTENT DESCRIPTORS[298]

ALCOHOL REFERENCE—Reference to and/or images of alcoholic beverages

ANIMATED BLOOD—Discolored and/or unrealistic depictions of blood

BLOOD—Depictions of blood

BLOOD AND GORE—Depictions of blood or the mutilation of body parts

CARTOON VIOLENCE—Violent actions involving cartoon-like situations and characters. May include violence where a character is unharmed after the action has been inflicted

COMIC MISCHIEF—Depictions or dialogue involving slapstick or suggestive humor

CRUDE HUMOR—Depictions or dialogue involving vulgar antics, including "bathroom" humor

DRUG REFERENCE—Reference to and/or images of illegal drugs

FANTASY VIOLENCE—Violent actions of a fantasy nature, involving human or non-human characters in situations easily distinguishable from real life

INTENSE VIOLENCE—Graphic and realistic-looking depictions of physical conflict. May involve extreme and/or realistic blood, gore, weapons, and depictions of human injury and death

LANGUAGE—Mild to moderate use of profanity

LYRICS—Mild references to profanity, sexuality, violence, alcohol, or drug use in music

MATURE HUMOR—Depictions or dialogue involving "adult" humor, including sexual references

NUDITY—Graphic or prolonged depictions of nudity

PARTIAL NUDITY—Brief and/or mild depictions of nudity

REAL GAMBLING—Player can gamble, including betting or wagering real cash or currency

SEXUAL CONTENT—Non-explicit depictions of sexual behavior, possibly including partial nudity

SEXUAL THEMES—References to sex or sexuality

SEXUAL VIOLENCE—Depictions of rape or other violent sexual acts

SIMULATED GAMBLING—Player can gamble without betting or wagering real cash or currency

STRONG LANGUAGE—Explicit and/or frequent use of profanity

STRONG LYRICS—Explicit and/or frequent references to profanity, sex, violence, alcohol, or drug use in music

STRONG SEXUAL CONTENT—Explicit and/or frequent depictions of sexual behavior, possibly including nudity

SUGGESTIVE THEMES—Mild provocative references or materials

TOBACCO REFERENCE—Reference to and/or images of tobacco products

USE OF ALCOHOL—The consumption of alcoholic beverages

USE OF DRUGS—The consumption or use of illegal drugs

USE OF TOBACCO—The consumption of tobacco products

VIOLENCE—Scenes involving aggressive conflict. May contain bloodless dismemberment

VIOLENT REFERENCES—References to violent acts

For those who want even more information, the ESRB provides "ratings summaries." As can be seen in the box below, these are brief but detailed overviews of the material in the game parents might find most objectionable. Parents can find these summaries by searching a game's title on the ESRB webpage (www.esrb.org) or via the ESRB mobile app.

EXAMPLES OF ESRB RATINGS, CONTENT DESCRIPTORS, AND RATING SUMMARIES

MARIO KART 8

This is a kart-racing game in which players compete with characters from the Mario universe. As players race against other drivers, they can use "cartoony" power-ups (e.g., bombs, turtle shells, fire balls) to impede opponents' progress. Some attacks result in vehicles spinning out, flipping into the air; comical yelps and colorful explosions accompany the action.

NANCY DREW: SEA OF DARKNESS

This is a point-and-click adventure game in which players assume the role of Nancy Drew, a young detective investigating a sailor's disappearance . . . Some text contains violent references (e.g., "[S]omething about her family line and ancient blood feuds and murders . . . "; "He's totally weird. Good-weird, not serial-killer weird"; and "Nothing says 'I love you' like a new murder tool."). One scene depicts small bloodstains in the snow. A limerick from a book briefly mentions grog.

GRAND THEFT AUTO V

In this open-world action game, players assume the role of three criminals whose story lines intersect within the fictional city of Los Santos . . . Players use pistols, machine guns, sniper rifles, and explosives to kill various enemies . . . Blood-splatter effects occur frequently, and the game contains rare depictions of dismemberment. In one sequence, players are directed to use various instruments and means (e.g., pipe wrench, tooth removal, electrocution) to extract information from a character . . . The game includes depictions of sexual material/activity: implied fellatio and masturbation; various sex acts (sometimes from a close-up perspective) that the player's character procures from a prostitute . . . Nudity is present, however, primarily in two settings: a topless lap dance in a strip club and a location that includes male cult members with exposed genitalia in a non-sexual context . . . Some sequences within the larger game allow players to use drugs . . . The words "f**k," "c*nt," and "n**ger" can be heard in the dialogue.

In addition to the information provided by the ESRB, many gaming websites feature extensive reviews of games and descriptors of their content. By reading a review, parents can get a pretty good sense of what to expect. Some of the more popular and useful websites are GameSpot (www.gamespot.com), IGN (www.ign.

com), Giant Bomb (www.giantbomb.com), and Polygon (www
.polygon.com). If a person wants to actually see the game in action,
he or she can hop over to YouTube and find hundreds of videos
of people playing it. Be careful, however, to note and consider the
source of any clips. News media often cherry-picks the worst clips
and presents them out of context to scare people. For parents still
worried about the games their kids want to play, we have a radical
suggestion: just play the game with your child! There are various
businesses and services—like Game Fly (www.gamefly.com) and
Redbox (www.redbox.com)—that allow people to rent games, so
you can try before you buy. Not only is playing a game the best way
to get a clear sense of its content, but this will give parents a better
understanding of what their child is actually *doing*. Some studies
even suggest that parents become less concerned about the content
of video games once they actually see them in action.[298] You never
know, you may even find it . . . fun.

VIOLENCE IN GAMES

The old adage, "fear sells," is true. Fear sells books (we'll see how this
one does, since we're basically telling you everything's OK), drives
clicks, gets grant money, gives politicians an easy way to win support,
and the list goes on. Anti-media watchdog groups, politicians, the
news media, and a vocal minority of scholars actively frighten, shame,
and guilt parents into a panic over video games. This isn't science, nor
is it good medical advice; it is simple moral advocacy. Groups like
the American Psychological Association and American Academy of
Pediatrics are essentially professional guilds, and identifying problems for their members to rush in and solve is just good business.
Fear is arguably an integral part of their business model. Anti-media
watchdog groups like Parents Television Council and Common Sense
Media survive on donations—donations generated by scaring parents

about the supposed dangers of violent video games. The Parents Television Council even has a helpful webpage where you can learn how to donate a car, stocks, or bequeath them money in your will![299] The financial motives of such organizations are arguably not much purer than those of the video game industry itself.

By this point in the book, it should be clear that society has nothing to fear from violent video games. These games are not responsible for real-world violence, and there is no reason for Veronica's mother to be worried that playing *World of Warcraft* is going to turn her daughter into a criminal or make her less sensitive toward the suffering of others.[300] That is not only the conclusion of this book—it is a conclusion endorsed by the majority of scientists who study the effects of media. In fact, one recent survey by an anti–video game researcher found that only 35 percent of scientists agreed with his belief[301] that media violence poses a danger.[302, 303] Other surveys of scholars and clinicians have produced similar findings, suggesting that only a trivial number of scientists (as low as 11 percent) actually believe that video games are a problem for society.[304, 305]

The fact that most scientists discount the notion that violent media causes real-world violence is a relatively new phenomenon. Surveys of media scholars conducted thirty years ago revealed that 90 percent of psychologists felt that media violence was among the primary causes of behavioral aggression.[306] This change in scientific opinion clearly indicates that the moral panic around violent video games, at least among scientists, has started to dissipate. One reason for this change is simple: during the past three decades, many older researchers have retired, replaced by younger scientists who grew up playing video games. In the past thirty years, as more and more research has been done on the effects of violent media, fewer and fewer scholars believe video game violence is something we should fear.

A note of caution: the fact that violent video games do not contribute to violent behavior does not mean that kindergarteners should be playing *Grand Theft Auto*. Parents might want to shield

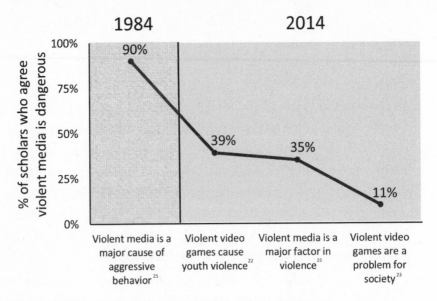

The changing scientific opinion about violent media

their children from such games for other valid reasons, including to prevent nightmares, help them avoid negative attitudes and outlooks and reduce anxiety, and to encourage them to feel that the world is a safe place. Adults themselves may choose to avoid violent games for similar reasons. Kids and adults alike are individuals, with individual sensitivities and personalities. Deciding at what age a child can play a certain game is going to be different for every family and every child. Parents ultimately hold the responsibility for making choices that are right for them and for their children.

Luckily, these choices aren't a matter of life or death—not even close. Deciding on appropriate media usage is well below the importance of other decisions such as "Should I vaccinate?" (yes), or "Should I spend more time with my kids or at work finishing a big project?" (choose the kids). When it comes to media in general and video games in particular, it's OK for parents to give a decision a try, see how it works out, talk with their kids about the experience, and readjust if necessary. As long as a child has a warm, structured, intellectually challenging home, things are most likely going to be

OK. Even the worst video games can't pierce that particular armor. It may not always feel this way, but parents have a lot more influence on their children than the media ever will.[307, 308] Parents should have confidence in their decisions, but they must also give themselves permission to make mistakes—because, inevitably, we all do.

KEEP CALM AND GAME ON

So, the idea that violent video games contribute to mass shootings, bullying, violent assaults, or other social problems (like depression or poor grades) is all but dead, at least scientifically. Just as dead as the idea that heavy metal, Harry Potter, pop music, or comic books contributed to these things. In fact, violent video games may have more of a role in preventing violence—by keeping young males busy—than in causing it. At the time of this writing, we're seeing signs that the moral panic surrounding video games is winding down. The US Supreme Court has given video games specific constitutional protections (and noted that violent games are not "harmful"), the Smithsonian has acknowledged games as art, and politicians seem to be a bit more hesitant to blame violence on gaming. Scholars are increasingly producing research that indicates games have minimal influence on behavior and, perhaps most importantly, the gamer generation is aging into the power structures of society.

Granted, we're probably not out of the woods yet: some people will still seize upon unfortunate acts of violence to promote their moral crusade against video games. Understanding the cyclical nature of moral panics can help us filter though the knee-jerk alarmism (and sometimes the exuberant claims of dramatic benefits) that so often greet new media. Although society's mistrust of video games seems to be ebbing, people will undoubtedly find something new to fear. Perhaps it will be the dangers of virtual reality, the rise of YouTube stars, or maybe it will be a technology we have yet to imagine (see Easter Egg 1). We're already seeing the beginning of a new panic around social media, with concerns that it is socially isolating and "brain draining."[309] People have even tied these fears to those of gun violence: in August of 2015, Vester Lee Flanagan, a forty-one-year-old former reporter, killed another reporter and cameraman during a live interview, then spread his own recording of the shootings via social media. This led some to worry that social media could motivate mass shootings, despite a lack of evidence that social media plays a role in gun violence.[310] Knowing that such arguments are forthcoming will help parents and the public keep these fears in perspective.

As with Fredric Wertham, who never flagged in his crusade against comic books, it's likely that anti-game activists and scientists will go to their graves insisting they've been right about video games all along.

But they aren't. So grab your controller—and game on!

EASTER EGG

1. One very real danger of virtual reality is looking like an idiot. Imagine yourself immersed in the virtual world of *Call of Duty*. In the game, you are firing your gun and throwing hand grenades like a super soldier. But in your living room, you are actually just waving your arms around at nothing while wearing giant ski goggles on your face—not your coolest moment. But again, we didn't grow up in the world of VR, so this might just be an example of two old folks not "getting" some newfangled technology. Now . . . get off our lawn!

NOTES

LEVEL 1

1   Trufant, J. (2014). "32 years later, Marshfield lets Pac-Man return to town." *The Patriot Ledger.* Retrieved from www.patriotledger.com/article/20140429/ NEWS/140426585

2   Kent, S. L. (2000). *The First Quarter: A 25-Year History of Video Games.* Bothell, Wash: BWD Press.

3   Ebert, R. (1975). "*Death Race 2000.*" Roger Ebert.com. Retrieved from www .rogerebert.com/reviews/death-race-2000

4   Romao, T. (2003). "Engines of transformation: an analytical history of the 1970s car chase cycle." *New Review of Film and Television Studies, 1*(1), 31–54.

5   Blumenthal, R. (1976). "'Death Race' game gains favor, but not with the safety council." *New York Times.* Retrieved from http://query.nytimes.com/gst/abstract.html?res =9404E1DC133FE334BC4051DFB467838D669EDE

6   *New York Times* (1981). "100 protest against L.I. pinball arcade." *New York Times.* Retrieved from www.nytimes.com/1981/03/27/nyregion/the-region-100-protes t-against-li-pinball-arcade.html

7   Kushner, D. (2003). *Masters of Doom: How Two Guys Created an Empire and Transformed Pop Culture.* New York: Random House.

8   Nuttycombe, D. (1994). "Pac-Man, Tetris—and Now It's Doom's Day." *Washington Post.* Retrieved from www.gamers.org/dhs/dmpblcty/wngtpost.html

9   Totilo, S. (2012). "Two video games. Two age ratings. What's the bloody difference?" *Kutaku.com.* Retrieved from http://kotaku.com/5901423/two-video-games-tw o-age-ratings-whats-the-bloody-difference

10 Totilo, S. (2007). "'Manhunt 2' developer finally talks about game, ratings controversy—much as it pains him." *MTV.Com.* Retrieved from www.mtv.com/news

/1572934/manhunt-2-developer-finally-talks-about-game-ratings-controversy-much
-as-it-pains-him/

11   Vella, M. (2008). "Electronic Arts tries to snatch Take-Two." *Bloomberg Business.*
      Retrieved from www.bloomberg.com/bw/stories/2008-02-25/electronic-arts-tries-to
      -snatch-take-twobusinessweek-business-news-stock-market-and-financial-advice

12   Ferguson, C. J. (2011). "Video games and youth violence: A prospective analysis in
      adolescents." *Journal of Youth and Adolescence, 40,* 377–391.

13   Federal Trade Commission. (2011). "FTC Undercover Shopper Survey on Enforce-
      ment of Entertainment Ratings Finds Compliance Worst for Retailers of Music
      CDs and the Highest Among Video Game Sellers." Retrieved from www.ftc.gov/
      news-events/press-releases/2011/04/ftc-undercover-shopper-survey-enforcement
      -entertainment-ratings

14   Kaiser Family Foundation (2002). "Rating Sex and Violence in the Media: Media
      Ratings and Proposals for Reform." Retrieved from www.academia.edu/2010783
      /Rating_Sex_and_Violence_in_the_Media_Media_Ratings_and_Proposals_for_
      Reform_Henry_J._Kaiser_Family_Foundation_

15   Schwartz, S. A. (1994). *Parents Guide to Video Games.* Roseville, CA: Prima
      Lifestyles.

16   Moby Games (2014). "*Grand Theft Auto* Reviews." *MobyGames.com.* Retrieved from
      www.mobygames.com/game/grand-theft-auto/mobyrank

17   McWhertor, M. (2015). "Grand Theft Auto 5 sells 45M copies, boosted by PS4 and
      Xbox One versions." *Polygon.com.* Retrieved from www.polygon.com/2015/2/3
      /7973035/grand-theft-auto-5-sales-45-million-ps4-xbox-one

18   Fall, S., Ed. (2014). *Guinness World Records 2015 Gamer's Edition.* New York: St.
      Martin's Press.

19   ESRB. (2016). "Rating category breakdown." Retrieved from www.esrb.org/about/
      categories.aspx

20   Ferguson, C. J. (2015). "Does media violence predict societal violence? It depends on
      what you look at and when." *Journal of Communication, 65,* E1–E22.

21   Ogas, O. & Gaddam, S. (2012). *A Billion Wicked Thoughts: What the Internet Tells Us
      about Sexual Relationships.* New York: Penguin Group.

22   McCormack, D. (2013). "Porn study had to be scrapped after researchers failed to
      find any 20-something males who hadn't watched it." *Daily Mail.* Retrieved from
      www.dailymail.co.uk/news/article-2261377/Porn-study-scrapped-researchers-failed
      -ANY-20-males-hadn-t-watched-it.html

23   Clasen, M. (2012). "Monsters evolve: A biocultural approach to horror stories."
      Review of General Psychology, 16, 222–229.

24 Vendel, C. & Goldberg, M. (2012). *Atari Inc.: Business is Fun.* Carmel, NY: Syzygy Company Press.

25 The International Arcade Museum (2015). "Shark JAWS." *Arcade-Muesum.com.* Retrieved from www.arcade-museum.com/game_detail.php?game_id=9509

LEVEL 2

26 "Hillary Hates on Video Games." *Youtube.com.* Retrieved from www.youtube.com/watch?v=x1udjd2Aq3E

27 Bushman, B. & Anderson, C. (2001). "Media violence and the American public." *American Psychologist, 56,* 477–489.

28 Ferguson, C. J. (2009). "Is psychological research really as good as medical research? Effect size comparisons between psychology and medicine." *Review of General Psychology, 13*(2), 130–136.

29 Brown v EMA (2011). Retrieved 7/1/12 from www.supremecourt.gov/opinions/10pdf/08-1448.pdf

30 Reinhold, R. (1990). "The Longest Trial—A Post-Mortem; Collapse of Child-Abuse Case: So Much Agony for So Little." *New York Times.* Retrieved from www.nytimes.com/1990/01/24/us/longest-trial-post-mortem-collapse-child-abuse-case-so-much-agony-for-so-little.html

31 Finkelhor, D. (2010). "The internet, youth deviance and the problem of 'juvenoia.' Presented at the Justice Studies Colloqium (October, 22, 2010)." Retrieved 10/2/11 from https://vimeo.com/16900027

32 Lewin, T. (2005). "Are These Parties for Real?" *New York Times.* Retrieved from www.nytimes.com/2005/06/30/fashion/thursdaystyles/are-these-parties-for-real.html

33 Kutner, L. & Olson, C. (2008). *Grand Theft Childhood: The Surprising Truth About Violent Video Games and What Parents Can Do.* New York: Simon & Schuster.

34 Kirschenbaum, M. (2007). "How reading is being reimagined." *The Chronicle of Higher Education, 54* (15), B20.

35 Trend, D. (2007). *The Myth of Media Violence: A Critical Introduction.* Malden, MA: Wiley-Blackwell.

36 Wertham, F. (1955). "Are they cleaning up the comics?" *New York State Education, 43,* 176–180.

37 Tilley, C. (2012). "Seducing the Innocent: Fredric Wertham and the Falsifications that Helped Condemn Comics." *Information & Culture, 47* (4), 383–413. doi:10.1353/lac.2012.0024.

38   Bushman, B. J. & Stack, A. D. (1996). "Forbidden fruit versus tainted fruit: Effects of warning labels on attraction to television violence." *Journal Of Experimental Psychology: Applied, 2*(3), 207–226. doi:10.1037/1076-898X.2.3.207.

39   Gosselt, J. F., De Jong, M. T. & Van Hoof, J. J. (2012). "Effects of media ratings on children and adolescents: A litmus test of the forbidden fruit effect." *Journal Of Communication, 62*(6), 1084–1101. doi:10.1111/j.1460-2466.2012.01597.x.

40   Wilkening, M. (2014). "30 Years Ago: An Ozzy Osbourne Fan Commits Suicide, Leading to 'Suicide Solution' Lawsuit." Retrieved from: http://ultimateclassicrock .com/ozzy-osbourne-fan-suicide

41   Cooper, J. & Mackie, D. (1986). "Video games and aggression in children." *Journal of Applied Social Psychology, 16*, 726–744.

42   Ivory, J. D., Oliver, M. B. & Maglalang, O. M. (2009, May). "He doesn't look like the games made him do it: Racial stereotype activation in estimates of violent video games' influence on violent crimes." Paper presented to the Game Studies Interest Group at the annual conference of the International Communication Association, Chicago, IL.

43   Cullen, D. (2004). "The Depressive and the Psychopath." *Slate*. Retrieved from www .slate.com/articles/news_and_politics/assessment/2004/04/the_depressive_and_the_ psychopath.html

44   Grossman, D. (1997). "Violent Video Games Are Mass-Murder Simulators." *Executive Intelligence Review*. Retrieved from www.larouchepub.com/other/2007/ 3417grossman_reprint.html

45   Fiore, F. (1999). "Media Violence Gets No Action from Congress." *LA Times*. Retrieved from http://articles.latimes.com/1999/nov/20/news/mn-35571

46   Anderson, C. (2000). "Violent Video Games Increase Aggression and Violence." Retrieved from http://public.psych.iastate.edu/caa/abstracts/2000-2004/00Senate .html

47   Gauntlett, D. (2005). *Moving Experiences: Understanding Television's Influences and Effects*. Luton: John Libbey.

48   Terkel, A. (2012, December 19). "Video Games Targeted by Senate in Wake of Sandy Hook Shooting." *Huffington Post*. Retrieved from www.huffingtonpost.com/2012/12 /19/video-games-sandy-hook_n_2330741.html?utm_hp_ref=technology&utm_hp _ref=technology

49   Sherry, J. (2001). "The effects of violent video games on aggression: A meta-analysis." *Human Communication Research, 27*, 409–431.

50   Fox News (2008). "Mass Effect Sex Debate." Retrieved from www.youtube.com/ watch?v=PKzF173GqTU

51   Strasburger, V. C., Donnerstein, E. & Bushman, B. J. (2014). "Why is it so hard to believe that media influence children and adolescents?" *Pediatrics, 133*(4), 571–573.

52   Anderson, C. (2013). "Games, guns, and mass shootings in the US." *The Bulletin of the International Society for Research on Aggression, 35*(1), 15–19.

53   Rich, M. (2014). "Moving from child advocacy to evidence-based care for digital natives." *JAMA Pediatrics, 168,* 404–406.

54   CBS *Face the Nation.* (2013). "Are video games, violence, and mental illness connected?" Retrieved from www.cbsnews.com/videos/are-video-games-violence-and -mental-illness-connected/

LEVEL 3

55   Rhodes, R. (2000). "Hollow Claims About Fantasy Violence." Retrieved from www .nytimes.com/2000/09/17/opinion/hollow-claims-about-fantasy-violence.html

56   Huesmann, L.R. & Eron, L. (2001). "Rhodes is Careening Down the Wrong Road." *American Booksellers Association Foundation for Free Expression.* Retrieved from http://web.archive.org/web/20101106190920/http://www.abffe.com/mythresponse. htm

57   Rhodes, R. (2000). *Why They Kill: The Discoveries of a Maverick Criminologist.* New York: Vintage.

58   Rhodes, R. (2000). "The He Hormone." Retrieved from www.nytimes.com/2000/04 /23/magazine/l-the-he-hormone-844799.html

59   Cooper, J. & Mackie, D. (1986). "Video Games and Aggression in Children." *Journal of Applied Social Psychology, 16,* 726–744.

60   Elson, M., Mohseni, M. R., Breuer, J., Scharkow, M. & Quandt, T. (2014). "Press CRTT to measure aggressive behavior: The unstandardized use of the competitive reaction time task in aggression research." *Psychological Assessment, 26,* 419–432.

61   Ferguson, C. J. (2013). "Violent video games and the Supreme Court: Lessons for the scientific community in the wake of Brown v EMA." *American Psychologist, 68,* 57–74.

62   Anderson, C. A., Shibuya, A., Ihori, N., Swing, E. L., Bushman, B.J., Sakamoto, A., Rothstein, H.R. & Saleem, M. (2010). "Violent video game effects on aggression, empathy, and prosocial behavior in Eastern and Western countries: A meta-analytic review." *Psychological Bulletin, 136,* 151–173.

63   Ferguson, C. J. (in press). "Do angry birds make for angry children? A meta-analysis of video game influences on children's and adolescents' aggression, mental health, prosocial behavior, and academic performance." *Perspectives on Psychological Science.*

64   Gallup News Service (2001). "Americans Divided on Whether School Shootings Can
      Be Prevented. *Gallup.* Retrieved from www.gallup.com/poll/1867/americans-divided
      -whether-school-shootings-can-prevented.aspx

65   Anderson, C. A. & Dill, K. E. (2000). "Video games and aggressive thoughts, feelings,
      and behavior in the laboratory and in life." *Journal of Personality and Social Psychol-
      ogy,* 78, 772–790.

66   Krahé, B. & Möller, I. (2004). "Playing violent electronic games, hostile attributional
      style, and aggression-related norms in German adolescents." *Journal of Adolescence,*
      27, 53–69.

67   Anderson, C. A. & Bushman, B. J. (2001). "Effects of violent video games on aggres-
      sive behavior, aggressive cognition, aggressive affect, physiological arousal, and
      prosocial behavior: A meta-analytic review of the scientific literature." *Psychological
      Science,* 12, 353–359.

68   Bushman, B. J. & Anderson, C. A. (2002). "Violent video games and hostile expec-
      tations: A test of the general aggression model." *Personality and Social Psychology
      Bulletin,* 28, 1679–1686.

69   Strasburger, V. C. (2007). "Go ahead punk, make my day: it's time for pediatricians to
      take action against media violence." *Pediatrics,* 119, 1398–1399.

70   Strasburger, V. C., Jordan, A. B. & Donnerstein, E. (2010). "Health effects of media on
      children and adolescents." *Pediatrics, 125,* 756–767.

71   American Psychological Association. (2005). "Resolution on Violence in Video
      Games and Interactive Media." Retrieved from www.apa.org/about/policy/
      interactive-media.pdf

72   American Psychological Association. (2005). "APA Calls for Reduction of Violence in
      Interactive Media Used by Children and Adolescents." Retrieved from www.apa.org/
      news/press/releases/2005/08/video-violence.aspx

73   American Psychological Association (2015). "APA Task Force on Violent Media."
      Retrieved from www.apa.org/pi/families/violent-media.aspx

74   Ferguson, C. J. (2015). "Clinicians' attitudes toward video games vary as a function
      of age, gender and negative beliefs about youth: A sociology of media research
      approach." *Computers in Human Behavior, 52,* 379–386.

75   Risen, J. (2014). *Pay Any Price.* Boston: Houghton Mifflin Harcourt.

76   American Psychological Association. (2014). "Statement of APA Board of Directors:
      Outside Counsel to Conduct Independent Review of Allegations of Support for
      Torture." Retrieved from www.apa.org/news/press/releases/2014/11/risen-allegations.
      aspx

77   Consortium of Scholars (2013). "Scholar's Open Statement to the APA Task Force
      on Violent Media." Retrieved from www.scribd.com/doc/223284732/Scholar-

s-Open-Letter-to-the-APA-Task-Force-On-Violent-Media-Opposing-APA-Policy
-Statements-on-Violent-Media

78 Australian Government, Attorney General's Department (2010). "Literature Review on the Impact of Playing Violent Video Games on Aggression." Commonwealth of Australia.

79 Swedish Media Council (2011). "Våldsamma datorspel och aggression—en översikt av forskningen 2000–2011." Retrieved 1/14/11 from www.statensmedierad.se/Publikationer/Produkter/Valdsamma-datorspel-och-aggression/

80 Cumberbatch, G. (2004). "Video violence: Villain or victim?" Video Standards Council: United Kingdom.

81 Gun Violence Prevention Task Force (2013). "It's Time to Act: A Comprehensive Plan that Reduces Gun Violence and Respects the 2nd Amendment Rights of Law-Abiding Americans." US House of Representatives: Washington, DC.

82 Common Sense Media (2013). "Media and violence: An analysis of current research." San Francisco, CA. Retrieved from www.commonsensemedia.org/

83 Zimbardo, P. & Coulombe, N. (2015). *Man (Dis)connected: How technology has sabotaged what it means to be male.* London: Rider Books.

84 Andrew Przybylski/Phil Zimbardo (2015). "Debate on video game effects." Retrieved from www.youtube.com/watch?v=8voQHnfOq7w&feature=youtu.be

85 Przybylski, A. K., Rigby, C. S. & Ryan, R. M. (2010). "A motivational model of video game engagement." *Review of General Psychology, 14*(2), 154–166.

86 Przybylski, A. K., Deci, E. L., Rigby, C. S. & Ryan, R. M. (2014). "Competence-impeding electronic games and players' aggressive feelings, thoughts, and behaviors." *Journal Of Personality and Social Psychology, 106*(3), 441–457.

87 Williams, D. & Skoric, M. (2005). "Internet fantasy violence: A test of aggression in an online game." *Communication Monographs, 72,* 217–233.

88 Durkin, K. & Barber, B. (2002). "Not so doomed: Computer game play and positive adolescent development." *Journal of Applied Developmental Psychology, 23*(4), 373–392.

89 Colwell, J. & Kato, M. (2005). "Video game play in British and Japanese adolescents." *Simulation & Gaming, 36*(4), 518–530.

90 Dominick, J. R. (1984). "Videogames, television violence, and aggression in teenagers." *Journal of Communication, 34,* 136–147.

91 Huesmann, L. R. (2007). "The impact of electronic media violence: Scientific theory and research." *Journal of Adolescent Health, 41*(6, Suppl), S6–S13.

92 Adachi, P. C. & Willoughby, T. (2011). "The effect of video game competition and violence on aggressive behavior: Which characteristic has the greatest influence?" *Psychology of Violence, 1,* 259–274.

93 Tear, M. & Nielson, M. (2013). "Failure to demonstrate that playing violent video games diminishes prosocial behavior." *PLoS One, 8*(7), e68382.

94 Engelhardt, C. R., Mazurek, M. O., Hilgard, J., Rouder, J. N. & Bartholow, B. D. (in press). "Effects of violent video game exposure on aggressive behavior, aggressive thought accessibility, and aggressive affect among adults with and without autism spectrum disorder." *Psychological Science.*

95 Sauer, J. D., Drummond, A. & Nova, N. (2015). "Violent Video Games: The Effects of Narrative Context and Reward Structure on In-Game and Postgame Aggression." *Journal of Experimental Psychology.*

96 Tear, M. J. & Nielsen, M. (2014). "Video games and prosocial behavior: A study of the effects of non-violent, violent and ultra-violent gameplay." *Computers in Human Behavior, 41*, 8–13.

97 Ballard, M., Visser, K. & Jocoy, K. (2012). "Social context and video game play: Impact on cardiovascular and affective responses." *Mass Communication and Society, 15*, 875–898.

98 Beuer, J., Kowert, R., Festl, R. & Quandt, T. (2015). "Sexist games—sexist games? A longitudinal study on the relationship between video game use and sexist attitudes." *Cyberpsychology, Behavior, and Social Networking.*

99 Charles, E. P., Baker, C. M., Hartman, K., Easton, B. P. & Kreuzberger, C. (2013). "Motion capture controls negate the violent video-game effect." *Computers in Human Behavior, 29*, 2519–2523.

100 Devilly, G. J., Brown, K., Pickert, I. & O'Donohue, R. (in press). "An evolutionary perspective on cooperative behavior in gamers." *Psychology of Popular Media Culture.*

LEVEL 4

101 Crowely, K. (2008). "Video Villains Come to Life." *New York Post.* Retrieved from www.nypost.com/2008/06/26/video-villains-come-to-life/

102 Rouen, E. (2008). "Six Long Island teens busted in 'Grand Theft'-style spree." *New York Daily News.* Retrieved from www.nydailynews.com/news/crime/long-island -teens-busted-grand-theft-style-spree-article-1.295664

103 Mercer, D. (2013). "Christopher Harris guilty of murder in beating deaths." *Huffington Post.* Retrieved from www.huffingtonpost.com/2013/05/31/christopher-harris -guilty-murder-beating-death_n_3367703.html

104 Cushing, T. (2013). "Researcher Tries to Connect Violence and Video Games During Murder Trial; Gets Destroyed During Cross Examination." *Tech Dirt.* Retrieved from www.techdirt.com/articles/20130531/19495123281/researcher-tries-to-connect -violence-video-games-during-murder-trial-gets-destroyed-during-cross -examination.shtml

105 Chapman, L. J. & Chapman, J. P. (1967). "Genesis of popular but erroneous psychodiagnostic observations." *Journal of Abnormal Psychology, 72*, 193–204.

106 Hamilton, D. L., Dugan, P. M. & Trolier, T. K. (1985). "The formation of stereotypic beliefs: Further evidence for distinctiveness-based illusory correlations." *Journal of Personality and Social Psychology, 48*, 5–17.

107 Anderson, C. A. (2001). "Heat and violence." *Current directions in psychological science, 10*, 33–38.

108 Cohen, J., Cohen, P., West, S. G. & Aiken, L. S. (2002). *Applied Multiple Regression/ Correlation Analysis for the Behavioral Sciences.* Mahwah, NJ: Lawrence Erlbaum Associates.

109 Anderson, C. A., Bushman, B. J. & Groom, R. W. (1997). "Hot years and serious and deadly assault: empirical tests of the heat hypothesis." *Journal of Personality and Social Psychology, 73*, 1213–1223.

110 Bushman, B. J. (2013). "Global warming can also increase aggression and violence." *Psychology Today.* Retrieved from www.psychologytoday.com/blog/ get-psyched/201307/global-warming-can-also-increase-aggression-and-violence

111 NewZoo (2015). "Top 100 Countries by Game Revenues." *New Zoo Games Market Media.* Retrieved from www.newzoo.com/free/rankings/top-100-countries-by-game -revenues/

112 IntelCenter (2015). "Top 10 Most Dangerous Countries: Country Threat Index (CIT) Based on Terrorist and Rebel Activity Over Past 30 Days as of 8 Mar. 2015." *IntelCenter.* Retrieved from http://intelcenter.com/reports/charts/cti/

113 United Nations Office on Drugs and Crime (2011). "Assault at the national level, number of police-recorded offences." Retrieved from www.unodc.org/unodc/ data-and-analysis/statistics/crime.html

114 Gaudiosi, J. (2012). "New Reports Forecast Global Video Game Industry Will Reach $82 Billion By 2017." *Forbes.* Retrieved from www.forbes.com/sites/john-gaudiosi/2012/07/18/new-reports-forecasts-globals-video-game-industry-will-reach-82-billion-by-2017/

115 Markey, P. M., Markey, C. N. & French, J. E. (2014). "Violent video games and real-world violence: Rhetoric versus data." *Psychology of Popular Media Culture.*

116 Donohue III, J. J. & Levitt, S. D. (2001). "The impact of legalized abortion on crime." *Quarterly Journal of Economics*, 379–420.

117 Associated Press (2010). "Call of duty breaks sales record." Retrieved from www.cbc. ca/news/ technology/call-of-duty-breaks-sales-record-1.949952

118 Leung, R. (2005). "Can a Video Game Lead to Murder?" CBS: *60 Minutes.* Retrieved from http://www.cbsnews.com/news/can-a-video-game-lead-to-murder-17-06-2005/

119 Hern, A. (2013). "Grand Theft Auto 5 under fire for graphic torture scene." The *Guardian*. Retrieved from www.theguardian.com/technology/2013/sep/18/ grand-theft-auto-5-under-fire-for-graphic-torture-scene

120 Edwards, R. & Martin, N. (2008). "Grand Theft Auto IV: Violence flares after launch." The *Telegraph*. Retrieved from www.telegraph.co.uk/news/1907172/Grand-Theft -Auto-IV-Violence-flares-after-launch.html

121 Murry, J. P., Stam, A. & Lastovicka, J. L. (1993). "Evaluating an anti-drinking and driving advertising campaign with a sample survey and time series intervention analysis." *Journal of the American Statistical Association, 88*, 50–56.

122 McCollister, K. E., French, M. T. & Fang, H. (2010). "The cost of crime to society: New crime-specific estimates for policy and program evaluation." *Drug and alcohol dependence, 108*, 98–109.

123 Messner, S. F. (1986). "Television violence and violent crime: An aggregate analysis." *Social Problems, 33*, 218–235.

124 Markey, P. M., French, J. E. & Markey, C. N. (2015). "Violent movies and severe acts of violence: Sensationalism versus science." *Human Communication Research, 41*, 155–173.

125 Dahl, G. & DellaVigna, S. (2009). "Does movie violence increase violent crime?" The *Quarterly Journal of Economics, 124*, 677–734.

126 Kutner, L. & Olson, C. (2008). *Grand Theft Childhood: The Surprising Truth About Violent Video Games and What Parents Can Do*. New York: Simon and Schuster.

127 Wegman, C. (2013). *Psychoanalysis and Cognitive Psychology: A Formalization of Freud's Earliest Theory*. Orlando, FL: Academic Press.

128 Hawtree, C. (1998). "News of the Weird: Stories from around the world that didn't make the headlines." The *Independent*. Retrieved from www.independent.co.uk/ arts-entertainment/news-of-the-weird-stories-from-around-the-world-that-didnt -make-the-headlines-1192419.html

129 Feshbach, S. (1984). "The catharsis hypothesis, aggressive drive, and the reduction of aggression." *Aggressive Behavior, 10*, 91–101.

130 Mallick, S. K. & McCandless, B. R. (1966). "A study of catharsis of aggression." *Journal of Personality and Social Psychology, 4*, 591–596.

131 Feshbach, S. & Singer, R. (1971). *Television and Aggression*. San Francisco: Jossey-Boss.

132 Bushman, B. J. (2002). "Does venting anger feed or extinguish the flame? Catharsis, rumination, distraction, anger, and aggressive responding." *Personality and Social Psychology Bulletin, 28*, 724–731.

133 Bushman, B. J., Baumeister, R. F. & Stack, A. D. (1999). "Catharsis, aggression, and persuasive influence: Self-fulfilling or self-defeating prophecies?" *Journal of Personality and Social Psychology, 76*, 367.

134 Feshbach, S. & Tangney, J. (2008). "Television viewing and aggression: Some alternative perspectives." *Perspectives on Psychological Science*, 3, 387–389.

135 Manning, S. A. & Taylor, D. A. (1975). "Effects of viewed violence and aggression: Stimulation and catharsis." *Journal of Personality and Social Psychology*, 31, 180–188.

136 Doob, A. N. & Wood, L. E. (1972). "Catharsis and aggression: Effects of annoyance and retaliation on aggressive behavior." *Journal of Personality and Social Psychology*, 22, 156–162.

137 Bresin, K. & Gordon, K. H. (2013). "Aggression as affect regulation: Extending catharsis theory to evaluate aggression and experiential anger in the laboratory and daily life." *Journal of Social and Clinical Psychology*, 32, 400-423.

138 US Department of Justice (1996). "Juvenile Offenders and Victims: 1996 Update on Violence." Office of Juvenile Justice and Delinquency Prevention. Retrieved from www.ncjrs.gov/pdffiles/90995.pdf

139 Levitt, S. D. (1995). "The effect of prison population size on crime rates: Evidence from prison overcrowding litigation." *The Quarterly Journal of Economics, 111,* 319–351.

140 Felson, M. (1994). *Crime and Everyday Life: Insight and Implications for Society.* Thousand Oaks, CA: Pine.

141 Snider, M. (2014). "Nielsen: People spending more time playing video games." *USA Today.* Retrieved from www.usatoday.com/story/tech/gaming/2014/05/27/nielsen-tablet-mobile-video-games/9618025/

142 McCord, J., Widom, C. S. & Crowell, N. A. (2001). *Juvenile Crime, Juvenile Justice. Panel on Juvenile Crime: Prevention, Treatment, and Control.* Washington, DC: National Academy Press.

143 Cunningham, S., Engelstätter, B. & Ward, M. R. (2011). "Understanding the effects of violent video games on violent crime." ZEW-Centre for European Economic Research Discussion Paper, 11–042.

144 Ward, M. R. (2011). "Video games and crime." *Contemporary Economic Policy*, 29, 261–273.

145 Ferguson, C. J. (2015). "Does media violence predict societal violence? It depends on what you look at and when." *Journal of Communication*, 65, E1–E22.

LEVEL 5

146 Lupica, M. (March, 2013). "Morbid find suggests murder-obsessed gunman Adam Lanza plotted Newton, Conn.'s Sandy Hook massacre for years." *New York Daily News,* Retrieved from www.nydailynews.com/news/national/lupica-lanza-plotted-massacre-years-article-1.1291408

147 Linkins, J. (2013). "Lemar Alexander Says Video Games Are 'A Bigger Problem Than Guns' But No, They Aren't." *Huffington Post*. Retrieved from www.huffingtonpost.com/2013/01/30/lamar-alexander-video-games-guns_n_2584837.html

148 Jaccarino, M. (September, 2013). "'Training simulation:' Mass killers often share obsession with violent video games." *Fox News*. Retrieved from www.foxnews.com/tech/2013/09/12/training-simulation-mass-killers-often-share-obsession-with-violent-video-games/

149 Bushman, B. J. & Newman, K. (2013). "Youth violence: What we need to know." Report of the Subcommittee on Youth Violence of the Advisory Committee to the Social, Behavioral and Economic Sciences Directorate, National Science Foundation. Retrieved from www.law.berkeley.edu/files/csls/NSF_(2013)_-_Youth_Violence_Report.pdf

150 Michigan Department of Education (2003). "Checklist: Preventing and responding to school violence." Retrieved from www.michigan.gov/documents/Checklist_Final_4-2-03_61305_7.pdf

151 Cherry Creek School District (2011). "Potential Warning Signs of Troubled Children: A Handout for Parents of School-Aged Children." Retrieved from http://www.cherrycreekschools.org/SafeSchools/Documents/WarningSignsSchoolAge.pdf

152 BBC News (September, 1999). Education: "Schools check for classroom killers." *BBC News*. Retrieved from http://news.bbc.co.uk/2/hi/uk_news/education/440803.stm

153 Troum, J. (October, 2013). "Hearing over autistic student's bomb drawing." *WBTW News*. Retrieved from www.wbtw.com/story/23694568/hillcrest-middle-hearing-wednesday-over-autistic-students-drawing

154 Langman, P. (2012). "School Shootings: The Warning Signs." *Forensic Digest, Winter-Spring*. Retrieved from www.schoolshooters.info/PL/Prevention_files/Warning%20Signs%201.2.pdf

155 CNN (March, 1998). "Judge orders boys held in Arkansas shooting." *CNN*. Retrieved from www.cnn.com/US/9803/26/school.shooting/

156 Sedensky, S. J., III (2013). "Report of the State's Attorney for the Judicial District of Danbury on the Shootings at Sandy Hook Elementary School and 36 Yoganada Street, Newtown, Connecticut on December 14, 2012." Retrieved from http://cbsnewyork.files.wordpress.com/2013/11/sandy_hook_final_report.pdf

157 Virginia Tech Review Panel (2007). "Mass Shootings at Virginia Tech, April 16, 2007." Retrieved from www.washingtonpost.com/wp-srv/metro/documents/vatechreport.pdf

158 Mikkelson, B. (January, 2005). "The Harris Levels." *Snopes*. Retrieved from www.snopes.com/horrors/madmen/doom.asp

159 Fein, R. A. & Vossekuil, B. (1999). "Assassination in the United States: an operational study of recent assassins, attackers, and near-lethal approachers." *Journal of Forensic Sciences, 44*, 321–333.

160 Vossekuil, B., Fein, R., Reddy, M., Borum, R. & Modzeleski, W. (2002). "The final report and findings of the Safe School Initiative: Implications for the prevention of school attacks in the United States." Washington, DC: US Department of Education, Office of Elementary and Secondary Education, Safe and Drug-Free Schools Program and U.S. Secret Service, National Threat Assessment Center.

161 Markey, P. M., Markey, C. N. & French, J. E. (2014). "Violent video games and real world violence: Rhetoric versus data." *Psychology of Popular Media Culture.*

162 Griffiths, M. D. & Hunt, N. (1995). "Computer game playing in adolescence: Prevalence and demographic indicators." *Journal of Community & Applied Social Psychology, 5,* 189–193.

163 Kutner, L. & Olson, C. (2008). *Grand Theft Childhood: The Surprising Truth About Violent Video Games and What Parents Can Do.* New York: Simon & Schuster.

164 Shedler, J. & Block, J. (1990). "Adolescent drug use and psychological health: A longitudinal inquiry." *American Psychologist, 45,* 612.

165 Tucker, J. S., Ellickson, P. L., Collins, R. L. & Klein, D. J. (2006). "Are drug experimenters better adjusted than abstainers and users?: A longitudinal study of adolescent marijuana use." *Journal of Adolescent Health, 39,* 488–494.

166 LaFontana, K. M. & Cillessen, A. H. (2002). "Children's perceptions of popular and unpopular peers: a multimethod assessment." *Developmental Psychology, 38,* 635–647.

167 United States Congress, House Committee on the Judiciary (2000). "Youth culture and violence: hearing before the Committee on the Judiciary, House of Representatives, One Hundred Sixth Congress, first session, May 13, 1999." Washington: US GPO.

168 Leary, M. R., Kowalski, R. M., Smith, L. & Phillips, S. (2003). "Teasing, rejection, and violence: Case studies of the school shootings." *Aggressive Behavior, 29,* 202–214.

169 Van Brunt, B. (2012). *Ending Campus Violence: New Approaches to Prevention.* New York: Routledge.

170 La Greca, A. M. & Santogrossi, D. A. (1980). "Social skills training with elementary school students: A behavioral group approach." *Journal of Consulting and Clinical Psychology, 48,* 220–227.

171 Funder, D. C., Ed. (1999). *Personality Judgment: A Realistic Approach to Person Perception.* Cambridge, MA: Academic Press.

172 Erikson, E. H. (1977). *Toys and Reasons: Stages in the Ritualization of Experience.* New York: Norton.

173 Vygotsky, L. (1978). *Mind in Society: The Development of Higher Psychological Functions.* Cambridge, MA: Harvard University Press.

174 Gottman, J. M. (1986). "*The world of coordinated play: Same- and cross-sex friendship in young children*." Cambridge, England: Cambridge University Press.

175 Connolly, J. A. & Doyle, A. B. (1984). "Relation of social fantasy play to social competence in preschoolers." *Developmental Psychology, 20*, 797–806.

176 Granic, I., Lobel, A. & Engels, R. C. (2014). "The benefits of playing video games." *American Psychologist, 69*, 66–78.

177 Przybylski, A. K. (2014). "Electronic gaming and psychosocial adjustment." *Pediatrics, 134*, e716–e722.

178 Roskos-Ewoldsen, D. R., Rhodes, N. & Eno, C. A. (2008, May). "Helping behavior in the context of video game play." Presented at the Annual Meeting of the International Communication Association (ICA), Montreal, Quebec, Canada.

179 Ferguson, C. J. & Garza, A. (2011). "Call of (civic) duty: Action games and civic behavior in a large sample of youth." *Computers in Human Behavior, 27*, 770–775.

180 Velez, J. A., Mahood, C., Ewoldsen, D. R. & Moyer-Gusé, E. (2014). "Ingroup versus outgroup conflict in the context of violent video game play: The effect of cooperation on increased helping and decreased aggression." *Communication Research, 41*, 607–626.

181 Zammitto, V. L. (2010). "Gamers' Personality and Their Gaming Preferences." Doctoral dissertation, Communication, Art & Technology: School of Interactive Arts and Technology.

182 Schreier, J. (2013). "*Minecraft* is Now 'Mine-Crack' Says Local News Everywhere." *Kotaku.* Retrieved from www. Kotaku.com/minecraft-is-now-mine-crack-says-local-news-everywhe-927656796

LEVEL 6

183 Mikelberg, A. (February, 2012). "Corpse of League of Legends player ignored at Internet cafe for nine hours." *New York Daily News.* Retrieved from www.nydailynews.com/news/world/corpse-league-legends-player-internet-cafe-hours-article-1.1017013

184 American Psychiatric Association (2013). "Diagnostic and statistical manual of mental disorders—5." Washington, DC: American Psychiatric Association.

185 Associated Press. (2011). "New Mexico mom gets 25 years for starving daughter." Retrieved from http://news.yahoo.com/mexico-mom-gets-25-years-starving-daughter-145411042.html

186 The Sun (July 2014). "Playing games as addictive as heroin." *The Sun.* Retrieved from www.thesun.co.uk/sol/homepage/news/5739475/Gaming-as-addictive-as-heroin.html

187 Griffiths, M. (2014). "Press to play: Is gaming really more addictive than heroin?" *Gamasutra*. Retrieved from www.gamasutra.com/blogs/Mark-Griffiths/20140715/221010/Press_to_play_Is_gaming_really_more_addictive_than_heroin.php

188 Sloan, J. (2011). "Are cupcakes as addicting as cocaine?" *The Sun*. Retrieved from www.thesun.co.uk/sol/homepage/woman/health/3913703/Are-cupcakes-as-addictive-as-cocaine.html

189 Koepp, M. J., Gunn, R. N., Lawrence, A. D., Cunningham, V. J., Dagher, A., Jones, T., . . . & Grasby, P. M. (1998). "Evidence for striatal dopamine release during a video game." *Nature, 393*, 266–268.

190 UCLA Integrated Substance Abuse Programs (2015). "Meth: Inside Out: Public Service Multi-Media Kit." Retrieved from www.methinsideout.com/assets/MIO_Public_Service_Multi-Media_Kit.pdf

191 Langlois, M. (2011). "Dopey About Dopamine: Video Games, Drugs & Addiction." Retrieved from http://gamertherapist.com/blog/2011/11/08/dopey-about-dopamine-video-games-drugs-addiction/

192 Charlton, J. P. & Danforth, I. D. W. (2007). "Distinguishing addiction and high engagement in the context of online game playing." *Computers in Human Behavior, 23*(3), 1531–1548.

193 Haagsma, M. C., Pieterse, M. E. & Peters, O. (2012). "The prevalence of problematic video gamers in The Netherlands." *Cyberpsychology, Behavior, and Social Networking, 15*(3), 162–168.

194 Desai, R. A., Krishnan-Sarin, S., Cavallo, D. & Potenza, M. N. (2010). "Video-gaming among high school students: Health correlates, gender differences, and problematic gaming." *Pediatrics, 126*(6), e1414–e1424.

195 Ferguson, C. J., Coulson, M. & Barnett, J. (2011). "A Meta-analysis of pathological gaming prevalence and comorbidity with mental health, academic, and social problems." *Journal of Psychiatric Research, 45*(12), 1573–1578.

196 Pontes, H. M. & Griffiths, M. D. (2015). "Measuring DSM-5 Internet Gaming Disorder: Development and validation of a short psychometric scale." *Computers in Human Behavior, 45*, 137–143.

197 King, D. L. & Delfabbro, P. H. (2013). "Video-gaming disorder and the DSM-5: Some further thoughts." *Australian and New Zealand Journal of Psychiatry, 47*(9), 875–876.

198 Skoric, M. M., Teo, L. L. & Neo, R. L. (2009). "Children and video games: addiction, engagement, and scholastic achievement." *Cyberpsychol Behav, 12*(5), 567–572.

199 Griffiths, M. (2005). "A 'components' model of addiction within a biopsychosocial framework." *Journal of Substance Use, 10*(4), 191–197.

LEVEL 7

200 Smith, B. (2013). "Violent Video Games Kill Self Control and Increase Unethical Behavior." *Red Orbit*. Retrieved from www.redorbit.com/news/health/1113012581/violent-video-games-self-control-unethical-behavior-112513/

201 Stenhouse, A. (2013). "Violent video games make youngsters pig out on chocolate according to US study." *Daily Mirror*. Retrieved from www.mirror.co.uk/news/uk-news/violent-video-games-make-youngsters-2863154

202 Grabmeier, J. (2013). "Teens 'Eat More, Cheat More' After Playing Violent Video Games." Press release from *The Ohio State University*. Retrieved from http://research-news.osu.edu/archive/selfrestraint.htm

203 Milgram, S. (1975). *Obedience to Authority: An Experimental View*. London: Tavistock Publications.

204 Milgram, S. (1963). "Behavioral study of obedience." *The Journal of Abnormal and Social Psychology, 67*, 371–378.

205 Slater, M., Antley, A., Davison, A., Swapp, D., Guger, C., Barker, C., . . . & Sanchez-Vives, M. V. (2006). "A virtual reprise of the Stanley Milgram obedience experiments." *PloS one, 1*(1), e39.

206 Klimmt, C., Schmid, H., Nosper, A., Hartmann, T. & Vorderer, P. (2006). "How players manage moral concerns to make video game violence enjoyable." *Communications, 31*, 309–328.

207 Hern. A. (2013). "Grand Theft Auto 5 under fire for graphic torture scene." *The Guardian*. Retrieved from www.theguardian.com/technology/2013/sep/18/grand-theft-auto-5-under-fire-for-graphic-torture-scene

208 Ingham, T. (2009). "Religious leaders slam Modern Warfare 2." *The Market for Computer and Video Games*. Retrieved from www.mcvuk.com/news/read/religious-leaders-slam-modern-warfare-2

209 Totilo, S. (2013). "Two Thirds of You Played *Mass Effect 3* As a Paragon. Mostly as Soldiers." *Kotaku*. Retrieved from http://kotaku.com/5992092/two-thirds-of-you-played-mass-effect-3-as-a-paragon-mostly-as-soldiers

210 Boyan, A., Grizzard, M. & Bowman, N. (2015). "A massively moral game? Mass Effect as a case study to understand the influence of players' moral intuitions on adherence to hero or antihero play styles." *Journal of Gaming & Virtual Worlds, 7*, 41–57.

211 Bushman, B. (2011). "The effects of violent video games. Do they affect our behavior?" *International Human Press*. Retrieved from http://ithp.org/articles/violentvideogames.html

212 Grizzard, M., Tamborini, R., Lewis, R. J., Wang, L. & Prabhu, S. (2014). "Being bad in a video game can make us morally sensitive." *Cyberpsychology, Behavior, and Social Networking, 17*, 499–504.

213 Tangney, J. P., Stuewig, J. & Mashek, D. J. (2007). "Moral emotions and moral behavior." *Annual Review of Psychology, 58,* 345–372.

214 Federman, J., Ed. (1995). "National television violence study: Executive summary." University of California, The Center for Communication and Social Policy. Retrieved from www.academia.edu/944389/National_Television_Violence_Study_Executive_Summary_Editor_University_of_California_Santa_Barbara_

215 Tookey, C. (2006). "Disgusting, degrading, dangerous." The *Daily Mail.* Retrieved from www.dailymail.co.uk/tvshowbiz/article-381294/Disgusting-degrading-dangerous.html

216 Bushman, B. J. & Huesmann, L. R. (2001). "Effects of televised violence on aggression." *Handbook of Children and the Media,* 223–254.

217 Rachman, S. (1967). "Systematic desensitization." *Psychological Bulletin, 67,* 93–103.

218 Fanti, K. A., Vanman, E., Henrich, C. C. & Avraamides, M. N. (2009). "Desensitization to media violence over a short period of time." *Aggressive Behavior, 35,* 179–187.

219 Cline, V. B., Croft, R. G. & Courrier, S. (1973). "Desensitization of children to television violence." *Journal of Personality and Social Psychology, 27*(3), 360–365.

220 Ramos, R. A., Ferguson, C. J., Frailing, K. & Romero-Ramirez, M. (2013). "Comfortably numb or just yet another movie? Media violence exposure does not reduce viewer empathy for victims of real violence among primarily Hispanic viewers." *Psychology of Popular Media Culture, 2,* 2–10.

221 Lake Research Partners. (2006) "Parents' Views on Fitness, Nutrition, and Overweight/Obesity among Delaware's Children and Teens." Retrieved from www.nemours.org/content/dam/nemours/www/filebox/service/preventive/nhps/publication/research.pdf

222 Centers for Disease Control and Prevention (2015). "Overweight & Obesity: Adult Obesity Facts." *CDC.gov.* Retrieved from www.cdc.gov/obesity/data/adult.html

223 World Health Organization (2015). "Obesity: Situation and trends." *Who.int.* Retrieved from www.who.int/gho/ncd/risk_factors/obesity_text/en/

224 Pollack, A. (2013). "A.M.A. Recognizes Obesity as a Disease." *New York Times.* Retrieved from www.nytimes.com/2013/06/19/business/ama-recognizes-obesity-as-a-disease.html

225 Centers for Disease Control and Prevention (2013). "One in five adults meet overall physical activity guidelines." *CDC.gov.* Retrieved from www.cdc.gov/media/releases/2013/p0502-physical-activity.html

226 St-Onge, M. P., Keller, K. L. & Heymsfield, S. B. (2003). "Changes in childhood food consumption patterns: a cause for concern in light of increasing body weights." *The American Journal of Clinical Nutrition, 78,* 1068–1073.

227 Reedy, J. & Krebs-Smith, S. M. (2010). "Dietary sources of energy, solid fats, and added sugars among children and adolescents in the United States." *Journal of the American Dietetic Association, 110,* 1477–1484.

228 Marshall, S. J., Biddle, S. J., Gorely, T., Cameron, N. & Murdey, I. (2004). "Relationships between media use, body fatness and physical activity in children and youth: a meta-analysis." *International Journal of Obesity, 28*, 1238–1246.

229 Robinson, T. N. (1999). "Reducing children's television viewing to prevent obesity: a randomized controlled trial." *The Journal of the American Medical Association, 282*, 1561–1567.

230 Markey, C. N. (2014). *Smart People Don't Diet: How the Latest Science Can Help You Lose Weight Permanently.* Boston: Da Capo Lifelong Books.

231 Sallis, J. F., Prochaska, J. J. & Taylor, W. C. (2000). "A review of correlates of physical activity of children and adolescents." *Medicine and Science in Sports and Exercise, 32*, 963–975.

232 Pearce M.S., Basterfield L., Mann K.D., Parkinson K.N., Adamson A.J., John J. Reilly on behalf of the Gateshead Millennium Study Core Team (2012). "Early Predictors of Objectively Measured Physical Activity and Sedentary Behaviour in 8–10 Year Old Children: The Gateshead Millennium Study." *PLoS ONE* 7(6): e37975.

233 Peng, W., Lin, J. H. & Crouse, J. (2011). "Is playing exergames really exercising? A meta-analysis of energy expenditure in active video games." *Cyberpsychology, Behavior, and Social Networking, 14*, 681–688.

234 Staiano, A. E., Abraham, A. A. & Calvert, S. L. (2012). "Motivating effects of cooperative exergame play for overweight and obese adolescents." *Journal of Diabetes Science and Technology, 6*, 812–819.

235 Staiano, A. E., Abraham, A. A. & Calvert, S. L. (2013). "Adolescent exergame play for weight loss and psychosocial improvement: a controlled physical activity intervention." *Obesity, 21*, 598–601.

236 George Washington University School of Public Health and Health Services (2013). "E-Games Boost Physical Activity in cChildren; Might Be A Weapon in the Battle Against Obesity." Retrieved from http://publichealth.gwu.edu/content/e-games-boost-physical-activity-children-might-be-weapon-battle-against-obesity

237 Wahi, G., Parkin, P. C., Beyene, J., Uleryk, E. M. & Birken, C. S. (2011). "Effectiveness of interventions aimed at reducing screen time in children: a systematic review and meta-analysis of randomized controlled trials." *Pediatrics, 165*, 979–986.

LEVEL 8

238 *How Games Saved My Life.* (2015). "How Fallout 3 Saved My Life." Retrieved from http://gamessavedmylife.tumblr.com/post/21795704943/how-fallout-3-saved-my-life

239 Reinecke, L., Klatt, J. & Krämer, N. C. (2011). "Entertaining media use and the satis-
     faction of recovery needs: Recovery outcomes associated with the use of interactive
     and noninteractive entertaining media." *Media Psychology, 14*(2), 192–215.

240 Sherry, J. L., Lucas, K., Greenberg, B. S. & Lachlan, K. (2006). "Video Game Uses and
     Gratifications as Predicators of Use and Game Preference." In Vorderer, P. & Bryant,
     J. (Eds.), *Playing Video Games: Motives, Responses, and Consequences* (pp. 213–224).
     Abingdon-on-Thames,UK: Routledge.

241 Przybylski, A. K., Rigby, C. S. & Ryan, R. M. (2010). "A motivational model of video
     game engagement." *Review of General Psychology, 14*(2), 154–166.

242 Rieger, D., Frischlich, L., Wulf, T., Bente, G. & Kneer, J. (2015). "Eating ghosts: The
     underlying mechanisms of mood repair via interactive and noninteractive media."
     Psychology Of Popular Media Culture, 4(2), 138-154.

243 Valadez, J. J. & Ferguson, C. J. (2012). "Just a game after all: Violent video game expo-
     sure and time spent playing effects on hostile feelings, depression, and visuospatial
     cognition." *Computers in Human Behavior, 28,* 608–616.

244 Ferguson, C. J. & Rueda, S. M. (2010). "The Hitman study: Violent video game
     exposure effects on aggressive behavior, hostile feelings, and depression." *European
     Psychologist 15*(2), 99–108.

245 Reinecke, L., Klatt, J. & Krämer, N. C. (2011). "Entertaining media use and the satis-
     faction of recovery needs: Recovery outcomes associated with the use of interactive
     and noninteractive entertaining media." *Media Psychology, 14*(2), 192–215.

246 Kowert, R., Festl, R. & Quandt, T. (2014). "Unpopular, overweight, and socially inept:
     Reconsidering the stereotype of online gamers." *Cyberpsychology, Behavior, and Social
     Networking, 17*(3), 141–146.

247 Lenhart, A., Kahne, J., Middaugh, E., MacGill, A., Evans, C. & Mitak, J. (2008).
     "Teens, video games and civics: Teens gaming experiences are diverse and include
     significant social interaction and civic engagement." *Pew Research Center.* Retrieved
     7/2/12 from www.pewinternet.org/PPF/r/263/report_display.asp.

248 Rosenbloom, S. (2011). "It's Love at First Kill." *New York Times.* Retrieved from www.
     nytimes.com/2011/04/24/fashion/24avatar.html?_r=0

249 Kowert, R., Domahidi, E. & Quandt, T. (2014). "The relationship between online
     video game involvement and gaming-related friendships among emotionally sensi-
     tive students." *Cyberpsychology, Behavior, and Social Networking, 17*(7), 447–453.

250 Rice, L. & Markey, P. M. (2009). "The role of extraversion and neuroticism in influ-
     encing anxiety following computer-mediated interactions." *Personality and Individual
     Differences, 46*(1), 35–39.

251 Shepherd, R. M. & Edelmann, R. J. (2005). "Reasons for internet use and social anxi-
     ety." *Personality and Individual Differences, 39*(5), 949–958.

252 Durkin, K. (2010). "Videogames and young people with developmental disorders."
     Review of General Psychology, 14(2), 122–140.

253 Anguera, J., Boccanfuso, J., Rintoul, J., Al-Hashimi, O., Faraji, F., Janowich, J., Kong,
     E., Larraburo. Y., Rolle, C., Johnston, E. & Gazzaley, A. (2013). "Video game training
     enhances cognitive control in older adults." *Nature, 501,* 97–101.

254 Peretz, C., Korczyn, A. D., Shatil, E., Aharonson, V., Birnboim, S. & Giladi, N.
     (2011). "Computer-based, personalized cognitive training versus classical computer
     games: A randomized double-blind prospective trial of cognitive stimulation." *Neu-
     roepidemiology, 36*(2), 91–99.

255 Landau, S. M., Marks, S. M., Mormino, E. C., Rabinovici, G. D., Oh, H., O'Neil, J.
     P., . . . & Jagust, W. J. (2012). "Association of lifetime cognitive engagement and low
     β-amyloid deposition." *Archives of Neurology, 69*(5), 623–629.

256 Basak, C., Boot, W. R., Voss, M. W. & Kramer, A. F. (2008). "Can training
     in a real-time strategy video game attenuate cognitive decline in older adults?" *Psy-
     chology and Aging, 23*(4), 765–777.

257 Stanford Center on Longevity. (2014). "A Consensus on the Brain Training Indus-
     try from the Scientific Community." Retrieved from http://longevity3.stanford.
     edu/blog/2014/10/15/the-consensus-on-the-brain-training-industry-from-the
     -scientific-community-2/

258 Ferguson, C. J., Garza, A., Jerabeck, J., Ramos, R. & Galindo, M. (2013). "Not worth
     the fuss after all? Cross-sectional and prospective data on violent video game influ-
     ences on aggression, visuospatial cognition and mathematics ability in a sample of
     youth." *Journal of Youth and Adolescence, 42*(1), 109–122.

259 Zimmerman, F.J., Christakis, D.A., Meltzoff, A.N. (2007). "Associations between
     media viewing and language development in children under age two years." *Journal
     of Pediatrics, 151*(4), 364–368.

260 Lewin, T. (2010). "'Baby Einstein' Founder Goes to Court." *New York Times.*
     Retrieved 12/22/11 from www.nytimes.com/2010/01/13/education/13einstein.html

261 Ferguson, C. J. & Donnellan, M. B. (2014). "Is the association between children's baby
     video viewing and poor language development robust? A reanalysis of Zimmerman,
     Christakis, and Meltzoff (2007)." *Developmental Psychology, 50*(1), 129–137.

262 Schmidt, M. E., Rich, M., Rifas-Shiman, S. L., Oken, E. & Taveras, E. M. (2009).
     "Television viewing in infancy and child cognition at 3 years of age in a US cohort."
     Pediatrics, 123(3), e370–e375.

263 Bleakley, C. M., Charles, D., Porter-Armstrong, A., McNeill, M. J., McDonough, S.
     M. & McCormack, B. (2015). "Gaming for health: A systematic review of the phys-
     ical and cognitive effects of interactive computer games in older adults." *Journal of
     Applied Gerontology, 34*(3), NP166–NP189.

264 Green, C. S. & Bavelier, D. (2003). "Action video game modifies visual selective atten-
     tion." *Nature, 423*(6939), 534–537.

265 Li, R., Polat, U., Makous, W. & Bavelier, D. (2009). "Enhancing the contrast sensitivity
     function through action video game training." *Nature Neuroscience, 12*(5), 549–551.

266 Bejjanki, V. R., Zhang, R., Li, R., Pouget, A., Green, C. S., Lu, Z. & Bavelier, D. (2014).
     "Action video game play facilitates the development of better perceptual templates."
     *PNAS Proceedings Of The National Academy Of Sciences Of The United States Of
     America, 111*(47), 16961–16966.

267 Feng, J., Spence, I. & Pratt, J. (2007). "Playing an action video game reduces gender
     differences in spatial cognition." *Psychological Science, 18*(10), 850–855.

268 Sims V. & Mayer R. "Domain specificity of spatial expertise: The case of video game
     players." *Appl Cognit Psychol.* 2002; 16: 95–115.

269 Hardy, M. S., Armstrong, F. D., Martin, B. L. & Strawn, K. N. (1996). "A firearm safety
     program for children: They just can't say no." *Journal of Developmental and Behav-
     ioral Pediatrics, 17*, 216–221.

270 Jalink M. B., Goris J., Heineman E., Pierie J. P. & ten Cate Hoedemaker H.O. (2014).
     "The effects of video games on laparoscopic simulator skills." *American Journal of
     Surgery. 208*(1), 151–156.

271 Rosser J. C. Jr, Gentile D. A., Hanigan K. & Danner O. K. (2012). "The effect of video
     game 'warm-up' on performance of laparoscopic surgery tasks." *JSLS: Journal of the
     Society of Laparoendoscopic Surgeons/Society of Laparoendoscopic Surgeons. 16*(1), 3–9.

272 Adams B. J., Margaron F., & Kaplan B. J. (2012). "Comparing video games and lapa-
     roscopic simulators in the development of laparoscopic skills in surgical residents."
     Journal of Surgical Education, 69(6), 714–717.

273 Ferguson, C. J., Garza, A., Jerabeck, J., Ramos, R. & Galindo, M. (2013). "Not worth
     the fuss after all? Cross-sectional and prospective data on violent video game influ-
     ences on aggression, visuospatial cognition and mathematics ability in a sample of
     youth." *Journal of Youth and Adolescence, 42*(1), 109–122.

274 Boot, W., Blakely, D. & Simons, D. (2011). "Do action video games improve percep-
     tion and cognition?" *Frontiers in Psychology, 2*, 226.

275 Millard H. A., Millard R. P., Constable P. D. & Freeman L. J. (2014). "Relationships
     among video gaming proficiency and spatial orientation, laparoscopic, and tradi-
     tional surgical skills of third-year veterinary students." *Journal of the American Veteri-
     nary Medical Association. 244*(3), 357-362.

276 Fleming, R. (2013). "Surgeons that play video games have better results." *Digital
     Trends.* Retrieved from www.digitaltrends.com/gaming/surgeons-play-video-games
     -to-prepare-for-surgery/

277 Anderson, C. A. & Bushman, B. J. (2001). "Effects of violent video games on aggres-
     sive behavior, aggressive cognition, aggressive affect, physiological arousal, and
     prosocial behavior: A meta-analytic review of the scientific literature." *Psychological
     Science, 12*, 353–359.

278 Anderson, C. A., Sakamoto, A., Gentile, D. A., Ihori, N., Shibuya, A., Yukawa, S., . . .
     & Kobayashi, K. (2008). "Longitudinal effects of violent video games on aggression in
     Japan and the United States." *Pediatrics, 122*(5), e1067–e1072.

279 Grossman, D. (2013). "Videogames as 'murder simulators.'" *Variety.* Retrieved from
     http://variety.com/2013/voices/opinion/grossman-2640/

280 Gentile, D. A. & Anderson, C. A. (2003). "Violent video games: The newest media
     violence hazard." In D. A. Gentile (Ed.), *Media Violence and Children* (pp.131–152).
     Westport, CT: Praeger.

281 Cognitive Training Data. (2014). "An open letter to the Stanford Center on Longev-
     ity." Retrieved from www.cognitivetrainingdata.org/

LEVEL 9

282 Haagsma, M. C., Pieterse, M. E. & Peters, O. (2012). "The prevalence of problematic
     video gamers in The Netherlands." *Cyberpsychology, Behavior, and Social Networking,
     15*(3), 162–168.

283 Desai, R. A., Krishnan-Sarin, S., Cavallo, D. & Potenza, M. N. (2010). "Video-gaming
     among high school students: Health correlates, gender differences, and problematic
     gaming." *Pediatrics, 126*(6), e1414–e1424.

284 Ferguson, C. J., Coulson, M. & Barnett, J. (2011). "A meta-analysis of pathological
     gaming prevalence and comorbidity with mental health, academic and social prob-
     lems." *Journal of Psychiatric Research, 45*(12), 1573–1578.

285 Przybylski, A. K., Rigby, C. & Ryan, R. M. (2010). "A motivational model of video
     game engagement." *Review Of General Psychology, 14*(2), 154–166. doi:10.1037/
     a0019440.

286 Ferguson, C. J. & Ceranoglu, T. A. (2014). "Attention problems and pathological gam-
     ing: Resolving the 'chicken and egg' in a prospective analysis." *Psychiatric Quarterly,
     85*,103–110.

287 Sillars, A., Koerner, A. & Fitzpatrick, M. A. (2005). "Communication and under-
     standing in parent-adolescent relationships." *Human Communication Research, 31*,
     102–128.

288 Jason, L. A., Danielewicz, J. & Mesina, A. (2005). "Reducing media viewing: Impli-
     cations for behaviorists." *Journal of Early and Intensive Behavior Intervention, 2*,
     194–206.

289 Coyne, S. M., Padilla-Walker, L. M., Stockdale, L. & Day, R. D. (2011). "Game on . . . girls: Associations between co-playing video games and adolescent behavioral and family outcomes." *Journal of Adolescent Health, 49,* 160–165.

290 Jackson, L. A., Witt, E. A., Games, A. I., Fitzgerald, H. E., von Eye, A. & Zhao, Y. (2012). "Information technology use and creativity: Findings from the children and technology projects." *Computers in Human Behavior, 28,* 370–376.

291 Kato, P. M., Cole, S. W., Bradlyn, A. S. & Pollock, B. H. (2008). "A video game improves behavioral outcomes in adolescents and young adults with cancer: A randomized trial." *Pediatrics, 122,* 305–317.

292 Ryan, R. M., Rigby, S. C. & Przybylski, A. (2006). "The motivational pull of video games: A self-determination theory approach." *Motivation and Emotions, 30,* 347–363.

293 Segrin, C., Woszidlo, A., Givertz, M. & Montgomery, N. (2013). "Parent and child traits associated with overparenting." *Journal of Social and Clinical Psychology, 32,* 569–595.

294 van Ingen, D. J., Freiheit, S. R., Steinfeldt, J. A., Moore, L. L., Wimer, D. J., Knutt, A. D., . . . & Roberts, A. (2015). "Helicopter Parenting: The Effect of an Overbearing Caregiving Style on Peer Attachment and Self-Efficacy." *Journal of College Counseling, 18,* 7–20.

295 Ferguson, C. J. (2011). "Video games and youth violence: A prospective analysis in adolescents." *Journal of Youth and Adolescence, 40,* 377–391.

296 Federal Trade Commission (2011). "FTC Undercover Shopper Survey on Enforcement of Entertainment Ratings Finds Compliance Worst for Retailers of Music CDs and the Highest Among Video Game Sellers." Retrieved from www.ftc.gov/news-events/press-releases/2011/04/ftc-undercover-shopper-survey-enforcement-entertainment-ratings

297 Kaiser Family Foundation. (2002). "Rating Sex and Violence in the Media: Media Ratings and Proposals for Reform." Retrieved from www.academia.edu/2010783/Rating_Sex_and_Violence_in_the_Media_Media_Ratings_and_Proposals_for_Reform_Henry_J._Kaiser_Family_Foundation_

298 Entertainment Software Rating Board (2015). ESRB Ratings Guide. Retrieved from www.esrb.org/ratings/ratings_guide.jsp

299 Parents Television Council. Retrieved from http://w2.parentstv.org/main/SupportUs/howtohelp.aspx

300 Markey, P. M., Markey, C. N., & French, J. E. (2014). "Violent video games and real-world violence: Rhetoric versus data." *Psychology of Popular Media Culture.*

301 Bushman, B. (2013). "Do violent video games play a role in shootings?" *CNN.com.* Retrieved from www.cnn.com/2013/09/18/opinion/bushman-video-games/

302 Bushman, B. J., Gollwitzer, M. & Cruz, C. (2015). "There is broad consensus: Media researchers agree that violent media increases aggression in children, and pediatricians and parents concur." *Psychology of Popular Media Culture, 4, 200–214.*

303 Ivory, J. D., Markey, P. M., Elson, M., Colwell, J., Ferguson, C. J., Griffiths, M. D., Savage, J. & Williams, K. D. (2015). "Manufacturing consensus in a diverse field of scholarly opinions: A comment on Bushman, Gollwitzer, and Cruz (2015)." *Psychology of Popular Media Culture, 4,* 222–229.

304 Ferguson, C. J. (2015). "Clinicians' attitudes toward video games vary as a function of age, gender and negative beliefs about youth: A sociology of media research approach." *Computers in Human Behavior, 52,* 379–386.

305 Quandt, T., Van Looy, J., Vogelgesang, J., Elson, M., Ivory, J. D., Consalvo, M. & Mäyrä, F. (2015). "Digital Games Research: A Survey Study on an Emerging Field and Its Prevalent Debates." *Journal of Communication, 65,* 975–996.

306 Murray, J. P. (1984). "Results of an informal poll of knowledgeable persons concerning the impact of television violence." *Newsletter of the American Psychological Association Division of Child, Youth, and Family Services, 7,* 2.

307 Ferguson, C. J., San Miguel, C. & Hartley, R. D. (2009). "A multivariate analysis of youth violence and aggression: the influence of family, peers, depression, and media violence." *The Journal of Pediatrics, 155,* 904–908.

308 Ferguson, C. J., Cruz, A. M., Martinez, D., Rueda, S. M., Ferguson, D. E. & Negy, C. (2008). "Personality, parental, and media influences on aggressive personality and violent crime in young adults." *Journal of Aggression, Maltreatment & Trauma, 17,* 395–414.

309 Marche, S. (2012). "Is Facebook Making Us Lonely?" *The Atlantic.* Retrieved from www.theatlantic.com/magazine/archive/2012/05/is-facebook-making-us-lonely/308930/

310 Denison, J. (2015). "More On-Air Shootings to Be Expected." The *Christian Post.* Retrieved form www.christianpost.com/news/more-on-air-shootings-to-be-expected-144238/

INDEX

ABOUT THE AUTHORS

DR. PATRICK M. MARKEY is a professor of psychology, the director of the Interpersonal Research Laboratory at Villanova University, and a former president of the Society for Interpersonal Theory and Research. Dr. Markey received his doctorate from the University of California (Riverside) in social and personality psychology, with a focus on behavioral statistics. Since receiving his degree, he has published over seventy book chapters and peer-reviewed journal articles and has made hundreds of presentations at universities and at national and international scientific conferences. Among his peers, he is widely recognized as an expert on how violent video games affect our behavior. For years, Dr. Markey has been involved in educating the general public and politicians about various psychological issues related to digital media. By giving talks at universities and elementary schools, he has been able to help parents, teachers, and school administrators better understand the complex research examining violent video games. Moving beyond the classroom, Dr. Markey has been invited to testify before numerous governmental committees, and he has served on various governmental task forces examining the effects of violent video games.

DR. CHRISTOPHER J. FERGUSON is an associate professor of psychology and department chair at Stetson University. Dr. Ferguson received his doctorate from the University of Central Florida in clinical psychology. His clinical work has focused on forensic psychology, including work with inmates, as well as juvenile detention and child protective services assessments. Since receiving his degree, he has published over 100 book chapters and peer-reviewed journal articles and has presented his research at numerous universities and scientific conferences. He is internationally recognized as an expert on the effects of violent video games. Dr. Ferguson was involved in the talks given by Vice President Biden's task force on gun control following the Sandy Hook shooting in 2012, and he also participated in the Institute of Medicine's hearings on the role of media violence in gun violence in 2013.